Hutchinson Social History of England

Life and Labour in England
1700 — 1780

Hutchinson Social History of England

Life and Labour in England
1700–1780

Robert W. Malcolmson

Associate Professor of History, Queen's University, Kingston, Canada

Hutchinson
London Melbourne Sydney Auckland Johannesburg

Hutchinson & Co. (Publishers) Ltd
An imprint of the Hutchinson Publishing Group
24 Highbury Crescent, London N5 1RX

Hutchinson Group (Australia) Pty Ltd
30—32 Cremorne Street, Richmond South, Victoria 3121
PO Box 151, Broadway, New South Wales 2007

Hutchinson Group (NZ) Ltd
32—34 View Road, PO Box 40-086, Glenfield, Auckland 10

Hutchinson Group (SA) (Pty) Ltd
PO Box 337, Bergvlei 2012, South Africa

First published 1981

Set in Garamond by TJB Photosetting Ltd
South Witham, Grantham, Lincolnshire

Printed in Great Britain by The Anchor Press Ltd
and bound by Wm Brendon & Son Ltd
both of Tiptree, Essex

British Library Cataloguing in Publication Data
Malcolmson, Robert W
    Life and labour in England 1700—1780.
    (Social history of England series).
    1. England — Social conditions
    2. Great Britain — Social conditions — 18th century
    I. Title   II. Series
    309.1'42'07   DA485

ISBN   0 09 144380 6 cased   0 09 144381 4 paper

In memory of a friend

David Sinclair

1942—74

Contents

Preface

'I much fear . . . the poor mans lot seems to have been so long remembered as to be entirely forgotten': So, on one occasion, wrote the poet John Clare.* People with little capital, and with no formal authority or apparent claims to individual distinction, have not, until recently, been accorded much sympathetic attention by historians of eighteenth-century England. Too often the labouring people have been both taken for granted and lost from sight: and it is indisputable that they have been largely excluded from most general (and textbook) accounts of the period. This book, essentially, is an attempt to make up for at least some of this neglect.

Numerous people have contributed, in some way or other, to the making of this study in social history. I would like, for a start, to emphasize my very considerable dependence on the work of many other historians, both the work of some decades ago and, in particular, the original research that has been published by social historians during the past fifteen years. Indeed, without this specialized work — in local history, in economic and demographic history, in the history of popular culture and public order — it would not, I think, have been possible to write such a book. I hope that I have adequately acknowledged my indebtedness to this varied literature in the notes to each chapter. Moreover, I have accumulated several debts of a more personal character. Five friends and fellow-historians each read at least half of the book in typescript, and I wish to record my especial appreciation to John Beattie, John Brewer, Patricia Malcolmson, Nicholas Rogers and Edward Thompson for their helpful comments, criticisms, and suggestions for change. Their advice — along with that of my publisher's readers — compelled me to see weaknesses that I otherwise would not have seen and to

*Clare: Selected Poems and Prose, ed. Eric Robinson and Geoffrey Summerfield (London: Oxford University Press 1966), p. 193.

correct misstatements and muddled thinking before they could get into print. I am particularly grateful to John Beattie both for his careful reading of the entire manuscript and for his encouragement of my work over a period of many years. Finally, it is a pleasure to thank Claire L'Enfant of Hutchinson for her editorial attentiveness; Elizabeth Wagner for her skilful typing of the final manuscript; Karen Donnelly, Becky Doyle and Barbara Latimer of the History Department at Queen's University for their efficient secretarial assistance; and the Canada Council and the Advisory Research Committee at Queen's University for timely financial support.

1 The labouring people in English society

'By the *Inferiour Sort* of *People*', wrote Guy Miege in 1707, 'I mean properly such as get their Livelyhood either in a mechanick, or servile way; as ordinary Tradesmen, Mariners, Husbandmen, Inferiour Servants, Labourers, etc.'[1]* Men of rank and fortune (and sometimes learning) in the eighteenth century had little difficulty in indentifying, to their own satisfaction, the labouring people. They were the 'poor', the people in 'low life', the 'lower orders', those in 'plebeian' society, the 'mob' — or simply the 'people'. Henry Fielding, for example, once spoke of 'that very large and powerful Body which form the fourth Estate in this Community', — the other three were the king, Lords, and Commons — 'and have been long dignified and distinguished by the Name of THE MOB'.[2] At another time he offered a definition of the poor: 'By THE POOR', he said, '. . . I understand such persons as have no estate of their own to support them, without industry; nor any profession or trade, by which, with industry, they may be capable of gaining a comfortable subsistence.'[3] (This definition apparently excluded many tradesmen and artisans.) And to John Brand, writing in the preface to his *Observations on Popular Antiquities* (1777), his subject was simply 'the *People*, of whom Society is chiefly composed'.[4]

There were numerous contemporary writers who attempted to situate the labouring people within the total social order. At the beginning of the century, for example, Daniel Defoe divided English society into seven broad categories, and while the first three of these groups do not directly concern us — these were '1. The Great, who live profusely. . .; 2. The Rich, who live very plentifully. . .; 3. The middle Sort, who live well' — his last four 'conditions of people' identify with reasonable precision the men and women whose experiences are the subject of this book. Defoe classified these groups as '4. The working Trades, who labour hard, but feel no want. . .; 5. The Country People, Farmers etc., who fare indifferently. . .; 6. The Poor, that

*Superior figures refer to the Notes and references on pages 161—201

fare hard . . . ; 7. The Miserable, that really pinch and suffer Want.'[5] (Many farmers were more prosperous than Defoe allowed, and these larger farmers — they could be freeholders, copyholders, or tenants with good leases — are more properly regarded as members of 'the middle sort' than as labouring people. Otherwise his classifications are acceptable.) There was, as Defoe's distinctions suggest, a considerable range of experience within this large body of people — not all of them, for instance, were considered poor, and the poverty that did exist was experienced in different ways and to varying degrees. However, to men of social standing — gentlemen, employers, literary figures — all these 'common' people, whatever their many individual differences, shared certain fundamental traits, traits that were considered to be of the first importance in the organization of social life.

To most genteel observers the fundamental distinguishing characteristic of the 'inferior sort of people' was their performance of manual, often menial, tasks, and their dependence on such 'laborious' tasks in order to live. Such work, of course, was not considered to be in any way 'honourable', and anyone who had sufficient property was certain to distance himself as much as possible from the necessity of manual labour. And yet, though lacking in prestige, this labour was widely considered to be essential for the welfare of society as a whole, and especially the welfare of the propertied classes. As a Member of Parliament, Mr Robert Nugent, said in May 1753 of the common people, addressing his remarks to an audience of fellow gentlemen, 'It is from their labour our quality derive their riches and their splendour; it is to their courage [in the armed forces] all of us owe our security.'[6] The rich, opined one writer in 1756, 'stand indebted' to the poor 'for all the comforts and conveniences of life'.[7] 'What would avail our large Estates and great Tracts of Land without their Labour', queried an essayist in 1739, 'it must be till'd and manured before Corn can be produc'd, and that must be afterwards threshed and baked before even a King can have Bread to eat.'[8] 'Were it not for these poor Labourers', thought Timothy Nourse in 1700, 'the Rich themselves would soon become poor; for either they must labour and Till the Ground themselves, or suffer it to ly waste.'[9] Similarly, John Bellers, writing in 1714, declared that 'regularly labouring People are the Kingdom's greatest Treasure and Strength, for without Labourers there can be no Lords; and if the poor Labourers did not raise much more Food and Manufacture than what did subsist themselves, every Gentleman must be a Labourer, and every idle Man must starve'.[10]

The social importance of the labouring people, then, was widely acknowledged. They were seen as the source of the nation's wealth. Labour was the foundation on which all riches depended. This emphasis on the value of labour in economic affairs was commonplace in contemporary thinking, as several historians have demonstrated.[11] John Millar, a Scottish social theorist, thought that the 'benefit resulting from every species of trade or manufacture, is ultimately derived from labour'; and the agricultural writer, Arthur Young, held that 'Agriculture, arts, manufactures, and commerce, are but so many aggregates of labour: Every circumstance that can affect the prosperity of a nation, is intimately connected, and even founded on labour.'[12] An anonymous author, in 1701, expressed very similar sentiments about the creation of the nation's wealth; and yet, as·he also noticed,

the laborious poor . . . for all their pains are allow'd oftentimes no greater share out of it, than what will keep them from present Starving . . . . those, who possess the greatest share of the riches of the World, are most indebted to those, that have nothing; . . . the faithful diligence of honest and ingenious Poverty is really the richest Treasure, and safest BANK OF CREDIT in any Nation.[13]

Poverty, in this writer's view, and in the view of most propertied observers, was socially necessary, for only as a result of their poverty would some men be prepared to perform those vital laborious tasks on which 'society' — that is, gentlemen, masters, merchants and the like — so obviously depended. Henry Fielding thought that there 'must be' poor people 'in any nation where property is — that is to say, where there are any rich'.[14] The poor, according to a clergyman in a sermon of 1684,

are necessary for the establishment of Superiority, and Subjection in Humane Societies, where there must be Members of Dishonour, as well as Honour, and some to serve and obey, as well as others to command. The Poor are the Hands and Feet of the Body Politick, . . . who hew the Wood, and draw the Water of the Rich. They Plow our Lands, and dig our Quarries, and cleanse our Streets . . .[15]

Similarly, Soame Jenyns claimed that 'the world could not subsist without' poverty, 'for had all been rich, none could have submitted to the commands of another, or the drudgeries of life; thence all governments must have been dissolved, arts neglected, and lands uncultivated, and so an universal penury have over-whelmed all, instead of now and then pinching a few'.[16] Poverty, then, was not only inevitable, it was also, in many respects, a good thing. In particular, poverty induced men (or so it was hoped) to work hard for the sake of their own survival, and in so working they would serve the greater interest of what was known as the 'public'. Poor labourers were highly valued — though only if their poverty could be converted into profitable labour. ('Idleness', the disinclination to work hard for this public, which was another possible attendant characteristic of poverty, was a source of widespread anxiety and disapproving comment. The poor had duties to perform, and the failure to perform these duties conscientiously was seen by others as manifest immorality.) And this profitable labour, it was widely assumed, could only be obtained (at least in many circumstances) by means of certain coercive interventions. The labouring people must be made to submit to those in authority; they must acquiesce in their positions of dependence and subordination; they must accept the discipline of poverty, hard work and low wages. They had, perhaps, something of a right to a basic subsistence, enough to let them survive; but it was doubtful if they should be allowed any more. It was clear, then, to people of property, that the majority of English men and women were destined to live lives of unremitting toil, in the service of the public good.[17]

Lest there were any anxiety concerning the apparent unfairness of this system of social relations — the stark inequalities of social opportunity, the harsh realities that loomed so unpleasantly over the lives of most labouring people — many social commentators were careful to demonstrate that this social order, rather than being a mere human construct, was, in fact, divinely ordained. For it was God, not man, that had created social inequality and assigned individuals to their various social positions. As one writer put it in 1681:

There is nothing more plain nor certain, than that God Almighty hath ordained and appointed degrees of Authority and Subjection; allowing Authority to the Master, and commanding obedience from the servant unto him; for God hath given express commands to Masters to govern their Servants, and to Servants to be subject to their Masters. . . . Christians in all Ages have asserted and owned this distinction; some of them having been placed as Masters, and others as Servants, and according to the Station which it hath pleased God to allot them, they have performed their mutual dutys. . . .[18]

Social inequality, according to another guidebook for servants, published in 1693, 'is not by chance, but by the Soveraign Disposer of the Lord of all'; and in the same vein a clergyman advised in 1708 that 'it is GOD's own Appointment, that some should be Rich and some Poor, some High and some Low'.[19] 'The Part that every Man is to act', counselled a guide to good conduct in 1720, 'is not fortuitously appointed him, but by the especial Designation of the great Disposer of all Things, that has set out to each of us the Part we are to act upon the Stage of this World.'[20] Similarly, in 1746 another moral writer asserted that

It has pleased the almighty Governor of the world to make a difference in the outward condition of his subjects here below; and though *high and low, rich and poor, one with another*, are all his *Servants*, yet in the course of his providence he has thought good to appoint various orders and degrees of men here upon earth. Some of these are placed by him in a high, others in a low estate. Some are born to rule, others to obey. Hence arises the necessity that some should be Masters, others Servants: and this constitutes a mutual relation and duty between them.[21]

This was the conventional wisdom among men of property: social distinctions were sanctioned by God, poverty and subservience were part of his master plan for mankind, and contentment with their lowly lot in life was expected of all labouring men. The social order was seen as a reflection of the 'Order of Nature', and any particular individual's social position was spoken of as 'that State of Life unto which it hath pleased God to call you'. These were commonplace sentiments. Moreover, an acceptance of such views was seen as a precondition of human happiness. As one writer counselled, 'The Boundary of true Felicity in this Life, is to be content in the Station which Providence has allotted us.'[22]

Although the will of God, in creating these social distinctions, was sometimes admitted to be not fully intelligible, many men claimed to be able to detect a good deal of sense and purpose in this divine ordering of human society. Perhaps the most important of these arguments about God's will concerned the presumed relationship between social inequality and stable, orderly government. This view was clearly outlined by Robert Moss in 1708:

there could be no Government without Subordination. And if, by the Disposition of Providence, all Men had been made as equal in Fortune and Condition, as they are in Nature, it would have been an eternal Dispute, who should obey, and who should govern: And it had been hardly possible to bring things, upon such a Basis, to any tolerable Order, or perfect Settlement. Whereas that Disparity of Circumstances betwixt Man and Man, which God in Wisdom hath appointed, serves to induce such as are mean and needy willingly to resign the Power to them who already enjoy the Advantages of Birth and Fortune: And it is no less an Inducement to the Wealthy and Honourable to cherish and protect the Poor, without the Assistance of whose Hands, the most plentiful Condition would be so far from being happy or easie, that perhaps it would be the most anxious, and the most laborious. And God's provident Care is very remarkable in making the Rich and Poor thus mutually needful and helpful to each other; that so they might be link'd together by the strongest Ties of Interest, and Both sufficiently encourag'd to act agreeably to the Station in which God hath placed them.[23]

'There can be no Society without Government', opined another clergyman, 'and no Government without a Subordination, or Submission of Inferiors to Superiors.'[24] The good order of any society depended, fundamentally and inescapably, on the preservation of these relations of domination and obedience. As one sermon put it, 'were all equally Rich, there could be no subordination, none to command, nor none to serve. But in such a case, the body Politick must dissolve'.[25] To strive for social equality, it was suggested, would be 'to make a perpetual War, many quarrelling about the same thing; as when one Bone is cast amongst several Dogs'.[26] 'The state of Servitude', according to William Fleetwood in 1705, 'is absolutely necessary, by the order and appointment of the wise Creator and Disposer of all things; the World cou'd not be govern'd and maintain'd without it; and it is fallen to their share [that is, those who are servants], to be instrumental to the publick good in that Station'.[27] Subordination, then, was essential to any orderly society, and such subordination implied the inevitable existence of a large body of lowly, materially poor people. This was all part of God's benign and rational plans for the world. Soame Jenyns was very pleased with this divine beneficence, especially as it was revealed to man in eighteenth-century England:

in the formation of the Universe, God was obliged, in order to carry on that just subordination so necessary to the very existence of the whole, to create Beings of different ranks; and to bestow on various species, various degrees of understanding, strength, beauty, and perfection; to the comparative want of which advantages we give the names of folly, weakness, deformity, and imperfection, and very unjustly repute them Evils: whereas in truth they are blessings as far as they extend, tho' of an inferior degree. They are no more actual Evils, than a small estate is a real misfortune, because many may be possessed of greater.

'The beauty and happiness of the whole' universe, he concluded, 'depend altogether on the just inferiority of its parts, that is, on the comparative imperfections of the several Beings of which it is composed.'[28] All things, then, were working for the best. And anyway, as many men must have thought — or at least those men who were well chosen — 'God is just and equal in all his Ways.'[29]

The poor, then, had no reason to be discontented with their lot in life. Indeed, it was often said that their lowly circumstances brought them certain important advantages, usually advantages of a spiritual nature. For labouring people were spared the anxieties, the pressing responsibilities and the moral temptations which were imposed on men of property. They were said to enjoy more peace of mind than their betters. According to one observer, 'Servants may have more of the Labours of Life, but then they have less of the Cares, than other People; their Bodies are more fatigu'd and exercis'd, but their Minds are less perplex'd: They are only concerned in one matter, to do the work that lies before them, whilst others have a world of things to look on, and look after.'[30] Similarly, Soame Jenyns held that 'poverty, or the want of riches, is generally compensated by having more hopes, and fewer fears, by a greater share of health, and a more exquisite relish of the smallest enjoyments, than those who possess them are usually blessed with'.[31] Moreover, labouring people were less likely than other men to be subjected to the menacing blandishments of worldly pleasure. One writer, in 1715, thought that they were 'in a nearer Disposition, *as Poor*, towards the Attainment of the Happiness of Heaven':

For Poverty shelters them from that Luxury and Vanity, from that Pride of Life, which is so contrary to the Spirit of Christianity, and which leads Men to Scepticism and Infidelity. It engages them by honest Industry to support the Necessities of Life; and consequently, frees them from the Temptations of Idleness, which corrupt so great a Part of Mankind. Poverty preserves the Purity of the Body, by keeping it at a Distance from Pleasure; and that of the Mind, by engaging it in a necessary Care for Subsistence. It discourages the Growth of the Passions, at least from the Despair of satisfying them; and seldom is tempted to enjoy Things forbidden, being accustomed to dispense with the Want of those that are allow'd. It disposes Men to Charity and Compassion towards their Neighbours, from the Experience of their own Miseries; and raises their Minds up to Heaven, in order to secure that Happiness they want here below.[32]

Poverty, then, was spiritually, as well as socially, functional. As one clergyman put it, 'Poverty is far from being any Hindrance to Virtue: It rather helps to awaken Consideration, to cure Mens Fondness for the World, and create a sort of Indifference towards it; and this naturally makes way for serious Thoughts, and raises the Affections towards better and higher Things.'[33] A poor man was certainly just as free to find true happiness as any rich man. Heaven, not earth, was of crucial importance to Christian people.

But where does all this evidence lead us with respect to a better understanding of the labouring people themselves? For our principal concern is to reconstruct *their* experiences, their own views of the world, their own modes of conduct, their actual relations with people in authority; and the social ideals and expectations of propertied people are not, surely, central to such an inquiry. Moreover, it might well be said that it should come as no great surprise to discover that men of rank and substance were satisfied with the social order as they found it, or that labouring people were conceived to exist largely for the service of other men, or that the will of God was, by long-standing convention, enlisted in support of these social arrangements. We do, certainly, obtain from this evidence a clear sense of one class's perceptions of another class: the expectations of a privileged culture as to how labouring people *ought* to think and behave, the constraints that were imagined to dominate their lives, the arguments and assumptions that served to legitimate a particular structure of social inequality. And this evidence cannot, I think, be entirely dissociated from the tasks at hand. For it is helpful to take account of the essential components of the orthodox wisdom of propertied people, partly in order to better appreciate, in subsequent chapters of this study, some of the discrepancies between these conventional genteel images of the labouring people and the actual realities of plebeian life. Moreover, in any historical study that might be attempted of the labouring people, it is inevitable, given the character of the surviving primary evidence (very little of which was produced by labourers themselves), that many of these plebeian experiences can be investigated only by paying close attention to the records produced by members of the dominant class; and this being so, it is wise to know something about the characteristic social commitments, biases and ideological dispositions of the authors of those sources on which we must so often and so heavily depend. The culture of propertied people, then, inevitably informs and intrudes into any discussion of non-propertied people; and some consideration of this privileged culture affords us a clearer sense of the contexts, both evidential and historical, within which the central questions of this book must be pursued. However, after allowing for all these influences, the central questions still remain. And these questions relate, not to the world as it was ideologically perceived by gentlemen, but to the world as it was *actually experienced* by labouring men and women.

Before entering this central terrain, however, one further question of importance remains to be considered, and that concerns the size of the plebeian population. How many labouring people were there? And what proportion did they represent of the total eighteenth-century population? In fact, as all historians would agree, no precise answers to these questions are possible. The relevant evidence is thin and spotty, and the social categories we work with are slippery and imprecise. No detailed and reliable information on the social characteristics of the English population as a whole is available for study, for no such information was ever compiled.[34] Evidence from particular localities is worth close attention, but its broader implications are not always clear, partly because of the marked regional variations in social structure. Moreover, while there is often no doubt about the social position of particular individuals or groups of people — ploughmen, sailors and shoemakers are clearly labouring people, while merchants, attorneys and most innkeepers are not — some signs of social identification are much less clear-cut. These ambiguities are especially pronounced around that social borderline where plebeian and petty bourgeois characteristics are closely interrelated: among such groups as husbandmen (farmers with small holdings), skilled artisans and petty tradesmen. Some of these individuals may have identified mostly with larger men of property, but others had too little property for any credible claim to 'middling' status. In sorting through these various problems, and in trying to estimate the number of labouring people in the population as a whole, I have found that the most useful and least suspect sources are the hearth tax returns of the 1670s. (This was a tax upon fireplaces: and in general the more fireplaces a household had the more prosperous the family that lived there.) Given that virtually all the occupiers of one-hearth households would have been labouring people, that the great majority of two-hearth households would have been occupied by slightly more prosperous labouring people, or by larger plebeian families (few 'middling' families would have lived in households with less than three hearths),[35] and that most of the indisputably non-plebeian households, those with three hearths or more, would have included one or more living-in servants of plebeian status, it is possible to establish on the basis of these records the approximate proportion of the population that especially concerns us. Although local variations are sometimes quite striking, a collation of the evidence from several counties suggests that at least 75 per cent of England's roughly 5.5 million people in the later seventeenth century were labouring people. My own judgement is that around 80 per cent of the population were labouring men and women, and that of the remaining 20 per cent no more than 5 per cent (and probably a little less) of the population were gentlemen, professional men and their ladies, the members of the governing class.[36] A very casual contemporary estimate, made in 1717, was probably not far off the mark: 'they of Great Britain who must work, beg, steal, or starve', according to this observer, 'are five times as many as those who have Estates, or Professions, whereupon to live without working'.[37] Our concern in this book, then, is with some four-fifths of the people of eighteenth-century England.

Several brief comments are in order before we proceed to the central substance of this study. First, when I speak of the 'eighteenth century', I almost always refer to the roughly 100 years up to the period of the American revolution. (Occasionally a source is used that dates from a slightly earlier or later period, but these are exceptions, and such sources are only employed, as a rule, when confirming evidence is available from within my chronological boundaries.) I am not, then (except in the final chapter), concerned with the last twenty to twenty-five years of the chronological eighteenth century. Indeed, it has struck me for some time that this last generation of the eighteenth century, with its noticeably accelerating processes of social change — the emergence of mechanized factory production, renewed and very rapid population growth, the development of a widespread popular political consciousness, a heightened pace of 'agricultural improvement' — is most logically and fruitfully reconstructed when it is studied in conjunction with the early decades of the nineteenth century. It makes little sense for a social historian to conclude his inquiries around the year 1800. And given that some chronological limits must be imposed, the period of the American revolution serves as a more defensible terminal point for a general social study of the eighteenth century than any other I can think of. At the same time, there is no reason why we should not begin this study in the later seventeenth century, since both the logic of the historical process and those practical considerations that relate to the state of the available literature argue in favour of such chronological elasticity. In fact, in the chapters that follow I shall refer, on occasion, to sources from as far back as about 1670. However, largely because of the relative thinness of the primary evidence for these early decades, the heart of this book concerns early Hanoverian England: the years between the second decade of the eighteenth century and around 1770.

A further general comment concerns my handling of the relationship between the static and the dynamic dimensions of historical analysis. Chapters 2-5 are fundamentally concerned with those elements of plebeian experience that were relatively stable and unchanging. They focus on recurrent experiences; on patterns of belief, behaviour and social relationships that were widely observed at all times during the eighteenth century. The emphasis in these chapters, then, is on the continuous aspects of social life. From time to time I allude to processes of social change, but a sustained examination of these dynamic questions, as they relate to the lives of the labouring people, is reserved for the concluding chapter of the book. Any author of a study of this kind must confront the serious problem as to how best to reconstruct the reality of a social world in which rapid change and virtually imperceptible change were intimately interrelated; whether my manner of dealing with this issue has merit or not must be left to others to judge.

Finally, in the course of this inquiry I have studiously attempted to avoid giving an undue emphasis to the peculiar social realities of the metropolis of London. London, of course, was very important and very populous; however, it represented only about 10 to 12 per cent of the total population, and approximately five out of every six eighteenth-century English men and women never laid eyes on their country's capital city.[38] The great majority of labouring people consumed all of their lives in the provinces — in villages or hamlets or isolated cottages; in a small market town, or a larger 'county capital' (Northampton, Bedford, Lincoln, Warwick) or one of the handful of 'great' provincial cities, such as Bristol, or Norwich, or Newcastle-upon-Tyne (and no such city, in 1700, had a population in excess of 30,000). Plebeian experiences, then, were overwhelmingly provincial experiences, and the design of this book is intended to reflect this essential fact. London is certainly not ignored in the chapters that follow: indeed, its distinctive characteristics, and its peculiar relationships with other parts of England, are often noticed and discussed. But I always try to see London within the broader social context, to situate it within English society as a whole, and thus to keep it in a properly proportioned perspective — the perspective of a predominantly non-urban, or only modestly urbanized, society.

These, I think, are the main cautionary considerations and authorial judgments that deserve to be kept in mind. Thus prepared, we can now proceed to an investigation of the actually experienced social world of the eighteenth-century labouring people.

2 Getting a living

In the mid 1840s, when Karl Marx and Friedrich Engels were formulating their social theories in opposition to the tradition of German idealism, they proposed a starting point for historical understanding that might seem to be virtually self-evident. 'The first premise of all human existence', they said, is 'that men must be in a position to live in order to be able to "make history". But life', they continued,

involves before everything else eating and drinking, a habitation, clothing, and many other things. The first historical act is thus the production of the means to satisfy these needs, the production of material life itself. And indeed this is an historical act, a fundamental condition of all history, which today, as thousands of years ago, must daily and hourly be fulfilled merely in order to sustain human life.[1]

Here was a clear and explicit statement of the material basis of all human history. Man has needs which must be satisfied if life is to continue; he produces, through labour, the means of survival; and the terms under which this subsistence is attained profoundly condition much of his culture and social experience. Getting a living, then, is the foundation on which social life is built.

Our concern in this chapter is to explain how, in the eighteenth century, people with little or no private property provided for their own subsistence. How did labouring men and women support themselves? And what were the principal determinants of their standard of living? It is clear that their sustenance came from many different sources and was produced in many different ways. Most men no longer lived as peasants, and the predominance of industrial employment lay in the future. But it is misleading to speak of this society as 'pre-industrial', for manufacturing was widespread and of vital importance. Yet at least three-quarters of the English people in 1700 still got a major portion of their living directly from some form of agricultural work. In order to appreciate the character of labour in this period it is best, I think, if we recognize the need to distinguish and describe both the actual tasks that people performed and the circumstances that conditioned the performance of these tasks. In most households an adequate subsistence depended on a complex of various forms of task-work and wage-labour: regular, full-time employment at a single job was not the norm. Occupational categories, then, as applied to particular individuals and social groups — farm labourer, weaver, housewife — should be treated with caution, for they tend to obscure the complexities and intricacies of the real world of labour as it was experienced by individuals and families. It is better to speak of the work itself — farm labour, weaving, housewifery — and to try to understand how such work contributed to a family's living. Moreover, labour of any kind was rooted in a particular local economy and derived much of its character from the specific opportunities and limitations of the local environment; and in the eighteenth century there was an immense diversity of local economies. The means of subsistence, then, varied markedly from place to place, and from family to family. But a recognition of diversity does not mean that useful generalizations are impossible. For underlying this diversity there were common patterns of living and widely shared social and economic objectives. What, then, were the principal conditions which constrained, or supported or enhanced the material circumstances of life? Which social and economic determinants were of central importance to the everyday subsistence of the labouring people?

The countryside and common rights

The productive enterprises in eighteenth-century England, the social units in which work was done, were mostly small in scale. Large units of production were exceptional. Factories were almost non-existent until the end of the century, and most coal pits, outside of the Tyneside region, were still modest undertakings, worked by a handful of men; only a very few enterprises, such as the naval shipyards and Crowley's iron works, could be regarded as undeniably concentrated units of production. Most work was done on a family farm, in a workshop, in the streets of a town, or in a household. In fact, the household was the central unit of production in the eighteenth century. A large proportion of manual labour, whether in agriculture, industry or service — probably the majority of such work — was directly implicated in the productive activities of the family household. The household was not merely a unit of consumption in which its members spent money that was earned elsewhere: an individual's actual work was normally done, not outside the household, but as part of the household's own productive economy. For most labouring people, then, the viability of the household economy was the crucial priority in life. An appreciation of the components of this economy is an essential prerequisite for our historical understanding.

In the first half of the eighteenth century, when about three-quarters of the English population lived in villages, hamlets, and scattered farmsteads and cottages, the viability of a working man's household economy depended heavily on the degree to which his family could gain some sort of (often partial) living from the land. The agrarian economy was of central importance to almost all of these families, but the specific character of this importance, and the particular benefits derived from the land, varied greatly from household to household and from parish to parish. Men with small farms — farms of perhaps ten, fifteen or twenty-five acres — enjoyed a modest degree of independence and prosperity. Some of them held freeholds; others enjoyed long leases, often by copyhold. They were usually known as husbandmen or, in later years, as smallholders. However, by the early eighteenth century the bulk of the rural working people held less land than this, and often no land at all, aside from a cottage garden. These people, the hundreds of thousands of cottagers, country labourers, and smallholders with one or two acres, usually owned no land and cannot be considered as members of the landholding class, if we understand this class to comprise men with, at the least, enough land, securely occupied, for a more-or-less self-sufficient farm. But even if most country people held no land in this sense, it does not necessarily follow that they were unable to get a major portion of their living from the land. In fact, the central concern of many of these families was, first, with rights of access to the use of land, and second, with the availability of employment on nearby farms. By means of the former they produced some of their own provisions and thus achieved a degree of domestic self-sufficiency; by means of the latter they obtained wages that allowed them to buy other necessities in the marketplace, pay the rent for their cottages, and purchase recreational pleasures. In this way an economy of self-reliance and an economy of wage-dependence could be linked together.

This economy of self-reliance was heavily dependent on the existence of common rights. It is important to appreciate that the notion of the absolute private ownership of land and its resources was not yet fully triumphant. Indeed, in many parts of the country — especially in regions where there were forests, or heaths and 'wastes', or simply unenclosed fields — no one landowner enjoyed exclusive rights to the use of particular tracts of land. In these areas numerous other individuals, most of them local men with little or no private property, claimed the right to make use of the land for certain customary purposes: purposes that were directly related to their own livelihoods. The rights these people claimed were usually supported by appeals to custom, by ideas of usage from time immemorial. 'Custome', as one writer put it around 1700, 'is a law or right, not written, which being established by long use and the consent of our ancestors, hath been and is dayly practised.'[2] Custom, in this context, was not simply the equivalent of 'tradition': custom had the power of law and could be enforced in the manorial courts. As the Webbs once remarked, these manorial customs, which were very widespread, 'were legally binding on both the Lord and his tenants'.[3] (A later eighteenth-century observer, sensing the tension between the older claims of custom and the newer claims of private property, whose 'real' rights the law was coming to favour, said of the poor around 1780 that 'though perhaps they have no real right to the commons, yet prescription and long usage seem to give them an apparent claim'.)[4] The conception of land appropriate to this discussion is one, not of landownership, but of land being used: used for different purposes by different people, none of whom was acknowledged to have absolute possession. A lord (or lords) would have rights to use such land — rights which, though they might be more extensive than those of other users, were never exclusive; and the poorer members of the community — or at least some of them, the 'commoners' — also had rights of access to the land for purposes that were sanctioned by customary practice. The land was there: nobody possessed it completely, many people enjoyed its material benefits in different ways and to varying degrees. To the commoners land existed to be used by those who needed it, not owned as private property.

What were the concrete advantages of these common rights to men of modest means? Most of the benefits of commons stemmed from two kinds of rights: grazing rights for livestock, and rights to gather, for household use, certain natural resources of the land. Grazing rights were particularly important for they allowed men with only tiny holdings, holdings too small for grazing, or with no holdings at all, to maintain a small number of livestock on the common lands and thus enjoy those direct and tangible rewards which stock-keeping generally involved. Although such commoners might be able to grow no grain of their own, their modes of sustenance were deeply implicated in some form of pastoral economy. Even very poor men could benefit from these common rights. As one writer put it in 1726:

there are in most Counties a Sort of Cottagers, that have Custom and Right of Commoning, tho' they Rent nothing but their Houses: And if it were a meer Hovel built upon the Waste, who would hinder a poor Man from keeping an Ewe and Lamb, or if he compass one, a little Heifer? For these can run upon a Green, or among the Lanes and Highways, till the Crop be ended; and then away with them into the common Fields, for the coming Season, as freely and unmolested as he that rents 100 1. per Annum, and by this Advantage in some Places divers poor Families are in good Part sustained.[5]

Access to common land for grazing allowed commoners to keep a cow or two, or some sheep or pigs — a labouring man who kept sheep could rent them to a farmer because of the value of their dung[6] — perhaps a few geese, or a horse which could be employed in the carrying trade. The specific nature and limitations of the rights enjoyed varied from place to place: stinting regulations were often enforced, pigs might be prohibited from feeding on parts of the common, grazing on certain unenclosed (but cultivated) fields would only be permitted during the months between the end of the harvest and the winter sowing. But whatever particular restrictions may have existed — and many of them were designed to protect the commons from exhaustion — substantial and widely enjoyed benefits always remained. In areas of wide expanse — the fens of East Anglia, Dartmoor and other moorland districts, the open field countryside of central England, forests throughout the country — cottagers and smallholders sustained a viable, if often tenuous, economy because of their ability to keep stock; and in many individual parishes in regions of intensive arable husbandry villagers enjoyed similar advantages from a local marsh, waste or other uncultivated piece of land, or from rights of access to unenclosed fields at times when no crops were growing.

Many examples could be selected to illustrate the value of these grazing rights. In Willingham, Cambridgeshire, for instance, an economy of smallholders, in which dairying was the principal activity, was only sustainable because of the existence of the spacious fen common, where the livestock of the cottagers and small farmers could be freely pastured. As the historian of Willingham remarks, 'the exercise of valuable common rights in a pastoral area was the equivalent of landholding in an arable area'.[7] A similar importance was attached to common rights in Myddle, Shropshire: for the labouring poor there, as David Hey has argued,

the wages they earned doing the many and varied tasks on the farm, from hedging and ditching, to sowing, weeding, reaping and harvesting, were supplemented by the profits of a small-holding. These consisted of just a few acres cleared from the woods, never big enough to grow corn for more than their immediate use, but sufficient to keep a few animals to care for their household wants. For these men, as for all cottagers in the woodland areas, their common rights, especially their rights of pasture, would be vital. (They were not illegal squatters, but had leases for their cottages, thus acquiring common rights.)[8]

There is similar evidence from the later seventeenth and early eighteenth centuries of the existence of common grazing rights in such diverse parishes as Powick in Worcestershire; Swingfield, Southborough and Lewisham in Kent; Ashby-de-la-Zouch and Wigston Magna in Leicestershire; North Frodingham in the East Riding of Yorkshire; Daventry and parts of the Soke of Peterborough in Northamptonshire; and Atherstone in Warwickshire.[9]

The importance of common fields for grazing livestock is widely attested.

In Croston, Lancashire, there was a common field of some 400 acres, known as 'Croston-Finney', and around 1725, when an attempt was being made to enclose this field, it was claimed by many of the parishioners that 'Great Numbers ... in Croston, by their Cattle pasturing on the Finney, and imploying themselves in making of Cheeses, Butter, etc. do now subsist themselves and Families very well, but would be utterly ruined, at least rendered incapable of so doing, if the same were allotted and divided'.[10] As one historian observes, 'even cottages with no land attached were partly self-supporting from the use of the extensive rough pastures'.[11] In the parish of Newport, Shropshire in the 1760s there was a piece of land, called 'the Marsh', 'on which every inhabitant who opens a door to the street hath the privilege of keeping a cow or other beast'.[12] In Burton Latimer, Northamptonshire, there was a common wold of some 800 acres, and right of access to this common, for pasturing cows and for fuel, 'was not attached to land but to residence in the parish as a "Housedweller" '.[13] In the 1770s a writer on Gloucestershire noted that, although 'great improvements might be made by inclosing the wastes and commons' of the parish of Yate, on the edge of the Bristol coalfield, 'yet it may not be expedient to inclose them, as it would incapacitate many poor families from pursuing their present business, who now employ themselves in carrying coal from the pits to sell round about the country, and depasture their horses on these commons'.[14] When the rights of the commoners in Raunds, Northamptonshire were being threatened by enclosure in 1797, 'under the pretence of improving lands in the same parish' (as the commoners put it), they responded by arguing the benefits of the commons: they were able to turn 'a certain number of their cows, calves and sheep, on and over the said lands', and they could thereby 'maintain themselves and their families in the depth of winter' and later sell their lean stock to graziers for fattening.[15] Several parishes enjoyed common rights of pasturage in the extensive waste of Otmoor in Oxfordshire, and it was said that 'the greatest benefit was reaped by the cottagers, many of whom turned out large numbers of geese, to which the coarse aquatic sward was well suited, and thereby brought up their families in comparative plenty'.[16]

In many places commoners also enjoyed rights to collect fuel, thereby saving themselves a major expense. According to a pamphlet of 1772, in addition to 'the privilege of common for cows and sheep many months of the year', many commoners 'have likewise a right to cut turf, roots, and furze in some places, which must be a great advantage to those who have not money to purchase any other fuel'.[17] It was reported in 1795 that in Waterbeach, Cambridgeshire, each commoner 'has ... a right to dig as many Turfs as shall be wanting for the fuel of his own Household, (but not to sell any out of the Parish) which affords a comfortable provision for the poor in this necessary

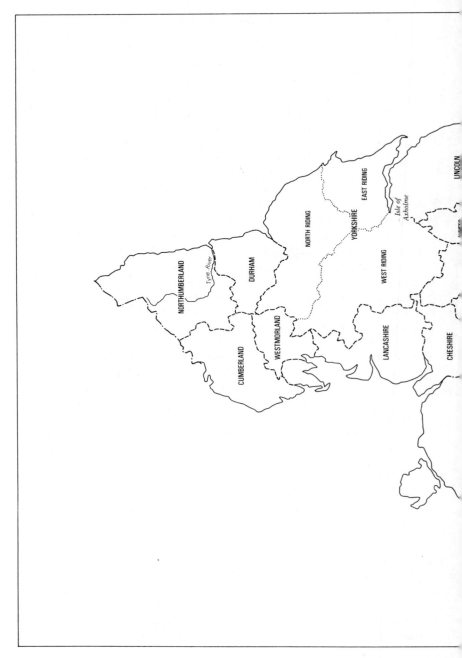

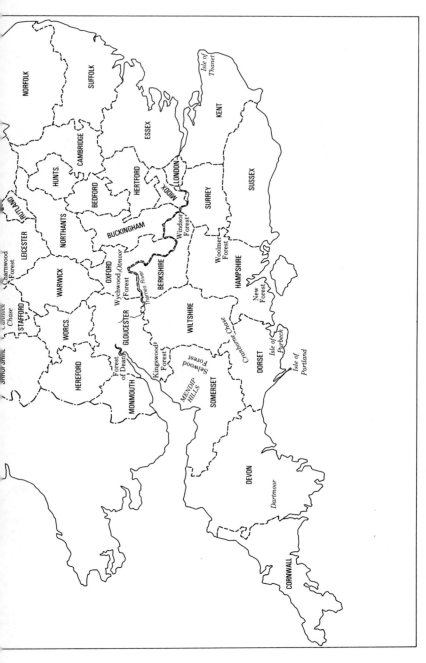

Counties of England *and various topographical features mentioned in the text*

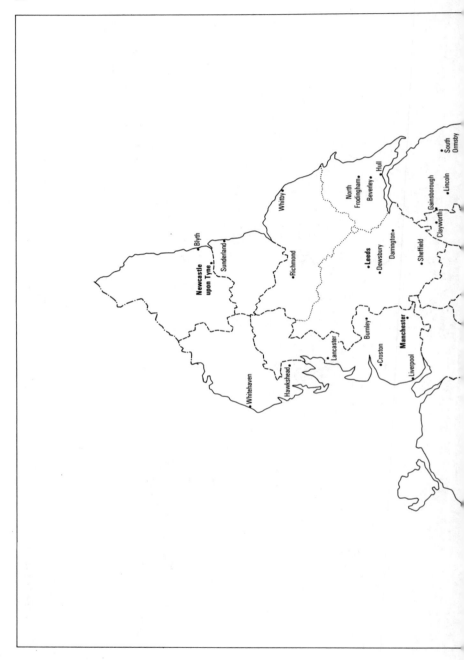

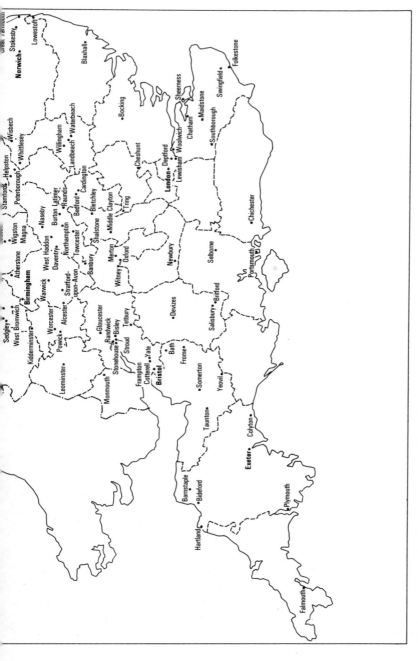

Cities, towns and villages *mentioned in the text*

article'.[18] A French visitor, in attempting to explain the popular disapproval
of enclosing common lands, noted in 1784 that 'the poor, from time
immemorial, have the right to cut the bracken and thickets for firewood';
and the Swedish visitor Pehr Kalm observed on several occasions the value
to the poor of the furze that was gathered from the common lands.[19] It has
been said that 'the high cost of bought fuel made the right to gather furze
from commons particularly valuable for poor commoners in Northamptonshire. Furze was used as firing in winter . . . it warmed cottages, [and]
fuelled bakehouses, limekilns, and brewers' pots'.[20] There is certainly extensive
evidence of the existence of fuel-rights of this sort — rights to obtain from
the commons peat, turf, bracken, furze, ling and brushwood. Even later
advocates of intensive commercial farming were able, on occasion, to
recognize the usefulness of these rights to the poor.[21]

Careful local research is beginning to reveal more clearly the widespread
importance of these various common rights. In a valuable study of common
rights and enclosure in Northamptonshire, a county that had much open
land, Jeanette Neeson has drawn attention to the extensive enjoyment of
these rights in 'champion' (that is, unenclosed arable) country and their
considerable value to so many of the county's smallholders, cottagers and
landless labourers.[22] She suggests that most household occupiers in unenclosed
parishes were commoners to some extent or other. Farmers, including many
small and part-time farmers, enjoyed substantial benefits from the common
rights — rights of access to the uncropped open fields (such as after the
harvest and during a time of fallow) and to the permanent pasture land — that
were attached to their landholdings: holdings that could be either leased or
owned as freehold. Similar, though usually less extensive, rights were attached
by law to a good many cottages. Moreover, in many open field parishes
completely landless inhabitants were also commoners, generally as a result of
their access to uncultivated pieces of land, the so-called 'wastes'. Even in a
county that was as intensively cultivated as Northamptonshire, a common
waste played an important role in the economies of a substantial minority of
open field parishes; and to these should be added the many other parishes
that had access to the thousands of acres of common grazing land in fens and
forests.[23] Common rights in open field parishes were also exercised over the
grass verges of roads and (according to one contemporary observer) the
'Baulks and Borders, and Slades and Bottoms, and other waste Places . . .
which the Farmer is never able to appropriate to himself or his sole using
(not even in the Years of Tilth, and much less in the Fallow-Season)'.[24]
Uncultivated land, then, was of considerable value to many labouring
households. Parishes that lacked such wastes 'could not provide the fuel, the
browse wood, the free range for pigs and poultry, the raw material for wood-

turning or rushwork, or the food (anything from nuts and berries to rabbits, hares and deer)' that were available, in varying degrees and according to the season, to the landless inhabitants of the county's forest and fenland parishes, and to those people who had access to 'the many woods and commons scattered along the western scarp and encircling Northampton'.[25]

Common rights were particularly prevalent and economically important in the forest regions of England. Indeed, almost all forests provided rich pickings for cottagers and smallholders, for they were areas of considerable 'openness': areas that were unenclosed and had never been fully colonized by the gentry and aristocracy, and access to which was both claimed and actually enjoyed by the majority of the people living in their vicinity. The forests served as well-stocked reservoirs of useful resources for families trying to sustain a subsistence economy. The naturalist Gilbert White, who lived on the edge of Woolmer Forest in Hampshire, noted that 'such forests and wastes . . . are of considerable service to neighbourhoods that verge upon them, by furnishing them with peat and turf for their firing; with fuel for the burning their lime; and with ashes for their grasses; and by maintaining their geese and their stock of young cattle at little or no expense'.[26] It was said that Cranborne Chase in Dorset 'afforded abundant material for firewood, fencing, hurdles, and spars for thatching'; in Sherwood Forest in Nottingham-shire, according to one traveller in 1755, 'the poor Inhabitants make a scanty Livelihood, by gathering the Fern and burning it, the Ashes of which they sell for making Soap' (a similar usage was observed in Cannock Chase in Staffordshire); and around 1779, when efforts were being made to enclose Needwood Forest in Staffordshire, some 250 cottagers, each of whom claimed the right to pasture two animals (usually cows) in the forest, asserted that these common rights 'are of great Importance to the Cottagers, for they, in a great Measure, contribute to the Support of their Families'.[27] Usages of this sort — and one could add others: the right to turn out pigs (known as mast or pannage), the right to collect nuts and berries, the right to take sand and gravel — were widespread in these forests and others, including Charnwood Forest in Leicestershire, the forests of Northamptonshire, the Forest of Dean in Gloucestershire, the New Forest and other forests in Hampshire, and Windsor Forest in Berkshire.[28] These use-rights were vital components of the household economy of the forest people. What one historian has said of the New Forest could be much more widely applied: 'the judicious exercise of rights of grazing and mast, supplemented by those of turbary [right to take turf for fuel], estovers [right to take wood for fuel], and marl, the cutting of bracken for bedding and litter, and gorse for fodder, enabled the small farmer or cottager to maintain himself in a state of independence or semi-independence, impossible of attainment without these rights'.[29]

Rights of direct access to the land, then, were highly valued by many country people. By means of these rights they could supply some of their own provisions and raise a few livestock for profit, and thereby reduce their dependence on both wages and purchased commodities. The right of women and children to glean — that is, the right to gather the unreaped and fallen grain from farmers' fields after the harvest — which was very widely claimed as a customary usage, frequently allowed families to satisfy their own grain requirements for perhaps two or three months of the year, and thus lessen their reliance on supplies from the marketplace.[30] Common rights afforded an important dimension of self-sufficiency in the household economy; they offered a basis for self-employment; and it is hardly surprising that the common lands themselves were sometimes known as the 'patrimony of the poor'. The resources available from the commons can be regarded as an extension of the productive economy of the cottage and the cottage garden, and as important supplements to the wages paid by employers. In Bisley, Gloucestershire, for example, the majority of the several hundred cottagers in the 1730s were principally employed in the woollen industry, as carders, spinners and weavers; but since there was a large common in the parish, of around a thousand acres, many of the workers' families were not completely dependent on wages, for they were able to keep cattle on these extensive wastes and thus better support themselves. This, at least, is what the commoners alleged when an enclosure bill threatened to deprive them of what they saw as their customary rights.[31]

However, important as common rights undoubtedly were in many districts, it should be recognized that in some regions they had probably never existed, in others they had already been partly eliminated, and in others still they survived only in an attenuated form. It has been said of Kent, for example, that

perhaps the greatest limitation of the commons in the agrarian economy of the county was the restricted areas which they served: in much of north Kent, especially towards the east, there was little or no waste, and in the Weald and even on the sandstone ridge there were many parishes where the commons were too small to be of much value to more than a handful of the poorer inhabitants.[32]

Kent, admittedly, was an extreme case, but in numerous other areas of intensive husbandry, especially the major grain-growing districts and the regions that were given over to large-scale sheep-farming — areas whose economies were dramatically different from those of, say, woodland districts — most of the land was under grass or active cultivation, often in already enclosed fields; commercial farming was in the ascendant and smallholdings had largely disappeared; and common rights, when they existed at all, were seldom of more than modest importance to the household economy. Common rights were certainly important in rural England, and their value and extent have too often been undervalued and depreciated by certain economic historians, especially by those whose enthusiasm for commercial farming sometimes runs away with them. But the fact still is that the actual economic value of commons varied greatly from place to place, sometimes to the point of irrelevance; and that wage-payment, in contrast, existed virtually everywhere and was probably the single most important means of support for the majority of labouring families in the early eighteenth century. Already in many parishes people relied almost completely on wages; and even in regions where common rights helped to sustain a partly self-sufficient household economy, the income available from wage-labour was normally an important component of the family's subsistence. Let us turn, then, to consider the sources from which these wages were obtained.

Wages in agriculture

In rural England the single most important source of wage-payment was farm labour. Since hardly any farming families were able to provide on their own all the labour needed on their farms at all times of the year, they were obliged to hire labourers to assist them with the tasks of the farming year — indeed, on the larger farms, labourers did almost all of the manual work. Arable and mixed farming, like most other forms of productive enterprise, was still very labour-intensive, and farmers depended heavily on their workmen to perform the large number of jobs that had to be done by hand. There were two main ways in which these workers were hired. Some of them, the 'servants in husbandry', were hired by the year and lived with their masters, where they received room and board in addition to an annual wage; they were regular, full-time agricultural labourers, continually under the authority of their employers to do whatever work was demanded of them. These farm servants were almost always unmarried, and most of them were less than 25 years old. They worked and lived in other people's households, not in their own or those of their parents. (I shall offer a fuller discussion of the character and significance of service in the next chapter.) Other workers, in contrast, were not hired as live-in servants but as wage-labourers who were paid by the day or the task as their services were needed to supplement the labour that was available from the farmer's own household. These men and sometimes women, who lived in their own (usually rented) cottages, were employed at the farmer's convenience, normally intermittently rather than regularly, to perform specific tasks according to seasonal demands.

The farming jobs for which labourers might be hired would vary, of course, from place to place, depending on the nature of the soils and the types of farming which were practised. In arable regions the seasons of ploughing and sowing, in autumn and spring, provided considerable opportunities for the employment of day-labourers. And at other seasons of the year workers would be hired, usually for short periods of time, for clearly defined purposes: threshing in the winter months; repairing hedges, building fences, digging and scouring ditches; felling trees, barking, chopping wood and faggoting in more wooded areas; mowing clover or grass, spreading manure, picking turnips, pulling woad; and in fielden parishes workers would be hired for such tasks as weeding, hoeing, harrowing and marling. In upland and sheep-corn districts men would be employed to help with the washing and shearing of sheep.

The season of easily the greatest demand for hired labour was the summer, the season of harvest. For each crop, as it ripened, there was just the right moment for harvesting, and when that moment arrived farmers wanted to get the job done as quickly as possible, while crop conditions were at their best and (they hoped) the weather stayed dry. Speed was of the essence, for delays could cause losses, and there was a great deal of work to accomplish in a short period of time. 'Esteem fair weather as precious, and mispend it not', recommended one authority, reflecting the conventional wisdom. During the wheat harvest, said Arthur Young of the farmer, 'Bad weather now greatly injures his profit: he must have many hands at work, to make the best use of fine seasons.'[33] A successful harvest, then, was only possible with the assistance of a large body of labourers hired especially for the occasion. So great was the demand for labour during the four or five weeks of the corn harvest that industrial workers often abandoned their ordinary labours in order to work as reapers, harvest gangs of skilled men were formed to negotiate favourable terms with farmers, and groups of Irishmen were commonly found migrating from farm to farm, some of whom may even have been grudgingly welcomed by farmers who desperately needed a few more hands. The overriding importance of getting in the crop ensured that this was a month of full employment. Similarly, though less intensively, haymaking, usually in July, afforded considerable short-term employment in many parishes; and in parts of Kent and Surrey hop-picking imposed at least as heavy demands upon the supply of labour as those experienced in corn-growing areas. Around 1790 William Marshall reported that 'whole families, indeed, the whole country, may be said to live in the fields during the busy season of hopping'. Even the daughters of tradesmen and other men of property, he claimed, 'are seen busy at the hop bins', and Maidstone 'is nearly deserted, in the height of the season. . . . Beside the people of the neighbourhood, numbers flock from the populous towns of Kent; and many from the metropolis; also from Wales; hop picking being the last of the summer works of these itinerants.'[34]

Wages from employment at farm labour, then, would have been an important component of the household economy of almost all country people, and even, because of harvest wages, of some town dwellers. Wage levels in the mid eighteenth century varied from region to region, but most of them probably fell within a normal range of 10 pence to 1s. 3d. per day; many employers gave their men allowances of beer (or cider in the West Country) in addition to money wages. Summer day-wages were often slightly higher than those in winter, partly because of the longer working day. The greatest rewards for labour were always received for harvesting: harvest wages were normally at least 50 per cent higher than those offered at other seasons, and farmers at this time of the year, recognizing the need to maintain good morale among their workers, were particularly inclined to be liberal with their provisions of food and drink — these, indeed, were perquisites which the labourers expected as a matter of customary right. When women were employed in the fields — and they sometimes were, especially at harvest, but also for such casual jobs as weeding and raking — they were usually allowed about half the wages given to men.

There were undoubtedly a few men who were employed more or less continuously at farm labour throughout the year: on the completion of one task they were hired again for different work, and by successfully linking together a series of seasonal jobs they were able to attain virtually full-time employment. But this was not the normal pattern of employment. Men who were hired as farm labourers for, say, 250 to 300 days of the year (a full working week comprised six days of labour), were considerably less numerous than those who were hired for less than 250 days, many of them for very much less. Winter, for instance, was a slack season; the demand for farm labour was low, and consequently many country people who had fairly regular employment between about March and November were unable to find enough work during the winter months.[35] Others still were only hired for the peak seasons of labour, in the spring and summer. Moreover, in pastoral regions there was a less active demand for hired labour throughout the entire year. Pastoral farming was not as labour-intensive as arable husbandry; sheep, in particular, required the services of only a small body of workmen. Consequently, in places where much of the soil was too poor for commercial cultivation — in upland regions especially — or where arable land had been converted to grass, families that did not occupy (even small) farms of their own, or had no access to common lands, would have been hard pressed to support themselves by relying largely on wages from farm labour. In both lowland and upland districts the irregularity of agricultural work might have been tolerable for families that enjoyed common rights, for then

the weight of wages in the equilibrium of the household economy would
have been rather more modest: they would have been supplements to the
partly self-sufficient modes of petty agrarian production which, as we have
seen, were sustainable when commons existed. But in many parishes there
were no commons at all. The result, then, was that agricultural underemployment, especially during the winter months, was a widespread and
basic reality of life. Wages from farm labour were important to the great
majority of rural households — indeed, they were probably vital, for harvest
wages alone were a tonic for most plebeian families in arable regions;
however, though necessary to a family's basic comfort and subsistence, they
were often insufficient by themselves. Further support had to be sought
through other, non-agricultural forms of employment.

These considerations help to explain why, by the early eighteenth century,
many rural households had come to be engaged in some form of industrial
by-employment. Agricultural underemployment forced people to look for
additional ways of getting wages: ways that would supplement the livelihood
they gained from agriculture, and that could be carried on in their own
cottages. At the same time merchant-manufacturers in a variety of industries
— such capitalists as clothiers, lace merchants, stocking masters, iron
masters, and button dealers — were searching for abundant supplies of cheap
labour, and they saw in the material circumstances of the countryside the
possibility of profit to themselves: profit that could be obtained without fear of
having to take account of the regulatory constraints of the trade guilds,
virtually all of which were city-based. There was a certain basic compatibility,
then, between the aspirations of these merchant-industrialists and those of the
country people. The former wanted labourers to do the actual manufacturing
— the 'working up' of the unfinished goods at the various stages of production
— that their numerous trades required; and the latter wanted to be able to earn
extra income by means of some employment that could be conveniently
grafted onto the traditional modes of subsistence associated with the rural
cottage economy. These were the roots of the domestic or putting-out system
of industry, a system in which cottage manufacturing was engaged in by
those families that were not fully and intensively employed on the land.

Rural industry

During the reigns of the later Stuarts the meshing of agricultural and
industrial employments was so pronounced in certain upland and pastoral
regions that some historians have spoken of the existence of an economy of
dual occupations: a household economy in which there was such an integral
relationship between farming (normally stock-keeping) and some kind of

cottage industry that it may be misleading to speak of 'by-employments' at all, for it is often the case that one means of livelihood cannot be clearly identified as predominant and the other as subsidiary. In rural south Lancashire, for instance, families frequently combined small-scale farming with textile work, especially weaving. Many men who were occupied as weavers also grew oats and potatoes or were otherwise employed in husbandry. When Richard Pococke was travelling in the Burnley area in 1751 he was told by a local youth, who was asked about his mode of living, 'that his father paid six pounds a year [for his holding], kept a horse, three cows, and forty sheep; that his father and he wove woollen both for their clothing and to sell'.[36] In the Rossendale region of south Lancashire, where there were no large landed proprietors, smallholdings were very common: families subsisted by grazing stock on the pasture and waste lands (little land was given over to tillage) and by making cloth; and the term 'yeoman', it is said, often indicated a 'landholder who divided his time between farming and weaving'.[37] A similar situation existed in many parts of the West Riding of Yorkshire, where families with modest landholdings were actively engaged in the woollen industry, many of whom worked independently of any large clothier. Here, according to Herbert Heaton, the 'alliance of land and loom was a great benefit to the clothing population, especially to the weavers, who often were compelled to lay aside the shuttle because of scarcity of yarn, but who were able to fill up this time by working in their garden, or by performing some necessary piece of work on the land attached to their house'.[38] Similarly, in south Yorkshire and the West Midlands during the late seventeenth and early eighteenth centuries many of the metalworkers - nailers, cutlers, scissorsmiths, scythesmiths - were also part-time farmers, some with only a few head of livestock, others with a much more substantial involvement in farming. By combining two occupations they were better able to cope with seasonal unemployment and other sorts of economic fluctuation, for a slump in one line of work did not necessarily spell complete disaster, and thus they were less likely to succumb to a condition of impoverishment, misery, and dependence. An economy of dual occupations, as Joan Thirsk has argued, 'was the best insurance that men with almost no savings and certainly no capital resources could have devised. If misfortune attended one activity, there was always the other to fall back on'.[39]

Even in places where dual occupations cannot be regarded as the norm, a significant minority of households often derived substantial benefits from both agriculture and some form of trade. Professor Hoskins found that in Wigston Magna, Leicestershire, 'there were at least a dozen tailors . . . in the late seventeenth century and nearly as many shoemakers. Almost without exception, they combined their trade with the cultivation of some land'.[40]

Around the same time in Middle Clayton, north Buckinghamshire, a parish completely owned by the Verney family, small-scale farming households were also engaged at various times in such diverse trades as building, blacksmithing, tailoring, innkeeping, carrying and carting, and making potash (a local specialty); one farmer took up weaving, another glove-making.[41] Around 1770 the woollen industry was well established in West Haddon, Northamptonshire, and at least one-fifth of these weavers and wool-combers also had small holdings of land.[42] Dual occupations were even found in some small country towns: until the middle of the eighteenth century the woollen weavers in Banbury, Oxfordshire, 'were mostly part-time workers, combining weaving with agricultural work'.[43] In the area of Frampton Cotterell, Gloucestershire, north-east of Bristol, a district that was full of rural industry, many men who were identified in contemporary documents as tailors, masons, weavers and other clothworkers, tanners, cordwainers, feltmakers and coal-miners can be shown from the probate inventories 'to have retained a substantial involvement in agriculture, in many cases equal in extent to that of yeomen and husbandmen..., in some cases so much so that, were it not for indisputable written attribution of their primarily non-agrarian occupation, one would have assumed they were either yeomen or husbandmen'.[44]

Occupational designations, then, can be seriously misleading, for in their apparent straightforwardness they often conceal much of the complexity of the household economies from which people supported themselves. A man was not always simply a farmer, or a weaver or a metalworker, or — the most difficult of all to interpret — a labourer, any more than most married women today could be usefully represented as 'simply' housewives. We want to learn about the actual activities in which people were involved. And people's livelihoods, even when they particularly depended on a single kind of employment, were usually derived from more than one occupational source. In the clay and heath regions of Dorset small farmers might be occupied in such by-employments as making ropes or nets, tanning, glove-making, and (on the Isles of Portland and Purbeck) the quarrying of stone.[45] Rural industry was common in the Arden district of Warwickshire by the early eighteenth century: some households were actively engaged in both farming and a craft, though others gained the bulk of their livelihood from some form of manufacturing (metalworking, weaving, woodworking).[46] Smallholders, commoners and cottagers in forest areas frequently found employment in carpentry, joining, sawing and coopering, as well as in such woodworking crafts as the making of rakes or ladders or hurdles.[47] In Kent fishermen 'might also be partly agricultural workers: thus in Thanet the mackerel season began in May when the barley sowing had ended, and the herring fishing took place between the end of the August harvesting and the wheat sowing in November'.[48] Such dovetailing of seasonal occupations was found as well among the miners in Cornwall, who often worked in the pilchard fishery during the peak autumn season,[49] and it was evidenced more generally in the priority that many industrial workers gave to harvest employment during the late summer, a season when the best wages were to be found in agriculture. Even a contrary piece of evidence reinforces our sense of these occupational interconnections: in July 1767, after a visit to Witney in Oxfordshire, famed for its making of blankets, Arthur Young reported that 'none of the manufacturers ever work for the farmers', but he regarded this as a 'remarkable circumstance'.[50] The iron industry probably offered less opportunity for ancillary employments than many other sectors of production — much of its labour was not organized under the putting-out system, for forges and furnaces required specialized work-places — but even here, according to T.S. Ashton, 'many labourers . . . held small plots of land which they cultivated in their spare time and which saved them from idleness when shortage of water, or other cause, brought the ironworks to a temporary stand'.[51]

In many corn-growing regions the character and extent of cottage by-employments were partly determined by the presence or absence of a large landowner in any given parish, and the authority that such a man could exercise. Many parishes in arable and lowland England were dominated by — indeed, sometimes completely controlled by — one large landlord. This was the parish of squire and parson — and, it is occasionally said, of quiescent and deferential parishioners — that is commonly regarded as the 'normal' village type. Such a dominant lord was not only concerned to ensure that what went on in the parish accorded with his own interests, he was also in a very strong position to successfully resist any uncongenial developments and to have his will obeyed. This was the classic 'closed' parish in which (normally) one man, by virtue of his overwhelming predominance as an owner of land, was able to control most of the locality's economic destinies and opportunities and the conditions under which people would be employed. Cottage industry was unlikely to take root in such parishes without the lord's approval.

Control of this kind, then, was potentially of great importance to the character of the local economy, for in closed parishes it was possible to restrict or even prohibit immigration, to disallow the construction of new cottages (the lord owned the land on which cottages would be built), and to prevent cottage industry from becoming established at all. Large landowners knew that labouring people in search of a livelihood tended to migrate to parishes where industrial employment could be found; that the population of these parishes usually increased very rapidly; and that as a result of this

growth in numbers the costs of poor relief, which were the sole responsibility
of the parish, not of any larger administrative unit — costs that had to be
borne largely by the parish's farmers, landowners, and other men of substance
— swelled to what were seen as intolerable levels. Rural industry, it was often
thought, was closely linked with rural poverty. It was just this concern that
induced the Dukes of Rutland to keep the hosiery industry out of Bottesford
in Leicestershire, a parish that they largely controlled.[52] All landowners
wanted a docile and dependent work force that was large enough to satisfy
their (and their tenants') demands for labour, just as they wanted to keep the
poor rates low; but only in closed parishes was it possible for landed
proprietors easily to attain these objectives — and attaining them often
involved prohibiting or strictly limiting the development of industry in their
parishes. By the early eighteenth century in South Ormsby, Lincolnshire, for
example, the 'up-to-date landowner, Burrell Massingberd, decided in future
not to have more cottages on his estate than he and his tenant farmers
required for their necessary labourers'.[53] Similar restrictions on the
construction of cottages were imposed by landowners in many closed villages
in the East Riding of Yorkshire.[54] Some large landowners even succeeded in
further minimizing the costs of poverty to themselves, for if an 'open' parish
was contiguous to their own — a parish in which landownership was
dispersed among a large number of smallish proprietors and immigration was
uncontrolled — they could allow their own cottages to become uninhabitable,
refuse to build new ones and thereby force some of their farm labourers, the
potential recipients of poor relief, to live outside the parish where other
ratepayers would be liable for their misfortunes.[55] In this way large landlords
and farmers could import labour as they needed it and export most of the
problems associated with seasonal fluctuations, unemployment and personal
distress. Not all large landowners were able to enjoy such a gratifying
imbalance of payments, but when they could they commonly worked
towards this goal. In closed parishes, then, industrial by-employments
among labouring men were often of little importance.

However, while large landowners might not have wanted their male
labourers and cottage tenants to take employment as weavers, framework-
knitters and the like, most of them did not object if the women and children
in these families earned modest incomes by means of some cottage craft. For
in this way the agricultural wages of the men could be supplemented by the
earnings of other family members, the household economy would thus be
made more resilient, and (it was hoped) there would be less need for
labourers to seek assistance from the poor law. For most landless families in
corn-growing districts — districts where both smallholdings and common
rights had long been in decline, and thus the opportunities for a substantial

degree of self-reliance based on access to land had been very much eroded — the earnings from the by-employments of women and often children were essential to the sustenance of their households. Landlessness inevitably led to a greater dependence on wage-payments, for both men and women, and underemployed women presented an attractive pool of cheap labour for merchant-manufacturers. Most of these women came to be employed in the making of textiles and wearing apparel. Undoubtedly the most widespread cottage by-employment was the spinning of yarn from wool or flax; indeed, the spinning-wheel may well have been the most ubiquitous industrial tool in eighteenth-century England, and spinning the most commonly practised industrial skill. Spinning was done almost everywhere, in both arable and pastoral districts, sometimes merely for a local market but often as part of a large-scale production for a mass market, as in much of East Anglia and parts of the South-west — usually at least six spinners were required to supply enough yarn for one weaver — and in many villages the majority of the women would have had part-time employment as spinners. Normally they were employed by clothiers or other middlemen and received on average perhaps three or four pence for a day's work. Other by-employments that women and often children took up were much less extensive than spinning and would have only been found in particular localities: hand-knitting in some villages, glove-making around Woodstock in Oxfordshire and in parts of Dorset and the counties bordering on Wales, button-making in a few places, straw-plaiting in southern Bedfordshire and northern Hertfordshire. Lace-making, which was much more common, was probably second only to spinning as a source of industrial employment for women and children in corn-growing regions: it was widely practised in Bedfordshire and Buckingham-shire, where it was the most prevalent form of industrial occupation, in parts of Northamptonshire, and in south-east Devon. In May 1714, when Ralph Thoresby was travelling through north-east Bedfordshire, an entirely rural district, he described it as a 'low moist country, abounding with willows, of which are made osier baskets, screens, etc. which, with bobbin-lace, seem the chief manufactures of these parts': and hardly any adult men would have been employed in such work.[56] In all these trades the work force was made up almost entirely of women and children.[57]

In most parts of central England rural industry — especially industry in which men were actively engaged — was likely to be much more highly developed in open than in closed parishes. For not all parishes were effectively dominated by one or two landlords who could rule with a commanding authority, subordinating all other interests to the maximization of their rent rolls. In some parishes the number of landowners was very large and no one lord exercised unchallenged authority; the ownership of land tended to be dispersed rather than concentrated, sometimes the soil itself was less suitable for intensive husbandry, and the institutions of social discipline, such as an active manorial court or a determined select vestry, were usually much less effective than in closed parishes. Open parishes, then, were much more accessible to immigrants, and as a result they experienced high rates of population growth. In time they became more densely populated than closed parishes, and since many of these people could not support themselves entirely (or even largely) from the available land, they were forced to seek a major portion of their sustenance from some form of domestic industry. Poverty and their tenuous involvement in agriculture made them turn to manufacturing in order to live.[58] These circumstances have received particular emphasis in the various accounts of the emergence of the framework-knitting industry in Leicestershire, Nottinghamshire and Derbyshire. This industry, which spread rapidly through the East Midlands from the late seventeenth century, tended to locate in those parishes that already had relatively large populations. As J. D. Chambers said of Nottinghamshire,

by the end of the seventeenth century, the industry of framework-knitting had taken root in many towns and villages of the region, its location being largely determined by the existence of cheap labour supplies in areas where population growth was encouraged by abundance of land for settlement or by the absence of institutional checks, such as the rigid control of settlement by landlords and parish officers.[59]

In Wigston Magna, Leicestershire, a populous village with no lord and many freeholders, about one out of every six households was largely dependent on framework-knitting by 1700; 'during the following century', according to W. G. Hoskins, the 'village became increasingly industrialized and its agricultural life correspondingly less important' (he estimates that at least one-third of the villagers were employed in manufacturing by the 1760s).[60] In the parish of Shepshed, Leicestershire, where there were many small proprietors and a major landlord who did not exert himself, the hosiery industry grew very rapidly in the course of the eighteenth century.[61] As in Wigston Magna, this industrial growth accounted for much of the village's expanding population. Population growth and rural industrialization were mutually reinforcing. So pronounced was the development of cottage industry in some open parishes that by 1800 a few of them had become heavily industrialized villages (not the same, it should be emphasized, as factory villages): parishes of dense settlement in which scores of households devoted themselves almost entirely to a cottage craft, and in which farming was already, or was rapidly becoming, a secondary occupation.

Self-sufficiency

In concluding this discussion of the modes of subsistence in rural England, we should emphasize, I think, the diverse character of most plebeian household economies. A labouring family around 1700 normally got its support, not from just one or two sources, but from a variety of activities. Its productive economy, one might say, was extensive rather than intensive. People tried to knit together a viable sustenance from a wide range of employments. We have already mentioned the value of common rights and the uses to which common lands were put. Even in places where few commons existed, many people had small cottage gardens where they could grow potatoes, cabbages, peas and beans; cottagers very commonly kept a pig or two, which could be fattened on almost anything; some had chickens or geese, a few kept bees. ('As the poorest family can often maintain a cat or a dog, without any expence', wrote Adam Smith, 'so the poorest occupiers of land can commonly maintain a few poultry, or a sow and a few pigs, at very little. The little offals of their own table, their whey, skimmed milk and butter-milk, supply those animals with a part of their food, and they find the rest in the neighbouring fields without doing any sensible damage to any body.')[62] Some of this produce they sold in the market, much of it they consumed directly. For most of them farm labour was an important source of income; and increasingly country people were taking up ancillary employments — spinning, weaving, knitting, glove-making, metalworking, and the like — to supplement the livelihood they gained from agricultural wages, a small-holding, or common rights. The returns from gleaning would provide some of the following year's bread, perquisites might be forthcoming from farmers and landlords (fuel allowances, cheap wheat, holiday treats and gratuities), a part of the wages from children in service would be returned to their parents, from a small plot of hemp or flax yarn could be spun (in 1776 Arthur Young noticed many hemp gardens between Wolverhampton and Shrewsbury),[63] and there were few deterrents against the casual 'poaching' of small game prior to the age of large game preserves and assiduous gamekeepers. It was standard practice for families to get their earnings from a variety of seasonal employments. In Selborne, Hampshire, for example, it was said by Gilbert White that 'besides the employment in husbandry the men work in hop gardens, of which we have many; and fell and bark timber. In the spring and summer the women weed the corn; and enjoy a second harvest in September by hop-picking.' They also did some spinning during the winter months.[64] A family's living, then, was usually obtained from a number of part-time and seasonal activities, and the more they could sustain this diverse economy, the better their security would be.

We can see as well, from evidence already presented and from many other sources, that plebeian households tried to attain at least a moderate degree of domestic self-sufficiency. The more they could produce directly for their own consumption, the less they would have to buy from the marketplace; and if their dependence on market purchases could be minimized, they would be less dependent for their livelihood and conveniences on the wages provided by employers. Providing for one's own needs by one's own efforts, without the mediation of wage-employment, made for greater self-reliance and independence, and these were goals that most people respected. They were also goals that many families were still able to satisfy, at least in part: getting a living outside the economic arena of contractual wage-payments was feasible and widely practised. Keeping a pig and some poultry, digging peat or collecting brushwood for fuel, having a plot of hay to provide fodder for a cow, growing potatoes or other vegetables in a cottage garden, collecting nuts or berries, making at least some of one's own clothing (shoes were always excepted, and thus the shoemaker was one of the most ubiquitous of craftsmen): these were some of the ways in which families would supply their own needs. It was said that in the Chichester area in the early eighteenth century 'spinning of household linen was in use in most families; also making their own bread, and likewise their own physic'.[65] In many places people made their own rushlights, by dipping rushes in animal fat, and were thus able to avoid buying candles. Gilbert White offered a detailed account of this — as he called it — 'very simple piece of domestic economy'. He was assured by an 'experienced old housekeeper . . . that one pound and a half of rushes completely supplies his family the year round, since working people burn no candle in the long days, because they rise and go to bed by daylight.' (In some places rushes were also used for plaiting mats or chair-bottoms.) This was the sort of economy that valued thrift and condemned waste: all resources were to be used for some purpose. White pointed out that the 'careful wife of an industrious Hampshire labourer obtains all her fat for nothing; for she saves the scummings of her bacon-pot' for dipping the rushes.[66] A similar sense of prudent resource management was found in parts of Lincolnshire, where, according to one Christopher Merret, surveyor of the port of Boston, who reported his observations in the 1690s:

the Country People gather up the Dung of Oxen and Cows, which they temper with Water, and spread on the Ground about Five Inches thick, and cut it out in oblong pieces of about a Foot, and call them Dithes, which they use for Fewel (but they smell strong); in some places they make Walls of them for Fencing . . . . They also gather up Hogs-dung and steep it in Water, and having well stirred it, strain it, and so use it to wash Cloaths, which, when bleached in the Summer, will become white and sweet; hence the Proverb, *Lincolnshire, Where the Hogs shit Soap, and the Cows shit Fire.*[67]

Urban occupations and mining

While most Englishmen got a major portion of their living from various agricultural employments, many others were already entirely (or almost entirely) detached from any direct involvement in the agrarian economy. They were employed in industry, trade and transport, and various forms of service and provisioning. Some of them were skilled craftsmen who commanded high wages or who worked independently; but most had specialized skills that were either in ample supply or were fairly easy to learn, and others were casual labourers, patching together a tenuous sort of existence from whatever jobs were available in the volatile economies of the expanding towns and cities. These were men and women whose household economies had come to be fully absorbed in urban and industrial modes of life — and their numbers were growing rapidly. In some parts of the country the human landscape was being dramatically transformed. In 1776, when Arthur Young was touring the area just north of Birmingham, he observed on the way to West Bromwich that 'the road for 5 or 6 miles is one continued village of nailers', and that around Wednesbury 'the whole country smoaks with coal-pits, forges, furnaces, etc. Towns come upon the neck of one another, and large ones too.' Agriculture was in a completely subordinate position: between Birmingham and Wolverhampton he 'saw not one farm-house, nothing that looked like the residence of a mere farmer'.[68] As manufacturing enterprises grew and prospered and came to be concentrated in particular regions, these local economies became predominantly industrial in character: metalworking in Sheffield and Birmingham, pottery in north Staffordshire, the making of linens and cottons in the towns of south Lancashire, coal-mining around Newcastle, a variety of specialized industries in the Bristol area (distilling, sugar-refining, glass-making, brass working), woollen manufacturing in various regions. In all these places there was a large and usually specialized industrial work force. The town of Stroud, for example, was a major centre of the Gloucestershire woollen industry, employing large numbers of workmen and dominating the local economy, as an account from the 1770s makes abundantly clear:

Many hands are employ'd in the various branches of the manufacture, as in cleansing the wool by picking and washing it; in scribbling and spinning it; spooling and warping the yarn; weaving the cloth; burling, milling, and rowing it; then in shearing and dressing it; and, if to be sent off coloured, in dying it; and lastly, in pressing and packing it; and most of these processes are carried on by distinct workmen. As spinning requires most hands, some of the clothiers send their wool to the distance of twenty miles or more, and the poor women and children, for that extent of country, work at this branch, which makes it difficult to ascertain the numbers employ'd in the manufacture. Most of the other branches are carried on at the mills, or at the clothiers houses; but the weavers work at home. There are in this parish eighteen clothing mills, and about thirty master clothiers.[69]

Industrial centres of this kind were, of course, producing their specialized goods for a national and international market, and as domestic consumption steadily increased and colonial markets expanded dramatically, employment opportunities in industry grew apace. This growth was uneven, both in time and space, and some older centres of industry fell upon hard times. But in general industrial expansion was much more prominent than industrial decline, especially in the Midlands and the North. Northampton became an important centre for the manufacture of boots and shoes; Leicester and Nottingham, both of which were quiet country towns around 1700, had developed into major centres of the hosiery industry by the end of the century. The Birmingham-Wolverhampton region was already becoming famous for its enterprising dynamism, the rapid growth of its population and the skill and inventiveness that were associated with its many thriving industries. Some of these trades employed skilled workmen, such as buckle-makers, locksmiths, gunsmiths, chapemakers, and scythesmiths — though nailers, who were relatively unskilled and poorly paid, were much more numerous than any of these more 'honourable' trades. In other industries a minute division of labour was emerging, usually under close managerial supervision. In 1755 a traveller to Birmingham inspected

the Manufactory of Mr. Taylor, the most considerable Maker of Gilt-metal Buttons and enamell'd Snuff-boxes: We were assured that he employs 500 persons in those two Branches, and when we had seen his Workshop, we had no Scruple in believing it. The Multitude of Hands each Button goes thro' before it is sent to the Market, is likewise surprising; you perhaps will think it incredible, when I tell you they go thro' 70 different Operations of 70 different Work-folks.[70]

Josiah Wedgwood was developing similar modes of assembly-line production in his Staffordshire pottery works, as were several of the manufacturers of pins, who employed mostly female labour.[71]

England has a long coastline in relation to its land mass, and given the long-standing importance of the sea in English commercial life and foreign affairs, it is not surprising that numerous jobs in coastal towns were directly related to the maritime economy. Employment geared to the sea was of four main types. First, there were the men employed in the fishing industry. Fishermen were found in most coastal regions — it is said, for instance, that all along the coast of Kent, from the mouth of the Thames, fishing 'gave a livelihood for some of the inhabitants of nearly every water-bound parish';[72] and in a few places it had already emerged as the most important local industry and a major source of employment. Fishermen were particularly prominent in such towns as Folkestone, Lowestoft, Great Yarmouth, Whitby and Bideford. Second, employment was available in the ship-building industry. Many of the private shipyards were small enterprises, employing only a few men; but the great naval dockyards at Portsmouth, Plymouth, Chatham, Deptford, Sheerness and Woolwich (the first three were the most important) were, by contemporary standards, very large undertakings, employing a multitude of shipwrights, caulkers, joiners, riggers, sailmakers, sawyers and various other workmen. Approximately 5000 men were at work in these royal dockyards in 1754.[73] Third, many men in port towns made their living as seamen; most commonly they were hired for voyages to other parts of Europe and for coastal shipping, such as the coal trade between the North-east and London. In the small port of Blyth in Northumberland, to take one local example, seamen were very prominent: of the 262 names entered in the burial registers between 1763 and 1799 for which occupations are given, 75 are of sailors, with 38 labourers the next largest group.[74] Employment as a seaman, however, did not necessarily preclude other kinds of work. As one authority has said, 'besides the regular sailors who gained their livelihood exclusively from the sea, there was a substantial fringe of men who came and went irregularly, making the odd voyage from time to time but taking other jobs in the interval'.[75] Fourth, an active port always provided distinctive forms of employment for the resident townspeople. It has been said of Hull, one of the most flourishing of the provincial ports, that 'the repair and maintenance of ships gave work for a variety of craftsmen, including ropers, block- and sail-makers, caulkers, holders, ship's-carpenters, and anchor-smiths, as well as custom for vendors of pitch, tar, sails, cordage, and other tackle'. Moreover, ships had to be supplied with foodstuffs, sailors and travellers required accommodation and entertainment, and the 'facilities in the port for the handling of cargoes provided jobs for wharfingers, keelmen, porters, and sledmen'.[76] Jobs of this kind — jobs that were ancillary to shipping and dependent on the port — were also common in other major coastal cities, such as Bristol, Liverpool and Newcastle.

Industrial and port cities were growing especially rapidly — the population of Birmingham, for instance, rose from around 10,000 to 12,000 in 1700 to about 45,000 by 1780, and that of Liverpool from around 6000 to almost 40,000 during the same period[77] — but the expansion of the urban population was a more general phenomenon, also affecting county capitals and many small market towns. And this urban expansion meant that more people came to be employed in trade and transport, in construction, and in

the victualling and distributive trades. With the emergence of a resident
gentry in many provincial cities — a new development in this period — more
employment was available in domestic service and provisioning. The expansion
of trade and manufacturing meant that more jobs were available for all sorts
of carriers, carters and boatmen, whether their burden was coal, corn,
pottery, textiles or people. The droving trade must have also increased. And
with this growth of traffic, combined with the greater disposable wealth of
propertied families in provincial cities, the public facilities for lodging,
victualling and entertainment expanded and became more elaborate. Public
houses, in fact, were extremely numerous. Around the middle of the
eighteenth century the small market town of Somerton in Somerset, with a
population of about 1000, had sixteen inns, some of them quite substantial
(like many other towns, Somerton had a brisk wayfaring trade); Devizes in
Wiltshire, with about 3000 inhabitants, had forty-one licensed public houses
of varying quality; and Tetbury in Gloucestershire, with a population of
around 2200, is said to have had forty-two licensed victuallers in 1755.[78]
Innkeepers cannot, of course, be regarded as members of plebeian society,
but their ample presence implies the employment of numerous servants
(ostlers, chambermaids, kitchen help) and the existence of a brisk local
market, usually a source of at least a modicum of casual and semi-skilled
employment.

In any town of, say, at least 1000 people, and even in some smaller places,
there was a distinct body of artisans and tradesmen who would have served
an exclusively local market. The most common of these craftsmen were
probably the shoemaker, carpenter, tailor, blacksmith, butcher, baker,
mason and wheelwright, though others may have been especially prominent
in particular regions. (While smallish villages often had one or two craftsmen
— perhaps a smith in one place, a thatcher or a joiner in another — specialized
crafts were more likely to be concentrated in market towns.) In most towns
around one-third of the working population were employed in trades
concerned with the three basic necessities of life — victualling, building and
clothing — and this estimate would exclude the workmen in any specialized
industry that a town may have had, such as the shoemakers in Northampton
or the wool-combers in a worsted district. Furthermore, in places of some
importance — a regional centre, a cathedral city, indeed any town to which
many people of property were disposed to resort — there would have been a
select group of very specialized artisans who offered skills that were less
likely to be found in smaller towns, and most of whom were heavily
dependent on the custom of prosperous families: the saddler, the watch-
maker, the upholsterer, the cabinet-maker, the harness-maker, the collar-
maker, the chandler and the stay-maker who served a fashionable market.[79]
The prosperity of the men in these diverse traditional crafts varied enormously.

A few of them had become masters, employing other men, and can thus be regarded as people of weight and substance. More commonly, though, they should be seen as members of the labouring elite, as men of independence and some degree of security who practised a marketable skill, but (as a genteel observer would have said) 'mechanics' all the same. Most of them were engaged in small workshop production for the local market, and they normally retailed their own wares. Such men would have qualified for membership in the group which Defoe described as 'the working Trades, who labour hard, but feel no want'. Others still, especially those in London, were only a little better off than common labourers, for they had no shop of their own and never advanced beyond being wage-dependent journeymen.

London, the largest city in Europe, was almost a world to itself. With a population of approximately 675,000 in the mid eighteenth century, it accounted for about ten per cent of the total population of England and Wales. No other English city was as much as one-tenth the size of London. It was a metropolitan giant; it was the focal point of many of the nation's political, social, and cultural activities; and it was a huge consumer market that required a multitude of services and supplies. London was a cosmopolitan city, with a complex and highly differentiated economy, and an extremely diverse labour force marked by many gradations of status, pay and security.

Tens of thousands of people found employment because of London's position as both a major port and a vast and concentrated market that had to be supplied with basic necessities. The city needed great quantities of grain, coal, fish and meat, vegetables, fruit and dairy products; and the transporting and distribution of these staples required much loading and unloading, hauling and carrying, storing and marketing — and all with virtually no mechanical assistance. Many men, then, were employed as coal-carriers, porters and wagon drivers, and as watermen and drovers; both men and women worked as street and market sellers (they hawked vegetables, fish, fruit and numerous other commodities), and as petty shopkeepers selling such cheap items as tripe, gin and old iron; some women found work as perambulating milk-sellers, some men were engaged to care for the horses employed in the carrying trade. London was easily the busiest and most important port in the kingdom: this importance was partly a function of the size of its consumer market (vast quantities of coal, for example, were shipped annually by water from Tyneside and Sunderland to the metropolis), and partly a result of its predominant role in overseas shipping. The port of London was at the centre of England's expanding overseas trade, both colonial and European; it was a great entrepôt for goods in transit, its docks were crowded (often overcrowded) with ships from abroad, and both sides of the Thames were alive with those trades and industries that depended on the port. London's port, then, was a vital source of livelihood for thousands of riverside workers: dockers, warehousemen, sailors, coal-heavers and lightermen, as well as the workmen in such industries as shipbuilding, coopering and sugar-refining.[80]

Since London was also the capital city, and the principal place of assembly and seasonal residence for the richest and most fashionable families in the country — those families that occupied the elegant houses in the newly developed residential estates in the West End — and also the normal place of abode for a large number of merchants, tradesmen and men of the professions, it presented a vigorous market for the kinds of services and specialized skills that depended on a concentration of wealthy consumers. The jobs dependent on such affluence were mostly of two types: those involved in the production of luxury goods and those involved in the provision of routine services to a leisured class. London, as the acknowledged source of high fashion and good taste, was the natural centre for the manufacture of all sorts of sophisticated consumer goods. In London gentlemen and their ladies could arrange purchases from jewellers, silversmiths, cabinet-makers, coach-makers, clock-makers, mantua-makers, haberdashers and the makers of musical and optical instruments. As a centre of the arts, and with its large reading public, London offered employment to compositors and engravers. Many of these skilled craftsmen pursued their trades in small workshops and earned good wages: they were the elite of London's workmen. In contrast, those employed in services were much more numerous and much less well paid. Some were employed as personal and domestic servants — as footmen, barbers, cooks, housemaids, scullery maids and ladies' maids; others found jobs in coffee houses, inns and taverns, and as carmen and chairmen; and others still were engaged — these were among the most menial and dreariest of jobs — as washerwomen, charwomen, seamstresses, milliners' assistants, chimney sweeps and scavengers.

Most of the rest of London's working people were employed in either the building trades or in some industry that was geared to a fairly broad consumer market. The construction workers included not only a variety of skilled craftsmen - bricklayers, carpenters, glaziers, plasterers and the like - who often received good wages when work was available, but also their many unskilled assistants, most of whom were casual labourers. Many of these building artisans were journeymen rather than independent masters, as were most of the men employed in the (comparatively) mass-oriented industries: tailors, shoemakers, hatters, stay-makers, chair-makers, chandlers, and breeches-makers. The work in many of these industries was already so subdivided into specialized and mechanical tasks that the qualities of individual craftsmanship had been substantially eliminated. The only large-scale industry for which London was still particularly noted (aside from shipbuilding), and which remained concentrated in the capital, largely in the Spitalfields district, was silk-weaving, a trade that was highly dependent on the winds of fashion in high society. Although a few of the silk-weavers worked as independent masters, the bulk of them were ill-paid journeymen in the employ of large capitalists. The material realities of life for most of these workers were very uncertain and full of tribulations. Except for a minority of highly placed servants and those skilled artisans in exclusive trades, and perhaps some of those fortunate younger men who as yet had few cares, most of the labouring people in London were of that class which Defoe described as 'the Poor, that fare hard', and a sizeable minority — the uprooted, the unemployed, the handicapped, the unskilled — were of the lowest social standing, those whom he represented (almost certainly correctly) as the 'Miserable, that really pinch and suffer Want'.[81]

The only considerable body of labouring men yet to be noticed are those who were employed in the various mining industries. Lead-mining was conducted in Derbyshire and the northern Pennines, tin- and copper-mining in Cornwall, and salt-mining in Cheshire. But the digging of coal was easily the most widespread and the most important of the extractive industries. The North-east (Durham and Northumberland), where thousands of colliers were at work, was certainly the leading region for coal-mining, but there were numerous other areas where the industry was important enough to employ at least 300 or 400 men, and sometimes many more: southern Yorkshire, the Derbyshire-Nottinghamshire border, north-east Warwickshire, south Staffordshire, east Shropshire, the Forest of Dean, sections of north-east Somerset and the area just east of Bristol, parts of south Lancashire and the Whitehaven district of Cumberland. Moreover, with the increasing demand for fuel, stemming from both urban and industrial growth, along with the complete inadequacy of wood and charcoal supplies for this purpose, coal production was rapidly expanding and the work-force in the colliery districts was increasing apace. J. U. Nef estimated the number of colliers in the late seventeenth century at 15,000 to 18,000 (with Scotland included),[82] and their numbers must have increased at least threefold in the course of the following century. In some areas, though, especially where coal could be easily dug from shallow pits, and thus little capital investment was required, mining was probably a part-time and often seasonal occupation, like many other forms of labour.[83]

Three general observations can be made of the labouring people in these mining regions. First, the wages of the actual pitmen were normally fairly high in relation to agricultural wages. Second, colliery villages, which were usually completely dominated by this one industry, tended to be socially distanced from the settlements around them. They were inclined to be

inward-looking, their members stuck closely together, and they had a strong
sense of their own distinctive culture. Third, and partly as a consequence of
the miners' social cohesiveness and cultural peculiarities, they were commonly
regarded by genteel observers as a strange, uncouth and rather frightening
breed of men — men who, in their manners and modes of life, seemed to be
about as far removed from the conventions of polite society as it was possible
to be.

As one can see, the variety of urban and industrial employments was great,
and because of this diversity in the circumstances of labour it is very difficult
to offer satisfactory generalizations about the character of work and the
common experiences of the workers themselves. For any discussion of this
large body of people might embrace nailers and servants in London, miners
and seamen, weavers and carriers, carpenters and street traders. Obviously,
the experiences of work, and the customs and consciousness associated with
work, would have varied dramatically from one trade to another. And yet,
underlying this diversity, there are certain features of labour that would have
been widely observed. First, employment in most trades was markedly
irregular, largely because of seasonal fluctuations in the demand for labour.
In the metropolis the 'London season' resulted in a brisk demand for a wide
range of services, provisions and specialized manufactures, but in the
summer and autumn, when many propertied families had retired to their
country houses, the capital's labouring people had trouble finding work. This
kind of seasonal underemployment was very common. Work on the docks
was always irregular, for overseas shipping was seasonal, and the winds that
moved the ships were capricious; transport difficulties in the winter affected
production patterns in numerous industries; and failures in the delivery of
materials, or periods of overproduction, or the sudden closing of foreign
markets would commonly put people out of work. Irregularity of employment,
in fact, was more likely to be the norm than the exception. Second, among
the workers in certain trades there was an intense consciousness of differences
in status: a closely observed gradation of privilege, authority and material
benefits. There was, for instance, a clearly perceived occupational hierarchy
among domestic servants, colliery workers and many of the skilled crafts in
London. One servant was not just like another, and in any trade some men —
men with the greatest experience, natives of a city, men who enjoyed the
'freedom' of a corporate body — took precedence over others. Third, in
numerous trades it seems that perquisites — that is, payments and benefits in
kind that were supplementary to normal wages — afforded substantial
additional earnings for many working people. Miners expected free fuel;
other workmen laid claim to the 'scrap' from their trade, commonly defining
this scrap in a generous manner. Servants claimed vails from visitors,

dockers and porters the 'sweepings' from spilt cargoes, shipyard workers the 'chips' from the leftover timber. Workers usually treated these sorts of perquisites as customary rights. Such customs, which employers came to condemn as 'embezzlement' or 'pilfering', were regarded by most workmen as the legitimate diverting of accessible materials into one's own possession: acceptable actions of 'helping yourself' to small portions of the commodities that passed through one's hands.[84] These are all aspects of labouring life that were widely experienced. Furthermore, and of particular importance, in discussing the experiences of work we must also attend to the question of the *control* over the conditions of labour: the relations between capitalists and workers, as revealed in the work place; the changes in these relations; and the conflicts that arose as a result of the changing terms and conditions of employment. These, indeed, are matters that will reappear more prominently in the last two chapters.

Concluding reflections

In the course of this discussion I have paid little attention to those nuances of chronology that help us to distinguish one generation from another and continually force upon our attention the reality of social change. And yet the kind of image that we might legitimately have in mind of the modes of production in, say, 1780, and the variety of positions in which the labouring people were situated, would be quite different from the sort of image that might be appropriate for the social reality of the late seventeenth century. If we try to blend together a collection of diverse evidence from a period of some four generations, and force it to march under one banner, the 'eighteenth century', we are apt to end up with too many analytical blurs. For the emphasis given to a particular characteristic of society at one period of time — perhaps the economy of dual occupations or the prevalence of customary sources of subsistence — might be inappropriate if applied outside its proper bounds. An adequate sensitivity to the processes of change, then, and their implications for plebeian society, is vital. Moreover, we require as well a proper sense of balance and discrimination in the task of social reconstruction. This sense of balance involves problems of composition and correspondence between art and external reality that are similar to those confronting, say, a portrait painter. And it involves as well an attentiveness to the 'weighing' of things in relation to one another that is inherently quantitative. Unfortunately, given the limitations of the primary sources and (with a few exceptions) their unsuitability for statistically conscious inquiries, quantitative statements can usually be no better than very rough estimates, and sometimes it is virtually pointless to estimate at all. We do not know —

and probably never will know — even the approximate number of men who made a significant portion of their living from fishing or from transportation, or the number of women engaged full- or part-time in spinning, and the relative weight of spinning in the household economy. In discussing a particular rural district around 1700 it may be extremely difficult — perhaps even impossible — to judge with any precision the relation between income from wages and non-monetary forms of sustenance, or the proportions of the 'mix' of agricultural and industrial employment. The possibilities for quantitative exactness are rare, especially at the national level. Many of our representations of social reality, then — representations involving such modifiers as 'many', 'some', 'a few', 'often', and the like — are inescapably matters of judgement and contextual understanding. All such representations are liable to be refined or revised, but whatever their fate the severe limits to the 'measurability' of social reality will continue to be a critical challenge to any attempts at such historical reconstruction.

However, the question still remains: what were some of the principal changes in the modes of plebeian subsistence between the later seventeenth and the later eighteenth centuries? There was certainly an indisputable movement of the labouring population — gauged in relative terms — away from the countryside. The movement, though, in aggregate, was not dramatically apparent: the rural population, which comprised approximately 75 per cent of the total population in 1700, still represented around two-thirds of the country's inhabitants in 1800. London accounted for about 10 per cent of the nation's population throughout the century, and the absolute numbers of the country dwellers continued to grow until the mid nineteenth century. But within this very broad framework of continuities major changes were at work. A growing proportion of the work force was becoming employed full-time in manufacturing: these people were found both in industrial villages — Shepshed and Wigston Magna in Leicestershire are two well-documented examples — and, more spectacularly, in those rapidly expanding centres of industry and trade that so impressed contemporary observers. Cities such as Birmingham, Liverpool, Manchester and Leeds, which were little noticed in the late seventeenth century, had grown to such heights by 1800 that they were a constant source of wonderment and commentary. A survey of the English economy in the earlier period might be excused for paying little heed to, say, the Birmingham area; by the 1780s or 1790s such neglect would be unthinkable. This process of industrial and commercial expansion in the provinces, which was especially pronounced in the second half of the century, was accompanied by the accelerated growth of an urban and industrial proletariat. Moreover, this increasing dependence on wages was becoming more marked in rural areas as well, for with the growing pressure of population on the available resources of land, the consolidation of farms into larger and more capital-intensive units, and the erosion of common rights, the kind of smallholder or cottage economy that was fairly prevalent under the later Stuarts became less and less sustainable. These are all themes that will warrant closer attention in our final chapter. For the moment it is sufficient to acknowledge, in the wake of a discussion that has been predominantly static and structural in character, the importance of appreciating the processes of change through which people lived and as a result of which their lives were altered, and to declare an intention to raise such questions below when they can be considered at greater length and against a more detailed background.

Finally, let us return to the theme of the household economy. For whatever the changing pressures that impinged upon, or even transformed, people's lives, the efficiency of the family economy continued to be the compelling priority in plebeian life. And this family economy was not normally centred around a single breadwinner: rather, it was assumed that the family's sustenance would depend on the productive contributions of all its members, each of whom helped to sustain the whole. A wife was always a working woman — indeed, marriage itself was, in part, an economic partnership — and children were usually put to work at an early age. Contemporary sources are full of references to the gainful employment of women and children. We have already noticed that women were actively engaged in a wide range of domestic industries — spinning, carding, knitting, lace-making, silk-winding, glove-making, the making of shirt buttons, the repairing of fishing nets; and in many of these trades children — especially girls — were expected, from an early age (perhaps at around 6 or 7), to help their mothers by performing such simple but necessary tasks as quilling, covering wire for the making of buttons or winding thread on bobbins. As they grew older these children would be taught the requisite skills of a particular handicraft, usually getting small earnings as they learned, earnings that were regarded as contributions to the family economy. William Hutton, whose father was a wool-comber, was born in Derby in 1723, and he recalled in his memoirs that in 1729 there was talk about sending him to work. 'Consultations were held about fixing me in some employment for the benefit of the family. Winding quills for the weaver was mentioned, but died away. Stripping tobacco for the grocer, in which I was to earn fourpence a week, was a second; but it was at last concluded that I was too young for any employment.' The next year, however, at the age of 7, he was sent to work in Lombe's silk factory in Derby.[85] In lead, tin and copper mining districts women and children were commonly employed at such jobs as breaking, sorting and washing the ore and pushing wagons and barrows; and young boys were normally hired to control the ventilation trap-doors in coal mines. Women were often employed in nail-making shops, and in London the wives of labouring men contributed to their families' sustenance by sewing and stitching, hawking goods in the streets or taking in laundry. In 1782 two-thirds of the housewives in Cardington, Bedfordshire, were engaged in a cottage handicraft, usually either lace-making or spinning, and many girls were similarly employed.[86] Female and child labour was not, for the most part, a matter of free choice: it was a matter of necessity. Few families could subsist for long from the earnings of only the head of the household. The smooth functioning of the family economy, then — an intimate economy of closely knit interdependence — was a fundamental preoccupation of almost all labouring people. And for most of them the family was also a central unit of social experience and personal relations: the small stage on which the everyday transactions of life were acted out. The phases through which families developed, the processes of personal development within these families, the passages in life that many people experienced, the hazards that threatened the security of families and individuals: these are all issues of considerable importance, and they are the principal concerns of the chapter that follows.

3 *Facts of life*

The brevity of life, the transience of human experience, has been a recurrent theme in poetic expression. In an episode from Bede's *Ecclesiastical History of the English People*, for example, the life of man was likened by one speaker to the swift passage of a sparrow in the winter time through the King's banqueting hall, 'coming in by one door and flying out through another'. It 'soon returns from winter back to winter again, and is lost to sight. So this mortal life seems like a short interval'.[1] Such metaphors have been commonplace in the creative arts. However, their representation of the passage of time, even at their most vivid and evocative, are usually of little assistance to the historical, as distinct from the religious, imagination. For the passage through life that they imagine normally omits, in the interest of poetic intensity, any sense of process or development, or any conception of the human relationships that are formed and nourished and extinguished in the course of an individual's life: and these processes of social change are clearly the historian's central concern. And at the centre of life, as experienced from birth till death, was the family: the family into which an individual was born and spent his or her early years, the frequently different families in which a person lived and worked as a youth, the new family that was established at marriage, and the changing character of the life of this family before death broke it up. At all times the family was a central focus for most people's experiences. Understanding the nature of these familial relationships, their dynamics over time, and the position of the family in the larger society are the principal objectives of the discussion that follows.

From childhood to adulthood

The experience of childhood in the families of labouring people is, unfortunately, almost entirely unknown to us. We have virtually no evidence concerning the treatment of babies, the practices of child-rearing, the familial sentiments involved in parent-child relations, and the expectations that children had of their parents and parents of their children. These are intimate aspects of life that were hardly ever documented, and it is unlikely that we will ever be able to say much about them. This lack of evidence has not prevented some writers from advancing rather large statements about the character of plebeian family life — statements that are too often wildly speculative and almost entirely unsubstantiated. In actual fact we are warranted largely to keep silent on these matters. About the only statement that can be offered with a high degree of confidence is that many infants died at an early age. It is probable that during the three generations before about 1750 the infant mortality rate (deaths during the first year of life) rarely fell below 150 per 1000 at risk: in most places about one baby in five died before its first birthday, and in some particularly unhealthy parts of the country, such as the metropolis of London, the infant death rate was even higher. Childhood, then, was an extremely precarious period of life. Even the children born to noble families in the first half of the eighteenth century had less than a 75 per cent chance of surviving until their fifth birthday. It is probably fairly safe to estimate that, among labouring families throughout the country at large, approximately 30 per cent of their children died before the age of five.[2] In contrast to contemporary industrial societies, where most deaths are among older people, infant deaths in the eighteenth century bulked large in the total profile of mortality. During the mid eighteenth century in London, for instance, nearly 45 per cent of all the recorded deaths were of children under 6.[3]

A high rate of infant and child mortality, then, was a fundamental reality of life. In numerous genteel families, families whose histories we can trace with reasonable ease, only half, or even a minority, of the children born to a husband and wife survived into adulthood — Edward Gibbon, for example, had five brothers and one sister who died in infancy, and Samuel Pepys, whose parents had had eleven children, was the only child in his family to live past the age of forty (three died in early middle age, the rest probably in childhood). Some fortunate families lost only one child, or perhaps none at all; others were decimated. There is no doubt as to the general cause of these manifold infant deaths. Babies and young children are particularly vulnerable to infectious diseases, and in any society where the nature of infection is not understood, where sanitary measures are primitive, where techniques of immunization are unknown, and where chemotherapeutic interventions are still mostly ineffectual, the rate of infant mortality is bound to be high. It was the prevalence of infant deaths that particularly depressed the expectation of life at birth: statistically, a new-born baby had a life expectancy of only 35 to 38 years, whereas a child of 5 could be expected to survive into his or her early fifties. Life was most at risk during the earliest years.

What were the principal social implications of this insecurity of infant life? Our view of how adults may have responded to, and tried to cope with, the high rate of infant deaths has to be based largely on inferential reasoning rather than direct documentation, and thus must be presented rather tentatively. Allowing for such caution, two points appear especially worthy of notice. First, given the significant probability that a particular infant would die young, parents may have been deterred from becoming intensively involved with their young child. The life of a baby was regarded as a provisional thing, for the chance of survival to adulthood was not that much better than the chance of an early death.[4] And a provisional life, a life that existed so tenuously, was not likely to warrant a major parental investment of emotional commitment, for such investments were too liable to be suddenly destroyed. It may be, then, that many parents distanced themselves emotionally from their infants, and only came to develop stronger bonds of affection when the children grew older and had thus passed through the most hazardous phases of physical development. (This argument, it should be said, may be more convincing for fathers than mothers. For the close and fairly continuous physical contact established between mother and infant during the first months of life, through suckling in particular, may have helped to forge stronger emotional bonds than is here allowed.) Second, high infant mortality militated against any serious efforts at family planning, for whatever may have been considered the ideal size for a completed family, no couple could feel any real assurance that this size could be actually realized. Three children might be born, all of whom could easily die in childhood; or in a family of six children it would be quite unremarkable for, say, five of them to live or five to die. Given such unfathomable realities, the kinds of predictive premises on which the disposition for family planning normally depends were largely unsustainable. Careful family planning made little sense in a world of such pronounced biological uncertainties.

A child who survived to the age of five or six might start, as we have seen, to contribute in some modest way to the household economy, or simply continue to spend a good deal of time in conventional childhood play. Alternatively, he or she might be sent to a local school in order to receive elementary instruction in reading, and perhaps later in writing and arithmetic as well. Many of these schools were short-lived and completely dependent on the presence of a specific individual — a widowed woman trying to support herself through teaching, a craftsman who could no longer practise his trade, a clergyman wanting to enlarge his income. Such 'schools' — or, perhaps more accurately, classes of primary instruction — enjoyed no endowment and no established physical fabric. Most of them were held in houses or shops, and their masters and mistresses received small fees from their students' parents — perhaps a penny or halfpenny per child for a day's instruction. At any given time in the first half of the eighteenth century there must have been many hundreds of these small private schools, commonly known as dame schools or petty schools, though very little is actually known about their conduct. There were also a large number of publicly financed parish schools: local schools whose funds came from private endowments or philanthropic subscriptions, and which normally provided elementary instruction free of charge. These 'free schools' were intended to cater largely to the children of labouring families. Most of them were closely associated with the Established Church and placed a considerable emphasis on religious teaching. It has been said that around 1740 in Leicestershire 'there were some eighty parishes with over sixty households and about half of these had some endowment [for education] — though usually small enough, providing the nucleus of a teacher's salary, or a few free places'.[5] Over seventy different parish schools are known to have existed in Cheshire prior to 1800, in addition to a considerable number of petty and dame schools.[6]

But how many children actually attended a school of any kind? Unfortunately, we do not know. School attendance was not compulsory; individual teachers came and went, and consequently the availability of teaching in any particular place was often sporadic; and the histories of most elementary schools are almost entirely undocumented. Given the thinness of the educational records and the loosely structured character of much contemporary schooling, confident generalizations are seldom possible. The best that can be offered at the moment is an inferential statement that, given what is known about the levels of literacy in England, perhaps about half of the sons of labouring families received some sort of elementary school education, and probably no more than one-third of the daughters.[7] Some children would have attended school fairly regularly for three or four years, emerging with at least a basic competence in reading the vernacular; others, who may have received only intermittent instruction, would have made little progress in their learning, for schools were liable to collapse, money was sometimes not available to pay a teacher's fees, and children were kept at home during certain seasons to help with the family's labour. Those who did receive any formal instruction probably began their schooling around the age of 6. Few of them remained in school beyond their tenth or eleventh birthdays; most probably left after two or three years of irregular instruction.

Children, for the most part, do not enter very clearly into the historian's range of vision until after their tenth year of age, for it is only then that they began, on balance, to be economically profitable and consequently to enjoy a modest degree of public recognition. In earlier childhood they almost always consumed more than they produced; by the age of approximately eleven to fourteen their earnings, or their productive usefulness, were starting to equal and then exceed the value of what they consumed. This was, for most of them, a major period of transition: a time when they would be getting their start in life — 'life' in the sense of full-time and self-sustaining labour. William Stout (born 1665), whose father was a small farmer in Lancashire (he held sixteen acres and had access to common grazing lands), recalled how his schoolboy days petered out in the 1670s. 'As we attained to the age of ten or twelve years', he said,

we were very much taken off from the schools, espetialy in the spring and summer season, plow time, turfe time, hay time and harvest, in looking after the sheep, helping at plough, goeing to the moss with carts, making hay and shearing in the harvest, two of us at 13 or 14 years of age being equall to one man shearer; so that we made smal progress in Latin, for what we got in winter we forgot in summer.[8]

(Few children of labouring parents would, of course, ever have been taught Latin.) Childhood, by present standards, ended early, but full adulthood was late to arrive — usually not until at least one's mid twenties — for until that time almost all young people continued to live in someone else's household, actively contributing to the productivity of that household, and thus remaining directly dependent on another person's will and subordinate to his authority. They had become full-time workers, then, but not 'free' and 'independent' labourers — that is, not heads of their own households.

Children of around eleven or twelve years of age might anticipate several possible immediate futures, though particular family circumstances usually determined the specific options (if there were any options at all) that would be considered as appropriate for any individual child. In the minority of families that had modest holdings of property, more often customary than freehold — normally craft workshops, or small farms or cottages with common rights attached — one son might expect to inherit the property from his parents, and small bequests might be made to the other children. Such practices were most prevalent in woodland and upland regions, and among independent craftsmen. However, in the majority of families there was little or no property to inherit, or at least not enough to offer much of substance to more than one heir. Consequently, the main objective of parents was to provide for their children suitable positions of employment: positions from which they could advance in life, in anticipation of future prospects, and by means of which they could support, or help to support, themselves on their way to full adulthood. Most plebeian parents were probably almost as concerned with finding suitable 'places' for their children as, on a grander level, were those better-known place-hunters of genteel status whose dedicated pursuit of family interest has been so often recorded.

Only a small minority of children, almost all of them boys, were apprenticed to masters outside their own families. Many fewer positions were available for young people as indentured apprentices than as farm and household servants — a reflection, in part, of the still modest role of artisan employment in a predominantly agricultural society. Moreover, apprenticeships were not available for nothing: a master almost always expected to receive an entrance premium along with a new apprentice, and this monetary prerequisite prevented many poorer families from apprenticing even one of their children. Some trades, those requiring premiums of ten or twenty pounds, were obviously out of the question for labouring families. In other circumstances, where a boy might be apprenticed to a master for around £2, £3 or £4, plebeian parents were sometimes able to find suitable positions for their sons — perhaps with a weaver, a shoemaker or a tailor. In many cases these apprenticeships must have laid the foundations for an adulthood of relative security and well-being — relative, that is, to the experiences of, say, casual town labourers and most agricultural labourers in corn-growing regions. However, it should also be recognized that, in general, only the least attractive trades were open to such boys: trades that tended to be overstocked, trades with rather uncertain career prospects, trades in which low earnings were usual, and trades that were dangerous or unhealthy. The more desirable the trade, the higher the entrance premium. Those pauper children whose apprenticeships were arranged by the overseers of the poor — and perhaps one-quarter to one-third of all apprenticeship indentures involved pauper children — faced even less happy prospects, for the local ratepayers were normally more concerned to see that such children were apprenticed outside the parish, to any masters who would take them, in order to spare the parish any further responsibility for their relief, than they were in trying to ensure that these children were adequately instructed in skills that would serve them well as adults. Apprenticeship in these cases was seen largely as a means of getting rid of burdens on the poor rates. Poor children who remained in their parishes were often apprenticed to 'husbandry' or 'housewifery' (the 'trade' for which most poor girls were destined), thereby providing cheap and relatively long-term menial labour for those farming households that could make use of such basic services. Apprenticeships generally began around the age of 13 or 14 and lasted, most commonly, for seven years.[9]

It was probably more common for the sons (and occasionally the daughters) of many industrial workers to be instructed in a trade by their parents or some other close relative, either with or without a formal apprenticeship. Weaving, for instance, was often taught to children by their fathers and elder brothers; after their training these children commonly continued to work in the family shop until, on the death of the father or at the time of their marriage, they set up their own households in which, as a rule, weaving was their principal means of support. Some parents may have helped their children to purchase a loom.[10] Lace-making was often taught by mothers to their daughters. Among the metalworkers in the West Midlands fathers and sons frequently worked in the same shops, and many workshops, it has been said, 'descended with the cottage from father to eldest son'. Here, as in other industrial regions, there was a noticeable continuity of family involvement in many trades: a study of the parish registers of Sedgley in Staffordshire suggests that the members of many families were 'more likely to change their place of residence than their trade.'[11] A similar sort of family continuity was found in various rural crafts.[12] In coal-mining districts, where alternative forms of employment were often scarce, the 'sons of pitmen worked in the mines from childhood', and 'generation followed generation in work underground'. In the North of England, according to one account,

the work of the collier was of so specialised a nature that a long apprenticeship was necessary . . . . in Northumberland and Durham it was necessary to ascend by the successive stages of trapper, foal, headsman, and half-marrow before one became an authentic pitman. Generally the training was given by the father, who carried his children to work with him from an early age.[13]

A position as a servant was one of the most likely prospects for the children of plebeian parents. In many parishes servants comprised between 15 and 20 per cent of the local population — in the nation at large they may have represented around 13 to 14 per cent of the total population[14] — and it is clear that the great majority of these servants, almost all of whom were unmarried, were less than 27 or 28 years of age. Children were usually sent out to service in their early teens, and they commonly remained in service for eight, ten, or twelve years, leaving only in order to get married and to set up housekeeping on their own. Service, then, as Ann Kussmaul has shown, was associated with a particular phase of life — with what would today be regarded as adolescence and young manhood (or womanhood); it was rarely a lifelong form of employment. Most of these young people were taken into other households, not as domestic servants, but as servants in husbandry: that is, as farm servants who boarded with the farmer's family, usually for a term of one year. Farmers needed regular and continuous labour for certain tasks, such as tending the livestock, and by employing servants they were able to supplement the often insufficient labour that was available from their own families, especially, perhaps, when their children were young. At the same time other country families — sometimes even other farmers with a surplus of children — looked to farm service as a means by which a child could become self-supporting, and learn some useful skills, and, it was hoped, save some of his or her wages for future needs. Men were hired as ploughmen, carters, shepherds and horsemen (caring for the draught animals was a major responsibility of male servants); women were employed as dairymaids and to perform a variety of lighter tasks associated with the farming household, such as weeding, managing the poultry, alemaking, and cooking. Most of these servants were drawn from the families of cottagers and small farmers: indeed, for the children of such families entering service was probably the principal reason for leaving home.[15] Only a minority of servants were employed as domestics. They usually worked in the country estate houses of the landed gentry or the town houses of the urban gentry; and it is probable that the positions available for young women — as chambermaids, cooks, scullery maids, nursemaids — were considerably more numerous than those available for men (footmen were the most common). Service, then, was one of the most common ways of launching a child into the world. And as Edward Thompson has remarked, 'Even among the rural poor (one suspects) the business of placing a son on a good farm, a daughter in service at the great house, occupied much effort and anxiety, and was part of the effort of transmitting to the next generation a "respectable" status, on the right side of the poor law.'[16]

Whatever the complaints that men of leisure may have lodged against servants — and they voiced plenty of complaints — it is clear that in most households, and especially in farming households, service involved few opportunities for self-indulgence, and that many masters and mistresses were intent on getting as much work out of their servants as circumstances would allow. On 10 October 1744 the mother of the bachelor squire in Shalstone, Buckinghamshire, wrote to the mother of a prospective servant maid, outlining the duties associated with the position available in her household:

She must milk 3 or 4 cows & understand how to manage that Dairy, & know how to boyll & roast ffowlls & butcher's meatt. Wee wash once a month, she & the washerwoman wash all but the small linnen, & next day she & the washerwoman wash the Buck [a large wash of coarser kinds of clothing]. She helps the other maid wash the rooms when they are done, she makes the Garrett beds & cleans them, & cleans ye great stairs & scours all the Irons & scours the Pewter in use, & wee have an woman to help when't is all done. There is very good time to do all this provided she is a servant, & when she has done her worke she sits down to spin.[17]

Similarly, William Ellis's account of the 'typical' dairymaid — an account that was not meant to be read by servants, unlike those guidebooks that were written explicitly 'for their benefit' and to help clarify their notions of gratitude and deference — left little doubt as to the sorts of burdens that were often associated with service in husbandry:

She may be known by her red plump Arms and Hands, and clumsy Fingers; for in most great Dairies they are forced to milk their Cows abroad, great Part of the Year; I may say, almost all the Year, even in Frosts and Snows, while their Fingers are ready to freeze in the Action; and sometimes while they stand in Dirt and Water .... And indeed it may be justly said of these, That their Work is never done; for where twenty or thirty Cows are Kept, they must begin about Four o'Clock in the Summer-time to milk, and at the same Hour next Morning; and between these times they have enough to do, to scald and scour their Utensils, and make Butter and Cheese; and thus are constantly employed throughout the Year. A good Dairy-Maid is a very valuable Servant; I mean, one that readily rises betimes; is diligent and skilful in making the best Butter and Cheese; is cleanly in the Performance of it, making the most of her Milk, and doing all in her Power to promote her Master's Interest .... [18]

In many households, in short, service was not an employment to be taken lightly.

Service and apprenticeship were not, of course, intended to last indefinitely, for it was expected that they would be succeeded by marriage and the setting up of an independent household. Indeed, most young people around 1700 assumed that a precondition for marriage was access to housing (usually rented) of their own: a place from which they could hope to construct a viable productive economy. Young married couples rarely chose to live with their parents; and rented rooms suitable for married couples, which held few attractions of any kind, were seldom found outside London and a few provincial cities, for they made little sense in a society where so much productive labour was associated with the actual household economy. A decision to marry, then, normally assumed that the bride and groom had found some suitable place, not simply to live, but also to work. As one historian has said, with particular reference to Stratford-upon-Avon, 'a man did not normally take a wife until he was able to maintain himself in an independent home'.[19] A couple disposed to marry would have been in search of, and they often had to wait for, an opening in the local economy — whether it was a small farm, or a workshop, or a vacant cottage with common rights; they always needed money to set themselves up — money for furnishings, and money to purchase handicraft tools and equipment or livestock for their smallholding; and this money could only be acquired, as a rule, from their mutual savings or as a result of a small family bequest. The process by which a man might become an independent housekeeper was described in a tract of 1785, which was attempting to explain the character of the economy of those cottagers who enjoyed common rights:

The children of these cottagers brought up under an industrious father and mother, are sent to yearly service amongst farmers, etc. and if in the course of a few years service, the young man can scrape up 20 1. or 30 1. and finds a young woman that he likes, possessed with nearly an equal sum, they strike a bargain and agree to marry as soon as they can find a cottage near the common; they then stock their cottage with cows, calves, sheep, hogs, poultry, etc. as much as their little fortunes will admit of. He then hires himself as a day labourer to a neighbouring farmer, and the wife stays at home to look after the live stock.[20]

It is clear, then, that there were various circumstances that could affect the timing of marriage — and most of them tended to delay it. An apprentice was not allowed to be married, and after 'his time' was up, usually when he was in his early twenties, he might work as a journeyman for a while, saving some money and perhaps hoping to get a workshop of his own before deciding to marry. Young people in service — or at least those youths of a prudent disposition — hoped to be able to save a substantial portion of their wages, and most of them would have been well into their twenties before they had accumulated sufficient savings to rent and stock a small farm. Stocking a farm of twelve acres, all in grass, would have cost, during the early years of George III's reign, around £65 in the first year; and it has been estimated that to save such a sum from service-wages would have required both partners to put aside two-thirds of their annual earnings over a period of about ten years[21] — obviously no easy task (the task would have appeared rather less formidable in areas where commons existed, for then a smaller holding might have sufficed). Moreover, small farms were not easy to find: they were much in demand; vacancies in any given locality were never very numerous; and it is clear that the supply of small farms was decreasing from the later seventeenth century, for landlords were increasingly consolidating small farms together in the hope that larger farms would be more commercially successful. (I shall return to this important theme in the final chapter.) Young people, then, often had to wait for a small farm, and waiting meant that marriages were postponed. The close connection between these two social realities is nicely illustrated by a remark in 1766 of William Cole, the rector of Bletchley in Buckinghamshire, who referred in his diary to the plight of a young man of 23 in the parish who aspired to become a small farmer:

Will Wood junr, who wants to be married to Henry Travel's Daughter, the prettiest Girl in the Parish, being uneasy with his Grandmother, (who can't afford to settle him), went away from her for 3 or 4 Days. The Times are so hard, small Farms so difficult to be met with, the Spirit of Inclosing, & accumulating Farms together, making it very difficult for young People to marry, as was used; as I know by Experience this Parish, where several Farmers' Sons are forced to live at Home with their Fathers, tho' much wanting to marry & settle, for Want of proper Places to settle at.[22]

These considerations help to explain, I think, what now seems to be an indubitable fact about English society in the later seventeenth and earlier eighteenth centuries: that is, the high age at first marriage. Research on this matter is still underway, and there may well have been more regional variations than have yet been recognized; but almost all of the evidence presently available points strongly in the same direction. In the mid eighteenth century in three south Warwickshire parishes the mean age at first marriage for women was approximately 27 years; in Shepshed, Leicestershire, between 1700 and 1749 it was 27.4; in Ashby-de-la-Zouch, Leicestershire, during the period between 1671 and 1695 it was 26.4; and taking together seven parishes whose populations have been reconstituted from their parish records — Colyton and Hartland in Devon, Banbury in Oxfordshire, Alcester in Warwickshire, Gainsborough in Lincolnshire, Aldenham in Hertfordshire, and Hawkshead in the Lake District — the mean age at first marriage for women was 27.0 in 1650-99 and 27.2 in 1700-49.[23] As a general rule men at the time of their marriage were slightly older than their brides — although occasionally, when the marriage age of women was exceptionally high, the grooms were on average a few months younger.[24] Circumstances induced young men and women to behave prudently, to delay marriage until they could become self-supporting. As David Levine has argued, given that economic independence was a 'necessary pre-condition to marriage, the age at marriage was kept high because of the inelastic demand for labour in the pre-industrial economy'. Vacancies in the local economy only arose, in many places, 'with the death or retirement of an older member of the community'. Consequently, it was common for a man to have to wait some time before succeeding to a cottage, a small farm, or a workshop. Moreover, older brides, he suggests, 'were often preferred', at least in part, 'because ... their experience in farmwork and domestic duties were economic assets of some importance' — assets that could likely be turned to productive advantage in the household of the newly married couple.[25] In addition, older women would have had more years to accumulate savings for the time when they became independent housekeepers. There were, then, major constraints upon early marriage, constraints that stemmed largely from the limited availability of economic opportunities. During the three or four generations before about 1750 late marriage made good sense for most labouring people.

After marriage the experiences of individual families would have varied enormously. Some families 'prospered': they were able to sustain a viable household economy, major misfortunes and disasters passed them by, they exercised prudence and foresight, and their children became helpmates rather than tiresome burdens. Others were less fortunate and in time became impoverished, weighed down with cares and frustrations, and in some cases even chronically destitute. In some families the requirements of dependent children did not exceed the parents' capacity to provide the necessary support, and thus family resources were not seriously overstretched: in others a large number of children posed a major peril to the household's tenuous economy. Some families succeeded in training their children for some useful employment or in placing them in suitable 'postions', perhaps as servants or apprentices; other children were left largely on their own to scratch a living as best they could. A small minority of couples, perhaps seven or eight per cent of the total, remained childless, for reasons of infertility. In the first half of the eighteenth century the number of births per completed family — a 'statistically average' family — was about five, and these births were spaced, on average, about two-and-a-half years apart. High rates of infant mortality normally ensured that not all of these children survived to adulthood: again, 'on average', around two of the five children would die before the age of 20. It was rare for a couple to have a very large number of children, in part because the high age at marriage reduced a woman's practicable child-bearing period by approximately 40 per cent from the potential biological maximum. With regard to the 'quality' of life experienced by these families, and especially the husband and wife, we can say virtually nothing of importance. There are hardly any records that shed light on the sentiments and values and consolations of plebeian family life — a regrettable but inescapable deficiency. Perhaps the best we can suggest is that marital life may have been dominated by the sort of stoical qualities which, very much later, George Sturt was to write about among the rural labourers in western Surrey. 'A kind of dogged comradeship', he said '— I can find no better word for it — is what commonly unites the labouring man and his wife; they are partners and equals running their impecunious affairs by mutual help.'[26]

Broken families as a result of 'premature' death were very common. In the later seventeenth and earlier eighteenth centuries the mean duration of marriage was only about twenty-one to twenty-three years, the median duration somewhat less. Some marriages, of course, remained intact for more than three decades, but most were prematurely broken by the death of one of the partners: the woman in childbirth, the man from an accident or infected wound, either of them from some kind of major infectious disease (tuberculosis, influenza, smallpox). Around 25 to 30 per cent of marriages were broken up by death within the first fifteen years; those couples who survived until all their children had grown up were almost certainly in the minority.[27] Family life, then, must be regarded as having been remarkably unstable and insecure, and this death-induced (rather than divorce-induced) impermanence had several notable consequences. First, few children were conscious of having grandparents, and only a minority of adults lived to have grandchildren. Given the high age at marriage, grandchildren could not normally be expected before the age of 54 or 55 at the earliest, and half of the persons who survived to young adulthood would be dead by then. Second, since so many people were widowed in early middle age, the prime of life, remarriages were very common. In 1688 twenty-six of the sixty-seven married couples living in Clayworth, Nottinghamshire, included at least one partner who had previously been married.[28] It has been estimated that around one-quarter of all marriages in England were remarriages for at least one of the partners.[29] Third, a substantial minority of children had lived or were living in families that had been broken by death. In both Clayworth, Nottinghamshire, in the later seventeenth century and Cardington, Bedfordshire, in the 1780s they comprised almost one-third of the total number of resident children. A few had lost both parents, others (whose surviving parent had remarried) were living with a stepfather or stepmother, but most of them were living in a household headed by a widowed parent, usually a widowed mother. In the 1690s approximately 30 per cent of the children living in Bristol had lost one or both parents.[30] The loss of a parent at a tender age, then, was a frequent occurrence. Conjugal family life — the life of a husband, wife and their immediate offspring — may have been the normal experience of domesticity for the majority of people, but it was a precarious form of experience that was continually threatened with dislocation and upheavals.

Mobility

The stages of life through which people passed, and the changing character of their occupational needs and expectations, inevitably involved a great many of them in frequent moves from place to place. Mobility of this sort was most pronounced during that phase of life between the end of childhood (around the early teens) and the establishing of one's own household. While some boys left home to become apprentices in other households, where they would normally stay for around seven years before moving on, easily the most common source of geographical mobility among young people was the high rate of turnover among farm and domestic servants. For servants did not normally continue in the same position for more than one year: indeed, it has been estimated that around three-quarters of the servants in husbandry took leave of their masters at the end of their annual contracts.[31] During the

hiring season every year, which was most often observed around Michaelmas
or Martinmas (or May in Lincolnshire), the country roads were full of
servants moving from one place to another; and those usually tranquil
market towns in which the hiring fairs took place were for a few days
exuberantly alive with large crowds of servants, masters and mistresses, and
often itinerant entertainers.[32] Servants, then, moved often, though most of
these moves were over short distances and within a small and familiar
district — a district that could be walked across in one day. Long journeys to
strange places were uncommon.[33]

There were several reasons for this high rate of mobility among servants.
First, servants expected to improve themselves as they grew older: they
looked forward to getting a more responsible position, or a position that paid
better, or a position in a more desirable household. A young servant maid
with very menial duties might hope to become in time a head cook or a
housekeeper; a young lad might aspire to be appointed the head man on a
substantial farm, and this would only be possible after he had gained
experience over several years as a ploughman for various masters. Service
was governed in part by hierarchical considerations, and young people
expected to move up in the service hierarchy.[34] And since the sort of
advancement a servant might want was not usually possible in the household
where he or she was employed at any particular time, for often no suitable
vacancy existed in that household, servants were induced to leave their
places and search out better prospects elsewhere. Much mobility, then,
resulted from these understandable ambitions of youths in service. (In any
given year, moreover, some older servants would be leaving their employments
in order to marry and set up housekeeping on their own; and these
departures from service would, of course, create new opportunities for
younger servants, who would move on to fill these vacant positions.) Second,
most farmers recognised that their own needs for labour were compatible
with this turnover of servants. As Ann Kussmaul has pointed out:

Most tasks on the farm were skill and age-specific. Small boys were not hired to
drive plough teams, and young adults were not hired to scare crows. Each farm
had a fixed set of tasks, but servants did not remain similarly fixed in their
capacities. They grew and expected their wages and the status of their tasks to
grow with them . . . . The little farms that Arthur Young described sometimes
hired a lad; they would not need the same growing lad, year after year, but rather
a succession of different lads.[35]

Mobility, then, was essential if the age of a servant was to be meshed
satisfactorily with the requirements of a particular position. Third, various
local and individual circumstances could encourage mobility. A master
might be dissatisfied with the work of a servant, and only too happy to see the

back of him at the end of a year. Similarly, a servant might be anxious to leave a disagreeable household. 'So much could be wrong with a servant's situation: the food could be stingy, the ale-house distant, the master or mistress vicious.'[36] Perhaps the farm was poorly run or the labour demands excessive; or maybe a servant was simply lonely or bored and thus hopeful that a change of scene would lift his spirits. Household and farm service, a full-time, confining, and seldom relieved form of labour, the functions of which were performed largely by adolescents and people in their early twenties, a time of life not noted for passivity, could easily involve hothouse and troublesome personal relations, and such strains were best handled by moving to another place. For all these reasons, then, servants comprised an unusually mobile group of people within the larger society.

There were other considerations as well that might have induced people to move. Marriage often involved mobility, for in many — perhaps a small majority of — cases the partners were from different (though usually nearby) parishes, and consequently at least one of them had to move. Sometimes too the cottage or shop or small farm that they had arranged to occupy was in another parish still — although again, usually a parish in the district. And just as servants and newly married couples moved in response to the availability of economic opportunities, so too other people might migrate as prospects arose or as necessity dictated — though it should be recognized that families and adult housekeepers never moved with anything approaching the frequency of single people. The most common pattern for such adult mobility among non-servants involved migrations from farming regions with static employment prospects to cities, towns, and industrializing villages. These were the places whose economies were expanding most dramatically, and the rapid population growth that went along with this expansion was seldom a function of natural increase — in fact, in most urban areas deaths exceeded births. Some of this movement to urban and industrial districts, especially that which involved artisans and tradesmen, may have been what Peter Clark has called 'betterment mobility': that is, migration which 'was not compelled by necessity but encouraged by the hope of social and economic improvement'. However, most of these migrants were more likely to be poor men who had failed to find a niche for themselves in any local economy, and consequently were shifting about in search of whatever work they could find. Clark refers to this as 'subsistence migration'.[37] These were the people who could have found their way to London or one of the larger provincial cities, or to a previously forested region where industrial work was available — the Forest of Kingswood, for instance, which was just east of Bristol, was growing so rapidly throughout the eighteenth century that its scattered settlements became more or less merged together into one

large and sprawling industrial suburb[38] — or to some other 'open' parish
where migrants were able to settle without fear of being restrained by a
powerful landowner or vigilant overseers of the poor. These migrants were
likely to find only casual jobs, at least initially, and casual employment was
more readily available in urban and industrial areas than in regions where
farming predominated. Some of them would have settled down somewhere,
perhaps in the East End of London or in an expanding provincial port or
manufacturing town. Others became more or less permanent transients,
leading lives of chronic uncertainty and frequent misery — we know little
about the experiences of such unsettled people prior to the nineteenth
century — lives which, I suspect, were often concluded with an early death.

We can see, then, that English society in the eighteenth century was by no
means immobile, with most people rooted in the same village for life. Indeed,
the person who lived in the same parish from birth until death would have
been in a distinct minority. At the very least there was a good chance that an
adult would have lived in a nearby parish, or in several nearby parishes,
during his or her years of service or apprenticeship. For most people mobility
was a normal expectation. In 1782 only about 30 per cent of the married
adults in Cardington, Bedfordshire, had been born in the parish.[39] For a
majority of people the parish of their death was different from the parish of
their birth. Families that preserved their roots in the same place for at least
three generations were exceptional. Indeed, if we were to compile a list of the
family names found in some randomly selected parish in, say, the later
seventeenth century, it is very likely that few of these names would still be
found there a century later. Many families disappear from the local records,
new names come in to take their place.[40] It should be noted too that most of
this migration was over short distances: at least 80 per cent of the migrants
moved less than fifteen miles. Mobility was for the most part local, or at most
regional, and many people who moved numerous times in the course of their
lives never lived more than a day's walk from the parish of their childhood.[41]
Long distance migration was exceptional, and much of what there was
probably went to London. The metropolis, in fact, was a great consumer of
men: it has been estimated that it had a net immigration rate in the
eighteenth century of around 8000 people per year, and these migrants were
drawn from many different regions. London was a magnet for many
uprooted or discontented provincial people, particularly youths and others of
adventuresome spirit, and for those whose patterns of migration took them
beyond their own district — certainly a minority of people — the capital was
more likely to be their destination than any other single place.[42]

Hazards of life

Much of life as experienced in the eighteenth century was hard, hazardous and unhealthy. Anyone acquainted with the period knows this to be so, and there is no need to dwell at length on what is beyond dispute. However, it may be helpful to devote some attention to the main sources of this precariousness: the basic conditions underlying suffering, uprootedness and the uncertainties of family life. Misery and destitution are found in any society and among many individuals, but societies have been distinguished from one another in the character and scale of the determinants of distress. There have been differences in the hazards that posed the most serious threats, the facilities for managing threatening conditions, and the uneven distribution of these hazards — along with the capacity to handle them — within the population at large. What, then, were the principal sources of suffering and dislocation in eighteenth-century England?

A great deal of distress stemmed from people's inability to exercise any significant control over the forces of nature. Given the primitive understanding of scientific regularities, and the consequent inadequacy of so many efforts at technological intervention for beneficent purposes, all men continued to be extremely vulnerable to disease, accidents, and various forms of natural calamity. People were very much aware of the destructive powers in the natural environment against which they could mobilize very few worthwhile defences. If one consults almost any substantial diary of the period, one cannot help being impressed by the frequent references to illnesses, serious mishaps and premature death. These seem, indeed, to have been almost regular, rather than extraordinary, realities of life. As D.E.C. Eversley notes:

We who live in the twentieth century can hardly imagine the significance of pain, disfigurement, and the loss of near relatives as a constant factor in everyday life. Slight wounds became infected and suppurated for weeks. Fractures healed badly. Minor irritations like toothache and headache became major pre-occupations, paralysing ordinary activity. Heroic figures like Josiah Wedgwood overcame the handicap of lifelong acute inflictions, most men did not. Against pain there was only opium, or drink. Neither means suppressed pain in a manner enabling the sufferer to lead a normal life. Surgery without anaesthetics, even where it was available, was dreaded, shattering in its impact, and uncertain in the outcome. Blood-letting could debilitate and kill an already weakened patient. Even where no acute injury or identifiable major disease was involved, common colds, gastric upsets from the consumption of rotten foodstuffs, and permanent septic foci such as those provided by bad teeth were common, if not universal. The myth of our ancestors, bursting with rude rustic health, given to manly out-door sports and taking their ease by limpid pools and in virgin forests, has long since been exploded.[43]

In early modern France, says Robert Mandrou — and exactly the same could be said of England — 'disease was rife ... the whole population was in a state of chronic morbidity, and ... medicine was helpless in the face of even the most common ailments'.[44] Life must have been, for large numbers of people, a continual struggle against the debilitating consequences of bodily infirmities.

The autobiography of William Stout (1665-1752) of Lancaster affords a vivid sense of the uncertainties of physical existence, and the volatile character of human relations to the natural environment, during one generation of the eighteenth century. For Stout wrote not only about his own problems, but also about those tribulations that affected the population at large. In 1716, for instance, he reported that the 'sharp frost last winter was succeeded by a sickly spring, when many died of strong fevers'; and in 1719 the 'beginning of this year was very foggy and wett, which caused many distempers and mortalety'. Late in the winter of 1721 there was 'much snow and frost, and the ground covred a month, which went hard with people. Turfe being lost in the late flood, and coles scarce, caused great mortalety and distempers by the extreame changes of the weather'. He pointed to 1723 and 1725 as years of general economic prosperity, but in the summer of the latter year there were outbreaks of smallpox and measles, 'of which very many have died in and about Lancaster'. 1728 was a very bad year.

We had a very wet spring and late seeding and cold summer, so that corn did not get its feeding, and a great blast in summer which scorched corn. It was also a very sickly summer, and great mortalety in the plaine country, much more than in the towns; and the buryalls were double this year to what they were last year, and corn proved dear .... So that the poor have a hard year.

The late 1720s, in fact, witnessed very high levels of mortality in almost all parts of the country — perhaps the worst in the entire century.[45] The following decade, in contrast, was healthier and more bountiful — though in early 1737, according to Stout, 'there was a generall distemper of violent coughs and coulds all over the nation, of which many died' — but in the winter of 1739-40 the country endured perhaps the longest stretch of severe weather that people of the century were ever to know. 'Sheep starved, the ground being covred with frozen snow a month together. Many trades men frozen out of their trades and imploy, and starved for want of fire; coles and turfe being at double prices.'[46] There was a general dearth through 1740, which, according to William Ellis, a farmer and writer in Hertfordshire, 'occasioned the Death of many poor People who wanted Heat and Victuals'.[47] Here was clearly a world of striking environmental hazards: a world in which personal security was very often conspicuously at risk.

Much suffering resulted from the hazards of people's working conditions, especially in urban and industrial employments. Many disabilities were related to the labourers' vulnerability to accidents in unregulated working conditions, where environmental hazards were common, and where inordinate stress was often placed upon the human body. Some very strenuous jobs — jobs requiring heavy muscular exertion, such as those of porters, seamen and dockers — were a source of frequent injuries and ruptures, and they commonly led to premature ageing and physical breakdown. Industrial accidents were very common among such workers as seamen and fishermen (from mishaps at sea), miners (from explosions, drownings and falls), and cutlery grinders (from the flying apart of the grindstone). Long-term disabilities were common in many trades. Lead or mercury poisoning was a major hazard for certain workmen (plumbers, glaziers, painters, various metalworkers); anthrax often afflicted leather workers, and bronchial and lung diseases were prevalent among wool-combers and flax-dressers. Stooped backs and other deformities were common among workers who spent long hours at jobs demanding unnatural and contorted postures, such as being hunched over some kind of machine. The loss of eyesight was widely found among tailors, seamstresses and lace-makers, for very close work was required in these trades. The sources of the period are full of scattered references to such occupational disabilities, and an examination of almost any industry would provide substantial evidence of the sufferings endured by its workmen. One traveller, for instance, who observed the unhealthy working conditions of the Mendip lead-miners and the Cornish tinners, seems to have been particularly disturbed by the conditions of work he observed in the copper industry in Cornwall. 'Nothing', he said,

can be more shocking than the appearance which the workmen in the smelting-houses exhibit. So dreadfully deleterious are the fumes of arsenic constantly impregnating the air of these places, and so profuse is the perspiration occasioned by the heat of the furnaces, that those who have been employed at them but a few months become most emaciated figures, and in the course of a few years are generally laid in their graves. Some of the poor wretches who were ladling the liquid metal from the furnaces to the moulds looked more like walking corpses than living beings. How melancholy a circumstance to reflect upon, and yet to how few does it occur, that in preparing the materials of those numerous utensils which we are taught to consider as indispensable in our kitchens, several of our fellow creatures are daily deprived of the greatest blessing of life, and too seldom obtain relief but in losing life itself.[48]

Other of the insecurities that people faced stemmed from the widespread irregularity of employment. I have already drawn attention to the seasonality and casual character of so many urban and industrial employments — the

fluctuations associated with maritime shipping, inland transport, the London
season, trade recessions, war and peace — and such seasonality was no less
prevalent in country districts. The demand for farm labour fell off sharply
during the winter months — this was a difficult season for other reasons as
well: fuel might have to be purchased, common rights for livestock would
have been of little value when snow was on the ground — and inclement
weather often restricted various kinds of outdoor labour at other times of the
year. Moreover, since most forms of production were labour intensive and
involved little fixed capital, the only effective ways in which a capitalist
could respond to a decreased demand for his product, or a period during
which the market was glutted, were by cutting the wages of his workers,
or the numbers of his workers, or by cutting both together: most capitalists,
in other words, had little incentive for actively trying to provide security
of employment. In such circumstances the burdens of trade slumps had
to be borne overwhelmingly by the wage-earning people. For all these
reasons, then, much labour was of an uncertain and somewhat hand-to-
mouth character. And all this irregularity meant that a family's income was
sometimes dramatically reduced, that for a period of time its members would
have to desperately scratch together whatever tenuous sort of living could be
found, and that such seasons of special hardship often resulted in malnourish-
ment, loss of energy and morale, and a heightened susceptibility to disease.
Sometimes these times of trouble even led to a complete collapse of the
household's viability: and the result would have been destitution (at least
temporarily, and sometimes permanently), perhaps dependence on alms and
poor relief, and in some cases the resort to vagrancy.

Two general observations can be offered about the character of such stark
impoverishment. First, the most extreme and unalleviated destitution was
probably found in London and the larger provincial cities. There were
several reasons for this state of affairs. As we have seen, uprooted and
dislocated people, the 'subsistence migrants', tended to gravitate, not to
predominantly farming regions, but to urban and industrializing areas,
where many of them came to live in chronic misery. In these rapidly
expanding centres more people were dependent on casual labour, which was
inherently very insecure; many people also depended very heavily on
industrial or transport-related employments, and because of the volatility of
many of these trades large numbers of workmen were periodically thrown
out of their jobs. Unemployed city-dwellers normally had fewer resources to
fall back on, for by-employments were less readily practised; and almost
everything had to be purchased in the marketplace, in contrast to country
districts where cottagers could often supplement their earnings from wages
by utilizing their rights of direct access to the land. Moreover, as a result of

urban population growth and these various circumstances that aggravated the scale of poverty in urban areas, the facilities for poor relief in the cities were often severely strained. Funds for the relief of the poor might become totally inadequate; paupers from outside the town (they were usually known as 'foreigners') were likely to be resented and sometimes persecuted (their presence was often a major source of generalized hostility towards the poor on the part of the property-owners); and local officials, even those with benevolent intentions, were often simply unable to handle adequately the formidable administrative problems that such extensive poverty produced.

The ineffectiveness of the relief measures in London is well known, and in many provincial cities the circumstances of impoverishment and poor relief were little different. As one recent study has concluded, 'by 1700 most of the dockyard and industrial towns had large numbers of paupers living in acute squalor, sleeping in cellars or on the streets. Poor relief was rudimentary and unable to cope with the wild fluctuations of economic activity'.[49] Labouring families in large cities 'live so poorly', according to Roger North in the late seventeenth century: they were 'in Want of all that is wholesome for Life', they lived 'in Cellars', had 'bad Diet', lived 'close packed', suffered 'Want of Exercise'. 'In the City, they are heaped up in nasty Holes, and lie and infect each other with Diseases and Immoralities.'[50] The wretchedness of the lives of so many people in London — the widespread begging, the homelessness, the very high rates of mortality, the abandoned infants and untended children — is abundantly documented. One contemporary, who recommended a programme of moral and social reform, said of the poor — and almost certainly the urban poor in particular — that they 'live more like rats and weazels and such like noxious vermine, than Creatures of humane race': and this was a view that appears to have been widely held by genteel observers.[51]

Second, in most parts of provincial England a high proportion of the dependent poor were widows and their children. Women were more liable than men to serious impoverishment. Indeed, prior to the mid eighteenth century few of the recipients of poor relief were able-bodied adult males. A woman on her own, for whatever reason, was less likely than a man to be self-supporting, for women's wages were seldom more than half those allowed to men (they were usually expected to be supplementary rather than central in a household's economy), and thus a woman who had to get by solely on her own wages would often find that these earnings were completely inadequate for a basic subsistence. This inadequacy was most pronounced if such a woman, usually a widow or a victim of desertion, had dependent children. Widows, moreover, comprised a rather substantial minority of the English people: they probably represented around 8 to 9 per cent of the total population, more than double the proportion that were widowers. It has been estimated that 12.7 per cent of all heads of households were widows and only 5.2 per cent were widowers. In Bristol in the 1690s 19.1 per cent of the households were headed by widows and 4.2 per cent by widowers.[52] (Men who lost their wives were more inclined to remarry quickly than women who lost their husbands. A widow in her thirties or early forties with several dependent children was not regarded as an attractive marriage prospect by the small number of eligible and available men who might know her. A widower, in contrast, was able to propose to a younger unattached woman.) Women, then, were much more liable than men to prolonged widowhood and its distressing economic consequences. So it is not at all surprising that the records bearing on the Poor Law show clearly that widows figured very prominently among those officially defined as paupers. In many parishes, in fact, around half of the recipients of poor relief were widows.[53] The rest of the recipients were mostly old and infirm people, orphaned children and those who were sick or physically disabled. (The problems of widowhood and old age, of course, often merged together.) For all these unfortunate and aged people the institution of the Poor Law did provide some genuine relief, especially in small communities where the poor were personally known and acknowledged to have a legitimate claim on the assistance of their neighbours. The people who were particularly vulnerable to impoverishment, then, must be strictly defined, for there is a danger that the labouring people as a whole might be crudely equated with the 'poor' — an equation that has too often been attempted. At any given time only a small proportion of the labouring people suffered from what William Cobbett later referred to as '*real want*, a real insufficiency of the food and raiment and lodging necessary to health and decency';[54] and, except for the largest cities, most of these impoverished people were widows, the elderly and the impotent. Labouring people enjoyed only basic material fare in their passage through life, but most of them were able to support their families in an average year without having to resort to the 'parish' for relief. The dramatic increase in the numbers of the dependent poor is largely a phenomenon of the years after 1750.

Human controls

It is clear that many of the tribulations people endured were rooted in a relationship with nature in which human controls and defences were still weakly developed. Major contagious diseases were both endemic and epidemic, and the delicate constitutions of infancy were especially vulnerable. When illness was not fatal it was often chronic or recurrent and sometimes incapacitating. And many kinds of labour were pursued in conditions that led to industrial diseases, accidents or premature physical decay. These were important sources of the fragility of personal and family life, and they help to account for many of the sudden social disruptions that must have so often intruded into the rough-and-ready equilibrium of plebeian existence. But not all distress stemmed simply from the pressures of the natural environment: unemployment, impoverishment, widowhood and old age were all, in part, conditions of life in which social and cultural variables were heavily implicated in determining the character and weight of the distress that was actually experienced. Some of the conditions bearing on suffering and personal sacrifice were as much social products as were enclosure bills or parsons' sermons; and conditions of this kind were not always simply accepted with quiet fatalism, or endured in a spirit of outward passivity and inward resentment. For there were some sources of distress which were clearly rooted in the structures of power in the broader society, which brought sharply into focus the complex relations between rich and poor, and which often resulted in manifest social conflicts and in various expressions of popular discontent, rebelliousness and direct corporate action. Such conflicts, in fact, as we shall see in Chapter 5, were remarkably prevalent. Moreover, the experience of distress was not simply a matter of sensations and 'natural' responses to 'natural' stimuli. Distress, like any other sort of experience, was always culturally mediated: its character was partly a result of the filtering of sensations through a complex of cultural mediators, and by means of these mediations the experience was interpreted and given value and significance. Pain, dislocations, and catastrophes had to be, in some way, 'understood' and situated within the total context of life. And just as life's sufferings had to be culturally understood and assimilated, so too the pleasures of life, and the possibilities for enjoyment and self-fulfilment, were components of a world of culture — a world of customs and rituals, values and mores, beliefs and identities. Popular culture, comprising numerous strands of consciousness, was just as much an integral, and often distinctive, reality of eighteenth-century life as the culture of tradesmen and merchants, whom Defoe and others so much admired, or the culture of aristocrats and landed gentlemen, whose outlook on life has been accorded so much sympathetic treatment by modern historians. An appreciation of the character and significance of the culture of the labouring people is the principal concern of the next chapter.

4 Beliefs, customs and identities

Just as a naturalist might view the world in a particular way, and a poet in another, each giving it different meanings, so too the diverse people of the eighteenth century understood their world in distinctive and sometimes divergent ways. The educated gentleman interpreted the world according to notions of ancestry, propriety, exclusive privilege and the social priority of landed property, and his ethical and political perspectives were partly informed by the literature of classical antiquity. The merchant, in contrast, was likely to see his environment in terms of calculation, risk, enterprise and adventure, and profit and loss. These two cultures associated with the ownership of property — the culture of gentility and the culture of commerce — have, of course, often been closely examined. But what about the culture of the mass of the population? What were the principal beliefs, outlooks, values and customary practices of the labouring people? How did they perceive the 'world', how did they cope with its hazards and harshness, and how did they organize and interpret their experiences? These are obviously important questions, but they are questions, it should be said, that can only be answered at present in a very tentative and qualified manner. The primary sources that shed light on such matters are thin, scattered and often fragmentary, so much so that some important questions may always be completely inaccessible to historical reconstruction; and partly because of these deficiences in the records few historians have attempted any serious inquiries into the nature of popular culture. Perhaps future research will bring to light important new findings. In the meantime, however, these questions deserve to be accorded whatever informed attention is presently possible, for a few relevant studies have been published in recent years, and an increasingly thorough search of contemporary sources has resulted in the accumulation of a growing body of helpful descriptive evidence. It is now possible, in fact, to offer at least an outline of some of the main strands of plebeian consciousness in the eighteenth century.

Religion and magic

The English labouring people perceived themselves and their environment within the framework of a largely pre-scientific culture. They had little understanding of the regularities of natural processes, especially of the various causal mechanisms underlying those material occurrences that inescapably determined so much of human life. The processes of nature *needed* to be explained, in some way or other, but as yet the physical and life sciences could contribute little to this necessary enterprise. (In polite society, in contrast, the impact of scientific thinking was already being widely felt.) Given these limits and constraints, it is hardly surprising that in the culture of the people — this predominantly oral culture that attached such importance to custom and tradition — the belief in the power of supernatural forces was profound and pervasive. The vision of reality that was commonly held posited the existence of a material reality and a spiritual (or supernatural) reality, and the latter was assumed to have a large and continuous impact on the operation of the former. Indeed, supernatural interventions in the secular affairs of human beings, whether for benign or malevolent purposes, were thought to be routine occurrences. Men were preoccupied with first causes: and first causes, it was widely held, had to be supernatural agencies. Consequently, many of the major events of human experience — disease, accidents, premature death, birth defects, a good or a bad harvest, timely or untimely weather, the destruction of property — were explained, at least in part, by reference to non-material forces. The world was a very mysterious place. So many apparently inexplicable things happened to people. Sudden catastrophes destroyed individuals, families and substantial sections of whole communities. Epidemics struck, crops failed, chronic pain and misery were endured, personal misfortunes cut down individuals in the prime of life. And what — they might well ask — was the purpose of it all? Why did people suffer in these ways? And how could a person try to cope with the harshness, the uncertainties and the tribulations of life?

Of course, the theology of orthodox religion addressed itself to many of these central concerns. If offered answers to such basic questions: answers that spoke of the (sometimes) inscrutable purposes of divine providence; of the Fall of Man; of the punishments for sin; of the happiness of the afterlife, when the sufferings of mortal existence would be ended; and of the solace available from faith during a man's stay on earth. These were fundamental messages of Protestant Christianity. But how widely were these messages believed? It is one thing for us to understand a theology: it is another matter to know the beliefs of the 'hearers' — the strength of their beliefs, the orthodoxy of their beliefs, the social significance of their beliefs. What, indeed, was the number of hearers? Perhaps many people were not (or were barely) hearers at all? These are obviously pertinent questions, but they are questions for which we have no satisfactory answers. The subject of popular religion is largely unexplored territory, and consequently very little is known about the religious faith of the labouring people during the century after the Restoration. Peter Laslett has claimed in *The World We Have Lost* that 'All our ancestors were literal Christian believers, all of the time', and that 'their world was a Christian world': but such grand assertions should not be taken too seriously.[1] In reality the evidence currently available on popular religion is so insubstantial as to hardly justify consideration. Although future research on the records of the Church may well remedy some of these deficiencies, at the moment there is precious little for the historian to say.

One matter, however, does deserve attention. For there is reason to think that the impact of orthodox religion on plebeian Englishmen was rather less powerful than has often been presumed. A recent study of the clergy in Leicestershire under the later Stuarts, for example, has revealed considerable evidence of religious apathy and indifference among the laity.[2] The Church itself, it should be recalled, suffered from numerous institutional deficiencies. During the 1680s William Sandcroft, Archbishop of Canterbury, became acutely aware of many of these inadequacies, as G. V. Bennett has recently observed:

Most of his clergy were quite desperately poor and reduced by the workings of the patronage system to dependence on the influential laity. Inequitable endowments, pluralities and non-residence resulted in a widespread and gross neglect of pastoral care. But what was perhaps most alarming was the almost complete indifference of the ordinary people to the distinctive features of Anglican churchmanship. The letters of the archbishop's suffragans indicated only too clearly that a continual pressure had to be exerted on lay people to attend services, receive the sacrament once a year, and send their children to be catechized or confirmed. In a land which had endured many religious changes and disruptions there was fierce protestant sentiment but Anglicanism as such was very far from having won the hearts of ordinary men and women.[3]

Orthodox religion could hardly be expected to flourish in such unpropitious circumstances. Moreover, other writers, including Christopher Hill and Keith Thomas, have pointed to the prevalence of popular irreligion in the seventeenth century: some labouring people were ignorant of the basic tenets of Christianity, many were apparently indifferent to religion and a few exhibited outright hostility and scepticism.[4] And there is no reason to suppose that orthodox beliefs became any more deeply rooted during the following century. Indeed, given the remarkable inadequacies of the eighteenth-century Church, irreligion may actually have grown in strength.

Established religion, then, had anything but a commanding presence in many English parishes.[5] Many clergymen performed their duties indifferently or negligently. Rich clergymen attended largely to the requirements of a genteel style of life; poor clergymen were preoccupied with the advancement of their careers and catching the eye of an influential patron, and they were liable to become embittered men if forced to endure prolonged penury. Few clergymen, it seems, devoted much time to pastoral labours. In the several cases of relatively prosperous clergymen whose lives are well documented, their everyday routine was dominated, for the most part, by socializing, leisure activities and the management of their own personal affairs. The rapid decline of the ecclesiastical courts from the late seventeenth century seriously handicapped the Church's efforts to enforce religious discipline and conformity. Clerical absenteeism and pluralism further undermined the impact of the Anglican faith. Moreover, in most areas of urban and industrial growth the Church was increasingly unable to cope with the expansion of the local population. In some forest settlements there was no church at all; in parishes that were geographically large, most of them in the North and other upland districts, many people lived at too great a distance from the parish church to enter regularly into its spiritual ministrations; and in London the facilities for worship and pastoral care were completely dwarfed by the vast size of the metropolitan population. In 1727 the Swiss visitor, César de Saussure, said of the London populace that 'It has no education and little fear of God. I am even persuaded that many of this class never go to church, and have no notion of religion, and are addicted to all manner of debauch.'[6] The early Methodist preachers were probably right when they pointed to the pervasiveness of infidelity and religious apathy in plebeian society. The Christian word, as John Wesley soon discovered, was not being heard in many parts of the Kingdom. (The Methodist movement was emerging and winning converts during the middle decades of the eighteenth century, and in some localities the impact of its evangelical teachings was by no means negligible. However, the followers of Methodism remained a tiny fraction of the total English population: the formal membership of the Methodist Connexion did not number 25,000 persons until 1770.[7] For this reason I have felt justified in omitting Methodism from this discussion of popular religion.) In 1733 an English peer remarked on the indifference to religion among some colliers he met in the West of England. They were asked by a gentleman 'whether they went to church. They replied, No. Why, then, said he, I believe you know nothing of the Commandments. They all replied they knew such a family living in their parts, but they did not know them personally'.[8]

We know as well that many labouring people held beliefs about the supernatural that were conspicuously non-Christian in character, and that they often tried to deal with these supernatural forces in ways that the Church vigorously condemned. Indeed, belief in the supernatural could be as actively manifested through the practice of magic as through the forms of worship provided by orthodox religion. Magic, in fact, was a vital component of plebeian culture. It attempted to explain important parts of human experience, especially the misfortunes people suffered, and to provide means of avoiding and managing (or coping with) these painful experiences; and in aspiring to these ends it was, of course, in direct competition with the approved forms of solace offered by the Christian faith. Magic, however, unlike religion, was not a broadly conceived system of belief. As Keith Thomas has said, magic did not provide 'a comprehensive view of the world, an explanation of human existence, or the promise of a future life. It was a collection of miscellaneous recipes, not a comprehensive body of doctrine. Whereas the faith of the Christian was a guiding principle, relevant to every aspect of life, magic was simply a means of overcoming various specific difficulties'.[9] Magic, then, had strictly limited, though still important, functions. It offered a wide range of practical techniques: techniques that were intended to alter men's relations to the natural and social environment. Occult practices — charms, rituals, modes of divination — were expected to afford concrete benefits for those who used them. Magic, in short, was meant to work.

In his very fine book, *Religion and the Decline of Magic*, Keith Thomas has drawn attention to the vitality and prevalence of magical practices and beliefs in the sixteenth and seventeenth centuries. Unfortunately, nobody has yet attempted a thorough study of magic in the eighteenth century. Consequently, we have no adequate appreciation of the character and prominence of magic during the period that especially concerns us. In the conclusion to his book, Keith Thomas considered the reasons for the decline of magical beliefs among propertied and educated Englishmen from the later seventeenth century, but he recognized, of course, the probability that these beliefs retained much of their potency among the labouring people, especially in rural areas. Indeed, when collectors of folklore began to conduct systematic field studies during the Victorian period, they almost always encountered abundant evidence as to the resilience of magic in plebeian society. Folklore studies from these years are full of references to the survival of beliefs in magic. One observer, for instance, found in the north-eastern counties during the mid Victorian years 'a vast mass of superstition, holding its ground most tenaciously'.[10] A recent study by James Obelkevich of religion in the Lindsey district of Lincolnshire between about 1825 and 1875 has pointed to the survival, among the rural labourers, of numerous magical observances and beliefs.[11] Such evidence of nineteenth-century survivals, seen in the light of Thomas's impressive findings for the years before 1700 — and most nineteenth-century evidence is remarkably similar to that from before 1700 — suggests that popular magic must have been widely practised during the eighteenth century. In fact, only by inferring such cultural continuity through the eighteenth century can the nineteenth-century evidence be satisfactorily accounted for. But is there any direct evidence on magical practices during the century or so after the Restoration? Given that there were hardly any students of folklore before 1800, investigators who might have at least observed popular behaviour and reported their findings, can anything worthwhile be said about the position of magic in eighteenth-century culture?

There are, in fact, three aspects of magic for which there is a modicum of eighteenth-century evidence: magical healing, divination and the practices of cunning men. Magical healing involved the attempt to deploy supernatural powers to combat illness. The central assumption underlying this healing was 'that disease was a foreign presence in the body needing to be conjured or exorcised out'.[12] Such exorcism might depend on charms, incantations, or efforts to draw out the evil spirits and transfer them to some other body. Amulets were often worn to help ward off sickness. To take one example of these magical practices, the bodies of executed men were thought to have the power to draw off the alien forces underlying certain ailments. After a public hanging in Gloucester in 1736,

several Persons having Wens in their Necks, made Application to the Sheriff to receive the Stroking or Laying on of the Dying Man's Hands, with the agonizing Sweats appearing thereon, in order to reduce the Swelling; and after bearing his Hands on their Necks whilst he hung, they seemed so well satisfied with the Apprehensions of a Cure, or some comfortable Relief by this Means, that at their Departure they severally returned Thanks to the Sheriff.[13]

Similarly, after a public execution in London in 1759, 'A young Woman, who had a Wen on her Neck, was held up in a Man's Arms, and the Hand of one of the hanging Malefactors was several Times rubbed over it, with much Ceremony.'[14] On the occasion of the execution of Nicholas Mooney in Bristol in 1752 it was said that a young woman had come 'fifteen miles for the sake of the rope from Mooney's neck, which was given to her, it being by many apprehended that the halter of an executed person will charm away the ague, and perform many other cures'.[15] There must have been many magical practices of this sort, attempted cures that depended on occult manipulations, though few were actually written down. One observance that was recorded involved the assumption of a sympathetic relationship between people and trees, and in 1776 Gilbert White recalled a ritual, involving a row of pol-lard-ashes in Selborne, which attempted to make practical use of this relationship.

These trees, when young and flexible, were severed and held open by wedges, while ruptured children, stripped naked, were pushed through the apertures, under a persuasion that, by such a process, the poor babes would be cured of their infirmity. As soon as the operation was over, the tree, in the suffering part, was plastered with loam, and carefully swathed up. If the parts coalesced and soldered together, as usually fell out, where the feat was performed with any adroitness at all, the party was cured; but, where the cleft continued to gape, the operation, it was supposed, would prove ineffectual.

'We have several persons now living in the village', he added, 'who, in their childhood, were supposed to be healed by this superstitious ceremony.'[16] It was believed that, as the tree healed and grew, so too the child would recover and grow in strength.

Plebeian culture also included numerous rituals intended to foretell the future, or even to affect future events. The practice of divination usually focused on the major issues of life: the identity of a future spouse, the prospective fortune of a child or the sex of an unborn child, the deaths that would occur in a parish during the coming year. Love divination seems to have been especially common, mostly among women. John Brand wrote in 1777 that 'our rural Virgins in the North, are said to use some singular Rites in fasting what they call St. Agnes' Fast, for the purpose of discovering their future Husbands'.[17] William Hutton recalled how a woman with whom his widowed father lodged in the 1730s, and who apparently wanted to marry him, resorted to various divinatory practices in order to foretell what would come of her ambitions.[18] Other rituals were designed to make a young woman dream of her future mate.[19] Such formal divinatory techniques should, of course, be distinguished from the widespread belief in omens and portents — that is, in unarranged and unsought prognostications. Such beliefs concerned the many small circumstances and (to our minds) chance occurrences of everyday life that were thought to presage good or bad fortune: the sudden loss of hair, finding a pod with nine peas, spilling salt, breaking a looking-glass, the appearance of a bird at a particular moment in life.[20]

While many magical techniques and rituals could be practised by anyone, it was often desirable, so numerous people thought, to seek out the services of a specialist in magic: a person who was thought to possess special powers in managing and interpreting the mysterious world in which people lived. These special individuals were known as wise men (or wise women), white witches, conjurers, or cunning men; and they were thought to possess a wide range of skills. They were often consulted for medical advice: they diagnosed a patient's ailments, commonly attributing them to supernatural causes, and they prescribed appropriate remedies, either 'natural' or supernatural. If a person was thought to be a victim of black magic, the advice of a wise man would probably be solicited, for he might be able to counteract black magic with white magic. In 1760 one writer spoke of a 'White Witch, who was referred to on Account of a young Woman, said to be afflicted with an uncommon Disorder, and pronounced to be bewitched'.[21] The cunning man was also considered to be an expert in the rituals of divination: he might, for instance, describe 'to young People of both Sexes what Sort of People they should marry, whether happy or unhappy in their Love Affairs'.[22] He was also reputed to be capable of helping to locate lost or stolen property. A man living near Leominster, Herefordshire, in 1731 was accused of 'taking on himself the Practice of Conjuration, pretending thereby to restore Goods stolen; or informing where they might be had, or giving a Description of the Persons who conceal'd or stole them'.[23] The fictional 'Countryman' in Daniel Defoe's *A System of Magick* (1727) said of the 'Cunning Man . . . hard by Northampton' that 'he can cast a Figure, tell Folks where their lost Cattle are, tell who robs them, and oftentimes help them to get their Goods again'. The 'Countryman' wanted to find out who (as he imagined) had cuckolded him, and he was confident that the cunning man 'will make me dream of the Man, and see him in my Sleep'.[24] Cunning men were also thought to be skilled in the interpretation of dreams and apparitions. The local wise man, in fact, offered advice on a wide variety of matters, and he often enjoyed a position of prominence in the local community. Many eighteenth-century villages must have had the sort of magical specialist that was still found in some places during the Victorian period, when his activities were more likely to get reported: there was, for instance, a noted cunning man in Darrington, Yorkshire before about 1850, and a later writer recalled his standing among his neighbours:

A few years before I knew anything about the village, there had died in it a person who must have been either the last, or one of the last of those strange characters, the Wise Men. He was known as Wise Man Wilkinson, and they used to tell me astonishing tales of his powers. He was credited with miraculous abilities by the people, and nothing that any clergyman or minister could say could alter the popular belief in him. The farmers used to give him a small annual payment to charm the fields, so that they might produce good crops, and they were all afraid of offending him lest he should put an evil spell on their cattle. In a certain degree he usurped the proper provinces of the veterinary surgeon and the doctor. If a cow was ill they would send it to the Wise Man for a charm; if a servant maid had toothache she would give him a shilling to write some cabalistic words on a scrap of paper, which was then tightly rolled up and placed in the hollow tooth. Whether it was because of their faith or whether the long arm of coincidence helped him it is certain that the Wise Man was firmly believed in. Everybody agreed that he had vast powers and that he was very rarely unable to exercise them.[25]

One finds as well scattered references to various other manifestations of magical beliefs: beliefs in ghosts, for instance, or in haunted houses.[26] Certain beliefs were associated with the dead, such as ensuring the soul of the dead person a contented afterlife, or enacting a proper rite of passage for a person at the time of his death. In 1762, when a man was about to be buried in Whittlesey, Cambridgeshire, 'some of the People observing the Bottom of the Coffin moist, to satisfy their Curiosity raised up the Lid, and to their Surprize found in the Coffin upwards of two Gallons of strong Beer, which has been put there by his Wife, who when she was asked the Reason, replied, That he loved Ale when alive, and she was willing he should not want it now he was dead'.[27] Several days after the death of a shepherd in Sussex in 1752, 'when the Corpse was to be interred, the Coffin was opened in the Room, though the Corpse smelt offensively, in order that the Country People, who were invited to the Burial, might have an Opportunity of seeing and touching the dead Body, a Circumstance which, according to their superstitious Notions, would prevent them from dreaming of their Acquaintance the Shepherd'.[28] In addition, popular beliefs in black witchcraft, which were perhaps the most conspicuous components of the culture of magic prior to 1700, persisted in many rural districts well into the eighteenth century. These beliefs, however, were no longer shared by most gentlemen, as they had been in previous generations; consequently, the prosecution of alleged witches noticeably declined and then ceased altogether, and the mobilization of popular hostility against witches came to be vigorously condemned by respectable opinion. Plebeian attempts to punish witches became rare, and one of the last public exercises in witch-hunting, at Tring in Hertfordshire in 1751, which resulted in the death of an elderly woman, received extensive negative publicity and was treated very seriously by the courts (one man was executed for his role in the witch-trial).[29] But whatever institutional restraints might have been imposed upon direct actions against witches, the underlying beliefs in witchcraft were harder to eradicate. The man to be executed in connection with the witch-trial at Tring had the sympathy, it seems, of most of the people: they declared 'that it was a hard Case to hang a Man for destroying an old wicked Woman that had done so much Damage by her Witchcraft'.[30] Similarly, after the 'trial' of a suspected witch near Frome, Somerset, in the winter of 1730/31, and her subsequent death, attempts were made by the authorities to prosecute some of the ringleaders for manslaughter, 'but tho' there were at least 200 Spectators, yet they cannot get Evidence against any of the principal Actors'.[31]

The prevalence of magical beliefs in eighteenth-century England was largely a function of people's inability to exercise effective technical control over their environment. Magical techniques compensated for the inadequacies of secular techniques. As Keith Thomas has argued:

it is the technological gap between man's aspirations and his limited control of his environment which gives magical practices their relevance. . . . their purposes were usually strictly practical. If contemporary doctors had been cheaper and more successful, people would not have gone to charmers. If there had been a police force to trace stolen goods there would have been no recourse to cunning men. If the Church had been able to cater for all practical needs there would have been no wizards. . . . The cunning folk discharged a limited number of functions: people went to them at times of need, for highly practical purposes and in a distinctly utilitarian frame of mind.[32]

But were magical rites effective? Did they produce any beneficial results? Recent writers have agreed that magic did achieve certain practical objectives. Divination, for instance, could be a means of helping a person to make a decision on some difficult matter by confirming and legitimizing, through ritual, what he or she was already inclined to do. Cunning men often functioned as professional consultants and personal advisers: they counselled people in distress or uncertainty, they offered sensible advice, they helped people to face the future more confidently. Their functions were akin to those of priests in some societies, of doctors in others. Their mystifying rituals, exotic props, and elaborate incantations were largely intended to impress their clients and reinforce their own authority, but the practical advice they offered was commonly based on more mundane considerations (such as shrewd questioning and good local intelligence), and the advice was often sound, or at least useful. Defoe recognized this, even as he condemned the 'fraudulence' of the cunning men and the credulity of their clients.[33] Take theft-detection as an example. Since society made virtually no useful provision for the recovery of stolen goods, a person who had been robbed might well consider resorting to a cunning man for help. The victim would have his suspicions, and probably reveal them; and the conjurer would probably know the local community well and have an informed opinion as to who the culprit might be. Conversation between the two would reveal a likely suspect, and the cunning man would then proceed to confirm, through ritual, the client's suspicion. This suspicion, of course, could well have been wrong. However, in a place where the cunning man's powers of detection were widely respected, simply the news that he was being consulted might induce the thief to restore the victim's property, for he was likely to fear exposure at the hands of the cunning man. This fear and respect were fundamental to the cunning man's effectiveness, as is suggested by an incident in Sheffield in 1788. A steelworker had been robbed of his life-savings of 17 guineas:

The poor man, almost in despair, employed the crier to make known his loss; and added, that if the money was not returned by such a day, he would next ways apply to the *Copper-street conjurer*, and proclaim the thief. In such high reputation, it seems, is the *Copper-street conjurer* for his knowledge in the *Black Art*, that the thief replaced eleven guineas of the money, the next night, which, it was supposed, was all he had left of the booty.[34]

Authoritative conjuring — conjuring that people took seriously — could, then, be a source of terror to wrongdoers (potential or actual): it was a means of deterring deviance, encouraging conformity and flushing out social offenders.

Magic, moreover, also gave people a sense of confidence that their problems could be overcome, and it was therefore psychologically valuable. It was one way of 'controlling', by means of the imagination and the ritualized expression of desire, what could not be mastered by technology. Magic could give men hope: the hope of mastering their hazardous environment and keeping trouble at bay, the hope that intense desire could be made into reality. (Hope could also help in healing, especially in cases of psychosomatic illnesses. Magic allowed a person to participate in his own cure, and the enhanced sense of confidence that stemmed from rituals and charms may have stimulated the patient's own healing mechanisms.[35]) Magic was one expression of the disinclination to do nothing when trouble struck: it reflected the need often felt to take some sort of action, to resist despondency and defeatism. As Malinowski once pointed out, an important function of magic 'is to ritualize man's optimism, to enhance his faith in the victory of hope over fear. Magic expresses the greater value for man of confidence over doubt, of steadfastness over vacillation, of optimism over pessimism'.[36] (Of course, magical beliefs were not always or entirely functional. Their implications could also be harmful and destructive. Unchecked superstitions could make people unnecessarily fearful, even terrified; 'evil omens', for instance, must have caused much unproductive anxiety. Some magical beliefs, such as those concerning witchcraft. heightened suspicions among neighbours and legitimized the ill-treatment of certain individuals, especially elderly women. A conjurer might be a rogue and an opportunist rather than a helpful counsellor. Magic, then, like almost any component of culture, can be seen in more than one light.)[37]

Finally, it is important to recognize that, from a popular perspective, magic and religion had many similarities. Both postulated the controlling power of the supernatural in everyday life, and both 'purported to help men with their daily problems by teaching them how to avoid misfortune and how to account for it when it struck'.[38] Religion and magic offered, in a sense, alternative means of coping with experience. However, in actual practice the distinction was often blurred, for Christian and magical beliefs were apt to coalesce in the popular mind. When evidence of popular religious expression can be found, it is usually discovered to have absorbed a good many highly unorthodox opinions and practices.[39] Moreover, the appeal of religion for many people depended less on its doctrines than on the power and efficacy of its rites and ceremonies. The Church baptized, married and buried: it highlighted and sanctified, through ritual and display, these major events in the cycle of life. The Church, in fact, was extremely well equipped to provide such ceremonial services. But the popular beliefs attached to these rituals were often well removed from the mainstream of Christian doctrine. The sacrament of baptism, for instance, which was held by the Church to be of strictly spiritual significance, was commonly credited by the faithful with physical power as well, and in the mid nineteenth century it was still being said of a sickly infant, 'Ah, there will be a change when he has been taken to church! Children never thrive till they have been christened.'[40] As many sources attest, popular belief concerning 'spiritual' matters was flexible, eclectic, and sometimes loosely construed, and it was seldom without some element of magic. And the benefits of belief, whether that belief was orthodox or unorthodox, were very closely related to the concrete imperatives of the secular world.

Identities

In a society that lacks the means of rapid transport and communications, local peculiarities are likely to be highly developed, and people's sense of identity will be powerfully affected by the distinctive traditions and circumstances of their local environments. In English society around 1700 a labouring man's sense of identity was largely determined by what he perceived and came in contact with in his own immediate locality — his own parish especially, but also the local market town and its hinterland — and by the particular cultural heritage of this parish and the region of which it formed a part. When, as a teenager, John Clare, the Northamptonshire poet and labourer, left his home parish of Helpston to seek employment 'abroad' (that is, more than a half-day's walk away) he felt as if he were entering foreign territory: 'I started for Wisbeach with a timid sort of pleasure & when

I got to Glinton turnpike I turnd back to look on the old church as if I was
going into another country. Wisbeach was a foreign land to me for I had
never been above eight miles from home in my life I coud not fancy England
much larger than the part I knew.'[41] Most labouring people in rural areas had
a closely defined sense of place: a place — both its landscape and its people —
that was known in minute detail; a place that was richly associated with its
own distinctive memories, relics, folklore, legends and customary practices.
The standardization of culture had not yet proceeded very far. There were
striking regional diversities associated with foodstuffs and culinary practices,
with drink (when so much brewing was done locally, ale and beer varied in
character from place to place, and in some localities the ordinary beverage
was cider or, less often, mead), with building materials and the traditions of
house construction, and with sports, festivities, and pastimes. These were
important sources of people's sense of personal identity: an identity that
included a firm attachment to the individuality, the concrete particularity, of
their own localities.

Perhaps the most compelling evidence as to the importance of a locally
defined plebeian consciousness was language itself, for there was no such
thing as a common English tongue. This was not merely a matter of different
accents: local dialects were so pronounced, especially in the countryside, that
a man from one region would frequently have been almost unintelligible to
the inhabitants of a village forty or fifty miles away. As one writer observed,
'every County has its peculiar Dialect, at least in respect to the vulgar
Language of their Rusticks, insomuch that those of Different Counties can't
easily understand each other'.[42] The widely travelled Daniel Defoe claimed
to be well acquainted with the common people and to have 'observ'd their
Language, that is, the several Dialects of it, for they strangely differ in their
Way of expressing themselves, tho' in the same Tongue; and there is as much
difference between the English Tongue, as spoken in the North of England,
and the same tongue, as spoken in the West, as between the French spoken in
Normandy, and that of Gasgogne, and Poictou'.[43] In another passage on the
same subject he suggested that 'the difference' between the speech in the
Dorset-Somerset region and that of London 'is not so much in the orthography
of words, as in the tone, and diction; their abridging the speech, *cham* for *I
am, chil* for *I will, don,* for *put on,* and *doff,* for *put off,* and the like'.[44]
Similarly, another traveller, William Stukeley, said of the Tyneside region in
1725: 'They speak very broad; so that, as one walks the streets, one can
scarce understand the common people, but are apt to fancy one's self in a
foreign country.'[45] Regional dialects were still deeply rooted in many rural
districts at the end of the century, and occasionally, as William Marshall
observed in Yorkshire, major distinctions in language were even to be found
within the same county.[46]

This linguistic diversity was partly a consequence of the substantial degree of illiteracy among the labouring people, for the inability to read common texts seriously restricted the possibilities for the standardization of language. But can one establish, with any sort of precision, the extent to which people could or could not read? Is there any useful way in which literacy can be measured? There are, of course, major hazards inherent in this area of inquiry: it is always necessary to posit some kind of meaningful relationship between the ability (or inability) to sign one's name, which can be directly observed, and the ability to read, which cannot be so observed; and the statistics concerning the ability to form a legible signature (or the necessity of making a mark instead) are of interest only in relation to their presumed significance for our assessment of the extent and social implications of actual functional literacy. Serious problems are still involved in interpreting the relevant primary sources; however, several helpful studies have recently been conducted on the history of literacy, and certain conclusions can now be reported with at least a modicum of confidence. It seems that, in the population at large during the 1750s, about 63 to 64 per cent of women and about 40 per cent of men were unable to sign their names in the marriage registers.[47] Illiteracy was always more common among women than men, and it was more pronounced in the countryside than in cities. In London, for instance, minimal literacy was very widespread: one study of thirteen parishes in the City between 1755 and 1759 found that 92 per cent of all men and 74 per cent of all women could sign their names. The rate of literacy was probably higher in London than in any other part of the country.[48] In contrast, in an entirely rural district of Bedfordshire between 1754 and 1785 only 52 per cent of the men and 28 per cent of the women could sign their names in the marriage registers.[49] The literacy rates in provincial towns were probably lower than those in London but higher than those in the countryside. In the 1760s in Northampton, for example, about 70 per cent of the bridegrooms and 44 per cent of the brides were able to write their names.[50]

What are some of the implications of this evidence for our understanding of popular culture? The widespread inability to read and write, especially in country districts, meant, of course, that oral communications were inevitably very highly developed. Traditions, stories, and practical knowledge were passed on by word of mouth, from generation to generation; and this oral tradition was the principal source of personal guidance, useful experience, imaginative expression, and helpful precedents. Wisdom was handed down from father to son and from mother to daughter; it was not learned from books. Consequently, the overwhelming emphasis in social conduct was on custom, on preserving past practices, on maintaining usages that had been observed 'from time out of mind'. The folk memory was the reservoir of the people's heritage: they looked to past experience to guide them in the present and future; they were concerned, not to innovate, but to ensure the continuity of life according to traditional standards. This involvement in an overwhelmingly oral culture may have sharpened and refined certain of their powers. It was said, for instance, that when few books were available, 'Men had to depend on their memories alone, and in consequence these were trained far more highly than they are to-day.'[51] But for many purposes memory is a weak tool, and a problematical source of authority; and the capacity of an oral culture to deal with an increasingly complex world is inherently limited, especially when the rulers of the people — the class of gentlemen, merchants and prosperous farmers — are themselves literate and well familiar with the keeping of records and the transmission through print of news and information. In most parts of rural England popular consciousness must have been markedly parochial and deprived of reliable information from distant places — though not, perhaps, quite as severely parochial as has sometimes been thought (newspapers were read aloud in some public houses, travellers brought news from the wider world, attending the weekly market broadened people's horizons). An oral culture was bound to restrict the development of a common plebeian consciousness; it also precluded any significant political mobilization that went beyond local grievances.[52] It is noteworthy that the evidence of popular political consciousness and responsiveness to political ideas relates almost entirely to London, a handful of provincial cities, and the elite of labour, such as skilled craftsmen and small tradesmen: those groups, in other words, that were most literate, most disposed to read and most likely to be informed about the activities of the nation's governing oligarchy. Almost all labouring people were sensitive to matters of social justice, but self-conscious radicals, for the most part, were bred only among readers.

Recreations

Much of the evidence presented thus far in this book tends to highlight the insecurities and sufferings of the labouring people: it points to the harsh reality of premature death, chronic illness, physical breakdown and grinding poverty. These were undoubtedly critical elements in the experiences of very many people. It is important, however, that we take care not to exaggerate their weight and significance in the full context of popular experience. For there was another, and quite different, dimension of popular experience that deserves to be accorded equal appreciation: the experience of play, of festivity and joyful celebration. It was through these experiences of recreation and free expression — music and dance, festivals and sports — that men and women were able to enjoy social and aesthetic pleasures and the satisfactions derived from ritual. These were the experiences that helped to satisfy the 'longing for amusement, distraction, sightseeing, and laughter', a longing that one modern writer considered 'the most legitimate desire of human nature'.[53] Play and festivity allowed people to fulfil some of their creative aspirations and to escape temporarily from the drabness of everyday routine, the tribulations of ordinary life. Perhaps the most satisfactory contemporary definition of such experiences came from Samuel Johnson, who spoke of 'diversion' as 'Sport; something that unbends the mind by turning it off from care'.[54]

During much of the eighteenth century the occasions for popular recreation were widely established and broadly accepted by all levels of society. Despite the earlier attacks on popular culture by the puritan reformers, most traditional forms of popular recreation continued to flourish during the century after the Restoration. The long-established holiday calendar, the character of which was determined largely by the seasonal rhythms of agriculture and the celebrations of the ecclesiastical calendar, offered an essential framework for the annual cycle of public festivities. Christmas, Shrovetide, Easter, May Day, Whitsuntide, the conclusion of the harvest: all these festive occasions were widely observed, and each one was marked by its own special customs, rituals and recreational attractions. In addition, annual parish feasts (or wakes) were held almost everywhere, generally in either the late spring or late summer-early autumn, and they served as major occasions for abundant eating and drinking, for sports and entertainments, and for the offering of hospitality to visiting friends and relations. In the early eighteenth century a feast was celebrated in at least two-thirds of the parishes of Northamptonshire; around 1730 Thomas Hearne recorded a feast day for 132 places in Oxfordshire or on its borders; and at least 122 places in Devon were reported to have a feast around 1750.[55] Country fairs were also very prevalent — in the 1750s there were some 300 fairs in the three counties of Essex, Suffolk and Norfolk — and some of them functioned at least partly as occasions for festivity, entertainment and sociability. There was also a considerable variety of sports and pastimes available to the common people: some were closely associated with a particular holiday, others were practised at various times of the year. Football was very common, cricket rather less so; wrestling and cudgelling (or backswords) were popular in some regions, and quoits and skittles were probably widely enjoyed. Bull-baiting and cock-fighting were the most common of the animal sports. And in many places some distinctive annual event was observed, a holiday featuring certain peculiar practices that were rooted in local custom and tradition: Bishop Blaze festivities among the wool-combers (on 3 February), the bull-running at Stamford in Lincolnshire (on 13 November), the 'Whipping Toms' at Leicester (on Shrove Tuesday), the Haxey Hood customs in the Isle of Axholme, Lincolnshire (on Twelfth Day). (These various sports, pastimes, and festivities are all examined in greater detail in my book *Popular*

Recreations in English Society 1700-1850.) The evidence available suggests
very strongly that in the mid eighteenth century traditional recreations in
England were thriving, deeply rooted and widely practised.[56]

The major public occasions for festive celebrations are, understandably,
the best documented of the various components of popular recreation. They
involved large bodies of people (including, in some instances, many gentlemen);
they were observed in most or even all parts of the country; and as very
special occasions in the yearly routine — occasions that exuberantly punctuated
and reinforced the rhythms of nature and of work — they attracted at least a
moderate amount of written commentary. But popular recreation was not
confined to these few annual holidays: much of it was of a more mundane
and unremarkable character, and it was fitted into those intervals of 'free
time' that punctuated the everyday processes of necessary labour. Moreover,
work and recreation were often so closely related that they were almost
indistinguishable. Traditional tales were retold by firesides at night, and
story-telling might accompany the work of spinners, harvesters or servants.
John Clare recalled how as a boy he sometimes worked in the fields at
weeding, 'which was a delightful employment, as the old women's memories
never failed of tales to smoothen our labour; for as every day came, new
Giants, Hobgoblins, and fairies was ready to pass it away'.[57] Among some
groups of workers one of their members was appointed to read aloud as the
others worked. The streets of towns were not simply business thoroughfares:
they were also the settings for a sort of public theatre, an often spontaneous
theatre of everyday life. In some regions, at appropriate seasons, men would
find time for angling, catching birds and hunting small animals. Collecting
nuts or berries provided social outings for women and children. Many
cottagers raised a pig or maintained a carefully cultivated garden[58] and a few
kept bees; these activities were a source of both pleasure and material
sustenance. Pleasure and business might also become meshed together on
market day, for the marketplace was a centre for social as well as economic
transactions. It was a place where news and gossip were exchanged, where
mountebanks and players might be seen and pedlars' wares inspected, and
where contacts could be made with a wider world.

But the focal point for everyday plebeian leisure was undoubtedly the
public house. (There were some 50,000 inns and alehouses in England.)[59] A
public house was the social centre of its community: people repaired to it for
companionship, warmth, games and entertainment and the exchange of
news. It offered a refuge from the harshness of labour and the drabness and
confinement of domestic life. It provided something of a sanctuary from the
intrusions of genteel tastes, and thus its cultural character could be very
much of the people's own making and fashioned to accord with their own

desires and traditions. The public house was the poor man's club: here he could find friends, conversation and a good fire. As well as being an everyday centre for ordinary conviviality, a public house often made special provisions for the diversion of its guests: these might include quoits, skittles, nine-pins, decks of cards or shuffle board. Publicans were also very active in promoting athletic events (wrestling, backswords, races), cock-fights, and special attractions on major holidays, for they knew that a festive or sporting crowd would assure them of a lively trade.[60] Some publicans organized their own petty fairs. Drink, of course, was regarded as an important social lubricant — a reinforcement of friendship, a stimulus to festive sentiments, a necessary accompaniment to joviality and sociability. Drink brought people together and provided a crucial underpinning to their recreational culture: and good ale was the social currency of public house life.[61]

Music was also an important element in the recreational culture of the labouring people, both in everyday life and on festive occasions. Music was the most accessible, the most public, the most democratic, of the creative arts. It was inherently non-exclusive: it could not be privately possessed, as could many of the products of the visual arts; and the material prerequisites for its practice and enjoyment were minimal, at least for singing and some kinds of instrumental music. The pleasure of music was not restricted to people of leisure and property and formal education. Everyone, no matter how poor, had a voice and hearing, the only pieces of equipment required; and all people, whatever their background, could understand the fundamental emotions of hope and fear, of love and aggression, the sense of jubilation or of sorrow, to which music gave expression. Music is accessible to the ear, and this was a fundamentally oral culture: a culture in which hearing played a larger role in people's awareness of the world than it does today. Communications were overwhelmingly by word of mouth, through face-to-face contacts; and since the culture of the written and printed word was weakly developed, especially in rural areas, literature was of negligible importance in most people's lives. The popular 'literature' that did exist was still, for the most part, unrecorded: it was transmitted orally from generation to generation, in the form of folk stories, proverbs and legends, and much of the poetry of the people was expressed musically, through the lyrics of ballads and songs. John Clare remembered how his father was 'fond of Ballads, and I have heard him make a boast of it over his horn of ale, with his merry companions, that he could sing or recite above a hundred; he had a tolerable good voice, and was often called upon to sing at those convivials of bacchanalian merry makings'.[62] Ballads were communicated in various ways: by fairground singers and travelling entertainers, by street minstrels, by workers moving from place to place. And in this culture of balladry there was sometimes no clear dissociation between the printed and the spoken word, for many songs had come to be printed and widely circulated, and thus they could have been read as well as heard — at least by those labouring people who had attained a minimal standard of literacy. Song-sheets were hawked in the streets of towns and, according to one authority, they 'were pasted up on the fireplace surrounds and high bench-ends' in country inns 'for the benefit of carters, ploughmen and others'.[63] The medium of print, in such circumstances, probably helped to reinforce, rather than reduce, the vitality of traditional folk song.

Music, in its various forms, was a central component of plebeian experience. Weavers sang at their looms, haymakers in the fields, mothers at their babies' cradles. When a farmer in Kent visited his oast house early one morning in September 1772 he reported: 'I heard my hop dryer (William Mace) sing very melodious several psalm tunes.'[64] Music could readily be a part of the everyday necessities of work: as one ballad put it, there were songs

Which every young swain may whistle at plough,
And every fair milk-maid sing at her cow.[65]

Dancing — and there were many occasions for dancing — assumed musical accompaniment; processions and ceremonials normally included some kind of musical participation; and public houses must have often afforded the sorts of convivial settings in which local singers were disposed to perform. Fiddlers were present at many times of festivity (at weddings, harvest dinners, village feasts, sheep-shearings, rush-bearings), town waits enlivened borough celebrations, and itinerant street musicians performed more routinely. Music from a violin and a horn even accompanied a body of rioters in Stonehouse, Gloucestershire in June 1734, as they set about destroying the local turnpike toll-gates.[66] Church choirs and (to a lesser extent) orchestras were established in many villages by the later eighteenth century, as is indicated by the presence of singers' and minstrels' galleries in parish churches (the church choir, according to one authority, was an 'established institution' which 'had become generally accepted in country churches by the middle of the eighteenth century'), and by the numerous references after about 1750 to the playing of musical instruments at Sunday services (especially bassoons, cellos and bass viols).[67] The compelling hymns of Charles Wesley were partly responsible for the popular appeal of early Methodism. Bell-ringing, both of church and hand bells, was widespread and popular, as numerous sources attest, and special societies were formed for the cultivation of the skill.[68] Music, of almost any sort, revealed the transforming potential of the plebeian imagination: it helped to tame a harsh reality, to assist people in coping with life; it offered hope and consolation; it gave expression to a sense of resilience and determination, and of the longing for a better life. Music, in short, must have been, for many people, one of the undeniable pleasures of life: a solace, a joy, the occasion for a sense of liberation, an accompaniment to laughter, or just plain entertainment.

Popular recreations served a great variety of purposes, some of them fairly obvious, others rather less apparent. Many festive events offered important occasions for courtship and sexual encounters. They provided young men and women with some of the best opportunities for establishing new contacts and for pursuing acquaintances already made; and because of their free and easy and relatively uninhibited social textures, they encouraged the kinds of gallantries, flirtation and personal displays that were not usually possible in everyday life. Ordinary sexual constraints were always relaxed during times of festivity. In many instances popular recreations also helped to foster social cohesiveness and group unity. Competitive team sports, for example — village against village, craft against craft — often reinforced the sense of solidarity of the communities from which the opposing players were drawn. The rituals that were observed on certain holidays — club day feasts, Plough Monday processions, weavers' parades, Bishop Blaze festivities — were affirmations of common interests and common sentiments, and always helped to consolidate group pride. Parish feasts encouraged social cohesiveness through their emphasis on fellowship, hospitality, good cheer, the entertaining of visitors and the renewal of the bonds of kinship and neighbourliness. Indeed, most festivities celebrated those ideals that transcended self; they reinforced the individual's consciousness of his group identity, his sense of social belonging. Furthermore, most popular recreations served to provide realistic opportunities for common people to acquire prestige and self-respect. Football, cricket, boxing, running, wrestling, cudgelling: all these sports afforded occasions for gaining personal recognition. It is clear, in fact, that one of the important implications of many recreations was that the accomplishments on the playground, and the ceremonial arrangements at a festival, and the display of fancy dress expected at a fair, provided substantial raw material for status evaluations. Persons were accorded criticism or applause, respect or shame, as a consequence of their success or failure in certain well established recreational roles. These, indeed, were among the few kinds of opportunities that labouring people had to perform publicly for the esteem of their peers.[69]

Recreation, in its various forms, was an important component of plebeian culture. It complemented the necessities of labour and offered distinctive satisfactions that were highly valued by labouring people. Festive occasions were very much times of freedom: they temporarily liberated men and women from many normal cares and constraints, they helped to alleviate the monotony and drabness of everyday life, they allowed opportunities for personal indulgence and provided moments of excitement, gaiety and spectacle — moments to enjoy, to look forward to, to be remembered. They were times of social suspension when the necessities of life could be subjectively transcended. It was said that during the Christmas season in Cumberland the country worker 'refuses to be governed by the cold and niggardly maxims of economy and thrift'.[70] Holidays were the principal plebeian occasions for cutting a figure, for living well (good food, lots of drink) and spending freely. Play and festivity offered, in a sense, an alternative reality to the reality of ongoing labour. A feast, a fair, a communal celebration, a major sporting event — indeed, most recognized holiday occasions — gave a labouring person, as one writer has aptly put it, 'the opportunity to be something other than what work made one'.[71]

Customary usages

At the root of many popular recreations, as of so much else of plebeian culture, were deeply held notions of customary practice and prescriptive right. Indeed, most of the people's activities were imbedded in traditions of customary usage, and the customs themselves were sustained by certain expectations about social behaviour for which there was a widespread popular consensus. Many traditional rights and customs flourished in the eighteenth century: the custom of gleaning in the fields, the right to gather fuel, the tradition of a rural feast that assumed the squire's patronage, the right to solicit (and obtain) donations on some annual holiday, the custom of sporting in a particular field (sometimes known as a 'football close' or a 'camping close': camping was the East Anglian version of football) at certain times of the year.[72] Around 1720 the rector in Landbeach, Cambridgeshire, was paying 'by custom' 2s. 6d. 'on Shrove Tuesday for the Football men'; at Beverley in the East Riding during the eighteenth century it was 'the custom, from time immemorial, for every Mayor of this town on his election, to give a bull to the populace, for the purpose of being baited, on the day of his being sworn into office'; and in Randwick, Gloucestershire, in the 1770s the people justified their annual revel by pleading 'the prescriptive right of antient custom for the licence of the day'.[73] Custom was observed in many different forms and served many different purposes: and many customs were seen by the people as having the force of law. In February 1766 there were severe storms in the area of Wychwood Forest in Oxfordshire that broke the tops and branches off many trees, and it was said that 'the neighbouring poor are extremely busy in sharing the spoil, [since] all falling wood is theirs by ancient custom'.[74] In some parts of the Midlands, according to William

Marshall, 'each labourer who has been constantly employed through the summer, has a right, by custom, to the carriage of a load of coals, in autumn. It is also a pretty common custom for farmers to let their constant labourers have their bread corn somewhat below the market price; more especially when corn is dear'.[75] The language of custom and privilege is a recurrent feature in contemporary sources, for the authority of custom — custom as a sanction, as a regulator, as a source of guidance — was a pervasive and inescapable reality in the culture of the labouring people.

One of the customs of the people — a custom that was not observed in polite or bourgeois society — was the so-called 'wife sale'. Edward Thompson has now succeeded in reconstructing the character and rationale of this plebeian practice.[76] A wife sale — whose particular rituals varied somewhat from region to region — was normally conducted in a clearly conventionalized manner. In one widespread form of the wife sale, a woman would be brought by her husband to the local marketplace, with a halter around her neck or waist. There she would be publicly exposed for sale. The sale was conducted in the manner of an auction — the husband might note some of his wife's recommendations, and then call for bids — and within a short space of time the woman would be sold to a man in the crowd who had offered to purchase her. The sale price was commonly fairly low, perhaps a shilling or half a crown, though sometimes the sum was larger. After the price was agreed upon the husband would often ceremoniously transfer the rope that held his (now former) wife into the hands of the purchaser, and the three parties to the transaction would sometimes retire to a public house to seal the bargain with a quart or two of ale, and perhaps some sort of written 'contract'.

The custom of the wife sale has sometimes been regarded as an exhibition of brutal and unfeeling social behaviour. However, Mr Thompson's examination of the practice has forced a reconsideration of these assessments. Several conclusions emerge from his study. First, the marriage under view had usually already broken down: the husband and wife were seriously at odds with each other and in some cases they were already living apart. Second, it seems that a wife sale, by popular custom, had to be conducted with the consent of the wife, not against her will. Third, the purchaser of the woman was not only normally known to her, he was often already her lover. The wife sale, then, was not done on impulse or in a random manner. In fact, it was a regulated ritual for the legitimation of divorce and remarriage. Given that legal divorce was in practice prohibited to almost all English men and women, the wife sale afforded certain people a publicly performed marital rite of passage that carried the recognition of the community. The wife sale was certainly regarded by many labouring people as a legitimate and lawful form of marriage, not in any way disreputable. To take just one example of the custom, in 1784 it was reported from Bristol that:

A man who had been some years abroad returned lately, and hearing that his wife cohabited with an acquaintance of his, a chimney sweeper, he went to their place of abode, and demanded her; but the sable knight of the brush, unwilling to part with what he considered a valuable acquisition, proposed a legal transfer by purchase, to which the husband agreed, and writings being accordingly drawn up, and presented to a lawyer for inspection, who pronounced them invalid, and advised the parties, as a mutual security, to have the woman taken by her husband, with a halter round her neck, to a public market, and there exposed for sale. In consequence of this, the woman walked in form to the beast market on Saturday, and was there purchased by her paramour for a guinea. This done, the parties retired, each seemingly well satisfied.[77]

Another custom that deserves to be noticed is the practice of 'trial marriage'. The prevalence and practical workings of this custom are still, it should be said, poorly understood. However, the evidence that has now come to light is sufficient to call for at least passing consideration. It is clear, for a start, that many women were already pregnant at the time of marriage: approximately one-third of England's eighteenth-century brides were pregnant on their wedding days, with a greater proportion pregnant towards the end of the century than at the beginning.[78] In attempting to explain this substantial incidence of pre-nuptial pregnancy, it is likely that a variety of circumstances will have to be taken into account, one of which will almost certainly be the custom of trial marriage. The evidence here, I admit, is thin, but what there is warrants attention. The social reformer Jonas Hanway, a very didactic writer but also a fairly well-informed observer of plebeian life, remarked on the practice at least twice. He regretted that the 'animal part of the villagers predominates so much, that the male and female often come together before marriage; and if the woman *proves*, as they term becoming pregnant, then the parties marry by a kind of honour and decency'. In country districts, he said, 'it is a common practice (not universal) to come together first, and if they *prove*, as they term it, then they marry. This is a law of honor'.[79] (Hanway and others recognized that some men did not choose to obey this law, thereby leaving their women in the lurch.) Perhaps the most explicit evidence concerning this customary practice relates to the Isle of Portland in Dorset, which was visited by the civil engineer, John Smeaton, in 1756. Smeaton was told by his guide that the local people never married until the woman was pregnant:

The mode of courtship here is, that a young woman never admits of the serious addresses of a young man, but on supposition of a thorough probation. When she becomes with child, she tells her mother; the mother tells her father; her father tells his father, and he tells his son, that it is then proper time to be married....If the woman does not prove with child, after a competent time of courtship, they conclude they are not destined by Providence for each other; and as it is an established maxim, which the Portland women observe with great strictness, never to admit a plurality of lovers at one time, their honour is no ways tarnished: she just as soon (after the affair is declared to be broke off) gets another suitor, as if she had been left a widow, or that nothing had ever happened, but that she had remained an immaculate virgin.[80]

The customary culture of the people also included practices that allowed for the ritualized expression of hostility towards individuals whose behaviour was judged to be flagrantly unnatural, unjust or otherwise deviant. Most labouring people held clear ideas as to the correct standards of moral conduct, and offences against these standards — especially serious and barefaced offences — were liable to result in public manifestations of popular indignation. Such widely felt hostility towards deviant individuals was often formally expressed, and the standard ritual for this purpose was a form of public denunciation known as 'rough music' (in certain districts it was known as the 'skimmington', or 'riding the stang').[81] Rough music was intended to humiliate the offender, to underline publicly his or her 'disgraceful' conduct and dramatically to censure this conduct. It might involve a great deal of raucous noise-making, accompanied by hostile chants and other forms of derision, outside the house of the offender; or it could involve a procession in which an effigy of the transgressor was prominently displayed, ritually abused and (at the end of the ceremony) publicly burnt. An essay of 1755 referred to rough music as a practice 'consisting of performances on cow-horns, salt-boxes, warming-pans, sheep bells, etc. intermixed with hooting, hallowing, and all sorts of hideous noises, with which the young wags of the village serenade their neighbours, particularly those families, in which (as the phrase is) the grey mare is the better horse'.[82] Many instances of rough music were directed against offences relating to marriage: excessive wife-beating (in these cases the women often staged the *charivari*), a marriage in which the wife was obviously the dominant partner, an old man contracting a marriage with a young woman. These were all regarded as very unnatural or improper forms of behaviour. On other occasions the objects of such public reprobation were persons who had misused their authority, or who had violated some deeply held popular sentiment. Paid informers, for instance, who were universally despised (popular suspicion of the machinery of the state was intense and very widespread), were sometimes subjected to the ordeal of a *charivari*; and occasionally a man in a position of authority — perhaps a magistrate or a parish official — was similarly treated when it was thought that he had shamelessly failed to do his duty and to conduct himself responsibly.

Customary practices were a powerful source of discipline and moral regulation within plebeian society. Any society needs means of enforcing its norms, of defending its moral standards, of inducing conformity to its conventional expectations: and the labouring people had various inherited ways of managing their own networks of social relations. These customs were often culturally distinctive — that is, many of them were not shared (or sometimes even approved) by people of property; and the values the people were intent on preserving were not necessarily the same as those favoured by their rulers and employers.[83] Moreover, customary practices assumed especial importance in relation to those branches of life for which the provisions of the law were thought to be inadequate or objectionable. Official sources of authority failed to satisfy many of the needs and desires that arose out of the actual experiences of ordinary existence. The official law afforded no means of divorce: the unofficial wife sale partially filled this vacuum. The official strictures concerning premarital chastity militated against certain useful forms of experimentation: trial marriage was intended to offer young people certain 'sureties' about each other (such as their ability to have children) before they set up lifelong housekeeping together. Rough music was a means by which certain deeds could be effectively sanctioned by the people themselves: deeds in which the law had little interest, or which it might even condone, but which the people regarded as serious offences. Rough music expressed the people's own moral sense, their sense of justice and injustice. It allowed them to affirm some of their own traditional values, to bring offenders into line (or force them out of the community), and to deter such deviance in the future on the part of others. Most customs were both restrictive and permissive: they specified what could be done and how to proceed on certain matters; they helped to clarify the boundaries between what was acceptable and what was unacceptable; and, as I shall argue below, custom provided a critical source of popular self-defence in a highly unequal society, for it was one of the normative weapons of the weak against the strong, one of the ways in which power was disciplined and concessions enjoyed. Customary practices, in short, were vital components of the people's cultural repertory.

Relations with authority

Most of the beliefs, identities and customs that I have examined thus far were rooted in the labouring people's relations with one another, not with members of the governing class. Popular culture was, in many important ways, substantially independent of the culture of polite society. The people had their own traditions, their own beliefs, their own modes of expression, their own priorities and aspirations. Much of their culture they made themselves: it did not trickle down to them from above. At the same time, however, it should be recognized that the lives of the people — or at least aspects of their lives — were inescapably affected by the realities of power in the broader society: the power of magistrates, landowners and local officials; the national power that was concentrated in Westminster. All labouring people had to confront the power of *authority*: its demands, its self-definitions, its capacity to shape people's lives. Chapter 1 described some of the expectations held by men of privilege and authority as to how the labouring people should behave. Working men were expected to know their place, to act with deference towards their superiors, to accept their lot in life in a spirit of dutiful resignation. They were charged with the obligation of labouring diligently for the public good; their personal rewards were to be postponed, for the most part, until the afterlife. These were the official definitions of the role of labour: but were these definitions accepted by the people themselves? Did they actually conform to these moral imperatives that enjoined them to be obedient, grateful, and respectful towards authority? In fact, it is now becoming clear, largely as a result of careful studies of a great many incidents of social conflict, that deference was a very conditional and sometimes calculating disposition, that official definitions of reality were often vigorously resisted, and that popular traditions of independence and dissent were deeply rooted in the cultures of many localities. Moreover, it is clear as well that the people had their own expectations as to how authority should be exercised: they had their own views about its limits and responsibilities, its functions and legitimacy, and these notions were often noticeably at odds with those that were held by the established authorities themselves. Our attention, then, must now be focused on the relations between the labouring people and the people of property and power: the tensions between them, the reasons for the outbreak of popular protests, the conflicts of value imbedded in these tensions and the consequences of the various collective expressions of popular discontent. Popular culture, to be fully appreciated, must be observed not only at moments of joy and exuberance and during periods of calm, ordered routine, but also at times of crisis and social conflict, when dissension had clearly triumphed over consensus. Let us turn, then, to examine this evidence of conflict.

5 Authority, legitimacy and dissension

The relations between the labouring people and people of authority have been variously represented. Some historians have spoken of the paternalism of the gentry, the deferential disposition of their tenants and labourers, and the generally cordial, or at least civil, social relations that were evidenced in most parts of the country. Such views of the past impart a strong sense of social consensus: of mostly harmonious social ties between rich and poor, privileged and unprivileged; of inequalities that were accepted with little fuss; and of a certain inertia and apathy, in regard to broadly 'political' issues, on the part of the labouring people. Other writers, in contrast, have been more impressed by the signs of social tension and disorder — by the frequency of 'popular risings', for instance, and the substantial evidence of plebeian disrespect for established authority. My own view is that such evidence of conflict deserves to be carefully considered. But this is little more than an elementary starting point. For the important issues at hand require a weighing of this evidence, a working out of its implications, and an attempt to place these relations of conflict, and to understand their meanings, within the broader social context.

Popular protest

Although respect for rank, property and authority was said by parsons and magistrates and most social theorists to be divinely ordained, and of fundamental importance to the unfolding of God's purposes on earth, many gentlemen who looked about them were made acutely aware of the large gap between this ideal of social tranquillity and the actual reality of widespread popular discontent and social disorder. Gentlemen complained of the levelling notions of many labouring people, of their 'licentious spirit' and their 'ungovernable appetites'. Social privilege, it appears, was often bitterly resented by the unprivileged, and duly constituted authorities were sometimes treated with derision rather than respect.[1] Servants, regretted one writer in

1693, especially those servants whose religious knowledge was deficient, were too inclined to be discontented with their lot in life. They

are apt to fret and fume at the narrow Portion allotted to them by Providence, to be laid in some cold out-House, or meanest Loft, of a poor Cottage, to have the leavings of the coarse fare there; hard work, cold blasts abroad, and, perhaps, hard words and unkind usage at home: this grates upon the Spirit, and makes them think their Life more miserable than any others; and they that know not God, will talk like Heathens, and rail at luck or Fortune, for placing them in such mean circumstances.[2]

Deference, it seems, could by no means be taken for granted. 'As for our Common People', remarked one observer in 1700, 'many of them must be confess'd to be very rough and savage in their Dispositions, being of levelling Principles, and refractory to Government, insolent and tumultuous.'[3] Some genteel observers attributed much popular discontent to outright envy and jealousy. Bernard Mandeville, for instance, was keen to demonstrate this connection:

In the rude and unpolish'd Multitude this Passion [of envy] is very bare-faced; especially when they envy others for the Goods of Fortune: They rail at their Betters, rip up their Faults, and take Pains to misconstrue their most commendable Actions: They murmur at Providence, and loudly complain, that the good Things of the World are chiefly enjoy'd by those who do not deserve them. The grosser Sort of them it often affects so violently, that if they were not withheld by the Fear of the Laws, they would go directly and beat those their Envy is levell'd at, from no other Provocation than what that Passion suggests to them.[4]

Lord Hardwicke, a prominent member of the Whig oligarchy, may have entertained similar sentiments, for in 1737 he was complaining that the 'people are always jealous of those in power, and mighty apt to believe every piece of scandal or reproach that is thrown upon them'.[5] Social subordination and quiescence were, of course, what such men wished for, but irreverence and insubordination were often what they actually had to face.

Much of the irreverence, unruliness and insubordination that gentlemen complained of was particularly situated in London. Indeed, many of the principal social anxieties of the age — the fear of crime, the concerns about drunkenness (especially cheap gin), the sense of the disintegration of paternalist restraints — were imbedded in the distinctive experiences of London life. London, to many gentlemen, seemed to be a place out of control — certainly out of *their* control. When such men thought of London they thought not only of Ranelagh, the theatre and fashionable society: their reflections also turned to the prevalence of theft, muggings in the streets and the insolence endured from porters, carters, beggars and the jostling crowds of London's busy thoroughfares. The literature of the period is full of a sense of the profound malaise of urban life. As Nicholas Rogers has observed of the literary consciousness of London, 'acute contemporaries were obsessed with the spectre of tumult and disorder. They were disturbed by the high incidence of violent crime, distressed at the comparative ease with which street robberies were conducted in open daylight within London itself, and dismayed by the insubordination of the common populace'.[6] London was seen as a great source of corruption: a centre of contaminating influences, of the destruction of innocence — usually thought of as 'rural innocence' — by vice and greed. Servants who came to London, it was thought, were quickly ruined. As one moralist claimed in 1746, in what was a commonplace charge, servants 'soon exchange the simplicity of the country, for the foppery of the town.... Here they lose their good principles; their morals are stained, their heart grows bad, and they stand ready prepared for the worst of crimes.... They are under no religious restraints, who then will vouch for their fidelity?'[7] In the city, moral evil and social disorder; in the country, innocence and order: this was a fundamental contrast in the minds of many gentlemen, a contrast that was repeatedly expressed. One observer in 1755, for instance — and there are many other almost identical observations — found that 'in London amongst the lower class all is anarchy, drunkenness, and thievery; in the country good order, sobriety and honesty, unless in manufacturing towns, where the resemblance of London is more conspicuous'.[8]

While London undoubtedly presented special problems for the preservation of social order, many country districts were much less tranquil and less easily governed than some of these London-oriented anxieties would suggest. Indeed, in many parts of England the exercise of established authority was tenuous, uncertain and often ineffectual. Everywhere, of course, some men had the legal right, reinforced by economic strength, to rule over other men, but the actual effectiveness of such authority in any particular place depended on a multiplicity of local circumstances. In one type of community — perhaps a small market town or a dominant squire's parish — we detect evidence of firm social discipline, outward deference and quiescence. In other places, however, we uncover a social reality of dissent, frequent social conflict and plebeian independence. In these latter districts the formal institutions of power were neither deeply rooted nor widely respected, and their populations were partly withdrawn from, and sometimes resistant to, the exercise of 'lawful' authority. These, then, were areas that had not been fully colonized by the nobility and gentry: official authority was weak, plebeian independence was prominent and relatively unconstrained. Such independence — gentlemen frequently saw it as 'lawlessness' — was normally associated with particular kinds of settlements: with places preserving abundant common rights, with recent settlements in forests and on waste-lands, with villages of smallholders, and with mining communities.[9]

Forest regions appear to have been particularly notorious for their unruliness: by common repute they were thought to be among the most lawless parts of eighteenth-century England. For in the forests of the country, whether they remained wooded or not, settled arable agriculture had not taken root; consequently, although the game of the forests was protected by law, there had been no economic basis for gentlemen, farmers, and ecclesiastics to impose their characteristic imprints of permanence (manor houses, substantial farmsteads, churches) on the local society. The exercise of parochial and manorial authority was either non-existent or very weakly felt. The forest-dwellers, as a result, were relatively unconstrained by the immediate presence of institutional authority, and they were only minimally involved in any relations of clientage with members of the governing class. They subsisted by a variety of (often makeshift) devices and were able to fashion their own distinctive modes of existence; their culture and conduct were often sharply in conflict with the imperatives of the established order around them. In the seventeenth century forest areas were noted for their religious nonconformity, frequent unruliness and general disrespect for established authority;[10] in the following century some of them became centres of serious social disorders, most of which stemmed from the efforts of royal officials and large landlords to impose more effective controls on the forests' inhabitants and to appropriate the forests' resources for their own exclusive uses. The turbulence in the forests of south-east England, and the tensions that arose of the competing claims to the use of game and common land in Cannock Chase, have been fully documented in recent studies.[11] Other forests exhibited similar signs of lawlessness — as seen by the lawmakers. Cranborne Chase in Dorset, for example, was noted in the eighteenth century for its social disorders: deer-stealing was common, smugglers sought refuge in the woods and the local inhabitants were said to be given to 'all kinds of vice, profligacy, and immorality' and to have contracted 'habits of idleness and become pests of society'.[12] Kingswood Forest near Bristol, which was occupied principally by colliers, was one of the most ungovernable districts in England; and the Forest of Dean, also in Gloucestershire, was frequently mentioned in connection with various incidents of popular disturbance.[13] Thieves were often reported to be working out of some forest area, waylaying travellers and sometimes terrorizing the residents of neighbouring villages. The Forest of Selwood, near Frome in Somerset, was said in the late eighteenth century to 'have been, within the memory of man, the notorious asylum of a desperate clan of banditti, whose depredations were a terror to the surrounding parishes. One of their evil practices, and which perhaps was far from being the worst, was that of coining money'.[14] Similarly, Arthur Young complained of the 'morals' of the people dwelling in and around Wychwood Forest in Oxfordshire: 'The vicinity is filled with poachers, deer-stealers, thieves, and pilferers of every kind: offences of almost every description abound so much, that the offenders are a terror to all quiet and well-disposed persons; and Oxford gaol would be uninhabited, were it not for this fertile source of crimes.'[15]

Popular assertiveness, then, whether it is seen as independence or lawlessness, was a vigorous reality in many of the 'open' parishes of England. These were settlements that were relatively withdrawn from the conventional forces of domination (most notably the active presence of a great landowner) that were prevalent in lowland and arable regions. However, the evidence of strained relationships between the propertied and the labouring people goes well beyond the confines of these notoriously open parishes. For there were, as well, times of actual crises of authority, usually during years of dearth, that were widely experienced — experienced in a great variety of places over concentrated periods of (normally) a few weeks or months. And there were also a large number of other expressions of popular discontent, stemming from a variety of circumstances, and from all parts of the country, that focused on such issues as the alleged abuse of magisterial authority, the destruction of certain traditional popular liberties or the imposition of some new claim on the individual by the state. But before attempting to understand some of these grievances it is first necessary to recognize and catalogue this manifold evidence of riot, rebellion, and the mobilization of popular collective action.

In eighteenth-century England the most common cause of social conflict was sharply rising food prices. Labouring families spent a high proportion of their income on food: at least 50 per cent, and sometimes as much as 80 per cent, of their earnings were spend on essential foodstuffs, of which bread (or grain to make flour) was easily the most important item. In good years, when grain prices were low or moderate, most of them could get by; however, in bad years, when prices suddenly shot up, increasing by 50 or even 100 per cent in the space of a few months, family budgets were seriously strained, many small consumers were no longer able to afford basic foodstuffs, and some families faced the immediate prospect of hunger and complete destitution. These conditions were especially prevalent during the following years: 1709, 1740, 1756/57, 1766/67, 1772/73, 1782/83, 1795 and 1800/1. And in all of these years there were widespread 'risings of the people': food riots in which people attempted to remedy some of the serious problems of subsistence that they faced.[16] The extent of these disturbances should not be underestimated. Food rioting affected at least sixteen counties in 1740, at least twenty-four counties in 1766.[17] An analysis of the food riots of 1756/57 has counted over 100 different disturbances in thirty counties.[18] And other recent studies have documented the seriousness and scale of food rioting at the very end of the century.[19] The marketing of food, then, was clearly a critical source of social dissension and of popular discontent.

Conflicts that were rooted in the processes of production were also common, though they were rarely found among agricultural labourers, and they were never as extensive as food riots — that is, during any given year they were always confined to particular localities, and to particular workers within these districts. Most of the disputes between masters and men focused on basic issues concerning the conditions of labour and standards of production: wage rates, payment in truck, the recruitment of new workmen, the means of assessing the quality of workmanship, the control of the actual work-place. These issues were confronted most frequently in England's dominant industry — the manufacture of woollen and worsted cloth — but they surfaced as well, from time to time, in many other trades and crafts. This is a subject on which, at present, general statements cannot be offered with any great degree of confidence, for little research has been conducted on industrial relations in the eighteenth century, and few serious attempts have even been made to draw together and synthesize the substantial body of evidence from regional studies and standard printed sources.[20] It appears, however, from the evidence now available that industrial conflicts were much more widespread than has sometimes been allowed. They were particularly common in the older textile districts of the west of England (Devon, Somerset, west Wiltshire and Gloucestershire), and occasional disturbances occurred in the more buoyant clothing towns of East Anglia and the West Riding of Yorkshire.[21] The various disputes in the cotton and linen industry of south Lancashire are now reasonably well documented.[22] Scattered reports are also found of incidents of collective action by a variety of other workers: Tyneside keelmen on several occasions; framework-knitters in Nottinghamshire in 1778/79; journeymen tailors in Newcastle and Norwich in 1753 and in Bristol in 1762; building workers in Manchester in 1753; nailers in the Birmingham region in 1738; female button-makers in Cheshire in 1737; journeymen needle-makers in the West Midlands in 1759; coal-miners in numerous places at different times in the century.[23] Industrial disputes were commonplace in the royal dockyards.[24] There is also abundant evidence as to the tensions between employers and workmen in many of London's trades.[25] In fact, few trading and manufacturing districts, whether urban or rural, avoided at least one or two major trade disputes in the course of the century.

The other manifestations of social conflict in the eighteenth century were less widespread, though some were especially important in specific regions at particular times. In parts of the south and east coasts affrays between customs officers and smuggling gangs were common, and smuggling was certainly thought to be no crime by the local residents, many of whom profited in a modest way from their periodic employment by the smuggling chieftains.[26] In other regions the Game Laws were a source of tension, though there were few serious conflicts over poaching until the second half of the century.[27] New taxes also caused occasional disturbances. Turnpike tolls, for instance, were sometimes vigorously resisted, mostly in Gloucestershire and Herefordshire during the second quarter of the century and in the West Riding of Yorkshire in 1753.[28] Popular hostility to impressment was frequently evident during times of war, and in 1757 there were widespread riots against the new statutory provisions for recruiting men to the militia.[29] In London many popular protests were at least partly informed by a consciousness of the politics of Westminster and the practices of the nation's ruling oligarchy: the Wilkite movement is the best documented case of these 'libertarian' sensibilities among the populace of London.[30] Finally, attempts to enclose common lands met with a moderate degree of determined opposition, almost certainly more than has sometimes been suspected, though because of the piecemeal impact of enclosure — it affected neighbouring parishes one at a time: one parish in a given year, nearby parishes ten, twenty or thirty years later — collective protests against enclosure were usually small-scale affairs, and they only became more broadly based when the common rights of an extensive region were being threatened, such as in areas of forest, fenland or substantial 'waste'.[31]

This, then, is an elementary inventory of the popular disturbances of the period. But such a summary hardly takes us very far. For our main objective, of course, is to try to understand at least some of the rationale of these protests and riots. How can we account for the people's grievances? And what did they hope to achieve by means of these protests, threats, and direct actions? Furthermore, how did the people regard 'authority'? What were thought to be its rights, its limits, its responsibilities? Finally, what do such disturbances reveal about the relations between the labouring people and the governing class? These, then, are the questions to which we must now direct our attention.

Food riots

Almost all popular protests and collective actions were informed by certain clearly defined moral concerns and social expectations: expectations as to the proper arrangement of economic affairs, the correct observance of priorities during times of hardship or the responsible exercise of magisterial authority. Direct actions, or 'riots', were not merely acts of unreflective impulse: they were disciplined and (at least partly) controlled by a complex of inherited values and sensibilities. Let us consider, for example, the people's ideas concerning the marketing of essential foodstuffs, for these ideas very much conditioned and directed their behaviour during years of dearth. According to these popular notions the public marketplace was the only fully acceptable setting for the buying and selling of grain and other agricultural produce. Farmers, as much as possible, should supply the marketplace directly, where consumers could purchase appropriate quantities of what they needed — a bushel of wheat, a peck of peas, a pound of cheese — from the actual producers. These transactions should be publicly conducted, open to scrutiny, as transparent as possible. Such openness, it was thought, would minimize the possibilites for cheating, profiteering and devious market manipulations. Appropriate officials should superintend the relations of the marketplace in order to ensure a fairness of exchange. The processors of farm produce, such as millers and bakers, should function as servants of the community rather than as profit-oriented entrepreneurs. They should receive a 'fair' return for their labours, not simply as much as the market would bear. From the people's point of view the activities of middlemen, such as badgers, dealers and cornfactors, were very suspect. These middlemen were inclined to circumvent the public marketplace, perhaps by contracting with the farmer for all of his crop before it was even harvested, or by purchasing grain from the farmer, not in bulk at the open market, but rather by sample in the parlour of some inn; non-public practices of this kind were not in accord with the customary notions of correct marketing procedures. Even when dealers did participate in the public marketplace it was felt that their behaviour should be closely regulated. In particular, small consumers should be allowed to make their necessary purchases at the start of the market, and only after a proper opportunity had been given for these needs to be met — often a bell would be rung to mark the beginning and end of this exclusive period of time — were dealers to be permitted to enter the market and purchase whatever provisions the farmer might have left. The central priority in this overall popular outlook was to supply the customary needs of the locality at affordable prices. Only after such needs had been satisfied could provisions be exported to distant places.

There was already, by the later seventeenth century, a large discrepancy between this popular ideal of marketing and the reality of marketing. In fact, a predominantly 'free' market in agricultural produce had already become widely established. The growing cities, most notably London, could only be adequately supplied through the efforts of dealers who purchased grain in many country districts and arranged for it to be transported to the urban markets where it would be sold for a profit. Moreover, after 1689 the government was offering bounties to encourage the export of English grain to foreign countries, and such incentives for farmers and traders were bound to undermine even further the traditional locally oriented patterns of marketing. In years of good or adequate harvests there was seldom any overt conflict between the interests of small consumers and those of traders and farmers. All markets were adequately provisioned, prices remained low or moderate (that is, within the normal range of previous experience), and customary standards of consumption could be readily maintained. However, in years of even modest dearth these customary standards were seriously threatened. Given that the demand for bread was highly inelastic, any shortfall in supplies inevitably meant that some expectations would not be satisfied and that prices, unless regulated, were liable to increase dramatically. In the view of the labouring people it was particularly at such times of deficiency that special care should be taken to enforce the traditional conventions of market relations. Strict priority should be accorded the needs of the small consumer, severe restrictions should be placed on the activities of dealers. No exports should be permitted from the local region unless local demand has been met. The laws against forestalling, engrossing and regrating should be enforced. Farmers should not withhold their supplies from the market, in expectation of higher prices; and cornfactors should not be allowed to speculate in grain and profiteer from its scarcity. In short, the grain market during such years should be closely regulated: regulated, that is, by the established authorities, normally the local magistrates, in the interest of the public as a whole. The justices were expected to protect the interests of the small consumers, to seek out and punish malpractices in marketing, to enforce the laws against profiteering and, if necessary, to regulate the prices of essential foodstuffs. It was thought that, as magistrates, they had certain responsibilities to fulfil, responsibilities of a paternalistic nature, and people of slender means had a strong interest in seeing that, during times of distress, these duties to the public were properly observed.

Although some magistrates undoubtedly did behave in conformity with these popular expectations and did attempt to regulate the marketing of food in the interest of 'fairness' as against profit, many local authorities neglected (or declined) to act in accordance with these standards of paternalism — standards that were manifested in particular laws, not simply in rhetorical ideals. As a result they were perceived by the people as making no effort to protect the interests of small consumers, as was expected of them, and such inaction invariably caused widespread anger and resentment. For if men in authority were to allow the allocation of bread, the basic staff of life, to be determined largely by the unconstrained forces of supply and demand, scarcity would inevitably lead to frightening price rises and severe hardships for many, perhaps most, labouring families. The experience of hardship does not, of course, necessarily lead to collective action. Some hardships may be seen as inescapable and beyond human control, and in these circumstances people may react to trouble with resignation and stoicism. But the hardships resulting from very high food prices were not regarded in this way: they were seen as at least partly a consequence of human greed, negligence and malpractice. Severe and sudden inflation was not accepted as necessary; the claims offered in favour of free market behaviour and the heavy stress placed on the rights of property — a farmer's right, for instance, to sell his crops when he wanted, to whom he wanted, at the price he could get — were thought to be illegitimate; and those magistrates who failed to recognize the rights of the poor to a basic subsistence and to protection against the threat of hunger were regarded as seriously remiss in their duties. But if the authorities failed to act, what could be done? In such circumstances, according to the people's views, it was legitimate to take direct and unofficial action in order to ensure that justice would be done and that the proper procedures for the marketing of food would be duly observed.[32]

These popular actions were intended to achieve several distinct, though related, objectives. Often their principal objective was to regulate prices: to force upon the sellers of food a 'just' or 'reasonable' price — a price that was considered by the people to be morally acceptable. Evidence has been collected of dozens of such cases of popular price-setting. A typical incident was reported from Taunton in Somerset, where, on the first market day in May of 1757, a year of general scarcity, 'a considerable Quantity of Wheat was brought to Town, and 8s. 6d. per Bushel was the Price set by the Farmers; on which a Number of our Tradesmen's Wives . . . assembled and met together, and, by Means of their united Vociferations and repeated Clamours, constrained the Farmers to bring down the Price to 6s. 6d. which the good Women were willing to pay'.[33] Similar incidents were occurring in other towns around the same period of time. At Newcastle-under-Lyne in Staffordshire a 'great Number of People, mostly Women, assembled in a riotous Manner in the Market . . . and seized several Bags of Corn and Oatmeal, which they obliged the Proprietors to sell considerably under the Market Price'; in the Salisbury marketplace 'a small Party of Women . . . laid violent Hands on some of the Farmers Sacks of Wheat and insisted on their selling it at 6s. per Bushel'; at the market in Yeovil, Somerset 'the People rose on account of the high Price of Corn, and obliged the Farmers to sell their Wheat for 10s. per Bushel'; and at Bewdley, Worcestershire, the

'Market . . . was put in a great Confusion by the Assembling of a Number of Women, who cut open some Bags of Wheat, and insisted on their being sold at 7s. per Strike, the Price Wheat sold at the Thursday before at Kidderminster'.[34] At Kidderminster in September 1766, 'some poor Women bidding Money for a Bag of Wheat in the Corn Market, a Baker came and offered more, and bought it from them, on which the People immediately became riotous, and obliged the Farmers to sell it at 5s. per Bushel'.[35] Market tensions of this sort were commonplace during years of scarcity. It was said, for example, that on a market day at Exeter in April 1757 'some Farmers demanded 11s. per Bushel for Wheat, and were agreeing among themselves to bring it to 15s. and then make a stand'. However, some of the townsmen, getting wind of this plot:

sent their Wives in great Numbers to Market, resolving to give no more than 6s. per Bushel, and, if they would not sell it at that Price, to take it by Force; and such Wives, as did not stand by this Agreement, were to be well flogg'd by their Comrades. Having thus determined, they marched to the Corn-Market, and harangued the Farmers in such a Manner, that they lowered their Price to 8s. 6d. The Bakers came, and would have carried all off at that Price, but the Amazonians swore, that they would carry the first man who attempted it before the Mayor; upon which the Farmers swore they would bring no more to Market; and the sanguine Females threatened the Farmers, that, if they did not, they would come and take it by Force out of their Ricks. The Farmers submitted and sold it for 6s. on which the poor Weavers and Woolcombers were content.[36]

Not all such actions were conducted by women. In early December 1757, for instance, about 100 labouring men marched on the market town of Richmond in Yorkshire,

forcibly rung the Corn Bell, and their Ringleader proclaimed the Price of Corn . . . ; which done, they seized the Sacks of the Farmers, and insisted upon having the Corn at the Price by them set, some of them paying, and others taking it without paying any Thing. Others of the Rioters set the Price on Oatmeal, Potatoes, etc. Some of the Town's People were as industrious as the Rioters themselves, in buying at the Price so set.[37]

One could go on with many more examples of this sort. Suffice it to say that in all such cases the 'rioters' are seen to be enforcing their own price standards: standards that (in their own minds) were determined by tradition, consumer need and basic notions of equity.

These collective actions in the marketplace were not formless, chaotic, undisciplined risings. Sometimes, it is true, price-setting could lead to straightforward looting, or involve incidents of looting, though it is often difficult to identify the provocations (as perceived by the people) that might help to explain such actions. In some cases, for instance, only those farmers who refused to accept the prices proposed by the people received nothing in return. But for the most part one is impressed, not by the 'plunder' of which some hostile observers loosely spoke, but rather by the orderliness and discipline of these so-called disturbances. (They were disturbances, that is, as seen by the authorities and by men of property; the common people, to whom hunger and injustice were greater enormities, viewed social problems and disorders rather differently.) It was said of a price-setting riot in Worcester in September 1766 that, 'notwithstanding the great Confusion there was for about two Hours, we do not hear of any personal Hurt being done. It does not seem to be the Intent of the Poor to plunder the Property of others, they only desire (for their ready Money) to be supplied with the common Necessaries of Life at a reasonable Price'.[38] In some of these actions a firm sense of correct procedure was revealed. In May 1795, for example, about 300 colliers from the Forest of Dean marched on Monmouth and, 'after waiting on the Mayor, informed him it was their intention to regulate the prices of provisions in the market'. They then took possession of the marketplace, where they sold butter for 8d. a pound and cheese for 4d. a pound. 'Their unexpected appearance in town created a temporary alarm', it was said, 'but as no personal violence was offered to any one, the fears of the inhabitants soon subsided; and after remaining about two hours, they returned home, without disturbance or molestation.'[39] Theft was not the objective of such rioters. A crowd who took over the market in Newcastle-under-Lyne in November 1757 and sold grain, butter, and cheese at their own prices afterwards 'render'd a just Account to the Farmers and returned them all their Money'.[40] Similarly, a farmer who was stopped by a crowd on his way to Tetbury (Gloucestershire) market in September 1766, and who had his produce forcibly taken 'and sold . . . to the Poor' (his own prices were considered too high), was paid right away for his goods.[41] These plebeian price-regulators could sometimes be remarkably fastidious about the rights of property in the course of their riotous conduct. At a market in Salisbury in September 1766 a crowd 'forced open the Farmers Sacks, and sold all their Grain at 5s. 6d. a Bushel; the Money for which, together with the Sacks, they returned to the Owners'.[42] And in August 1766, according to another report, the

Price of Wheat was raised so high in the Market at Barnstaple, that the Poor, who are in the utmost Distress, joined in a Body, and compelled the Farmers to sell it at Five Shillings per Bushel. Some of the Farmers refusing to take the Money, the Poor were honest enough to tie it up carefully for them in their Sacks. And as soon as they had taken it at a low Price sufficient to supply their Necessities, they dispersed, leaving the Farmers to make what Price they could of other People.[43]

If one central objective of food riots was to regulate prices, another was to ensure that local markets were adequately supplied. For what would prices matter, even regulated prices, if there was not enough to buy? Here the main concern of the people was that provisions might be, or were being, withheld from the market: withheld by farmers, or stockpiled by millers and dealers, in expectation of rising prices. Collective action was intended to make some of this withheld produce available for immediate sale, often by means of intimidating visits to farmers' houses. Such popular initiatives were fairly common, for example, in the tin-mining districts of Cornwall.[44] In parts of Devon in the summer of 1766 rioters seized 'what Wheat they could meet with in the Granaries of the Farmers, which they carried immediately to Market, and sold openly from four to five Shillings per Bushel'. (They 'afterwards returned to the several Owners, and carried them the Money which they had thus raised from the Sale of their Grains, together with the Sacks'.)[45] There was a disturbance in Northampton in the winter of 1726 'on Account of the Farmers keeping up their Corn in the Inns, and not bringing it into the Market, in order to raise or keep up the Price', though after a skirmish during which some sacks were cut open and 'a considerable Quantity of Corn was spilt', the public market was once again properly supplied; 'and in order to prevent the same [disorder] at Towcester, the Cryer made Proclamation for the Farmers to sell their Corn publickly in the usual Place, which had the proposed Effect'.[46] Popular action, then, could achieve some concrete results. After a price-setting riot in Newcastle-under-Lyne in November 1757 the farmers were told by the people that 'if they did not immediately thresh their Corn, and bring it to the publick Market, they would take that Trouble upon themselves, which has had such an Effect upon all the Farmers . . . that they are all very busily employ'd in getting their Corn ready for Market'.[47]

Many risings were particularly intended to prevent the export of grain to foreign markets at times when local needs had not been adequately met. Exports should only be permitted, according to this popular view, when there was no danger of shortages or price increases in local markets. It was said of a riot in the region of Dewsbury in the West Riding in April 1740 that the people's objective was 'to prevent the Badgers from making Wheat Meal or Flower, to send into other Countries, alledging that such Practice would cause a Scarcity in Yorkshire, and much advance the Price of Corn'.[48] Similarly, rioters in Devon in the summer of 1766 claimed that the 'vast Quantity of Corn exported, had been the Occasion of all the Calamities under which the Poor labour, by the exceeding high Price of every Necessary of Life'.[49] Attacks on wagons and boats loaded with grain, and 'visits' to the premises of millers and mealmen known to have flour stored for export, or to the docks and wharves of coastal and inland ports, were frequently reported during periods of scarcity in local markets. To take a typical example, in May 1737 a wagon-load of wheat belonging to a farmer in Britford, Wiltshire, was stopped about six miles away, on the road to the coast, by about sixty people, 'who first knock'd down the fore-Horse, then cut the Waggon and Wheels to peeces, cut the Sacks, and strewed about the Corn, and threaten'd they would serve all Persons after that Manner, who should offer to carry any more Wheat for Exportation'.[50] In June 1753 at Taunton, Somerset, several hundred women assembled in a body to destroy the weir belonging to several grist mills and thereby prevent corn from being ground at the mills (the men, it was said, 'stood as Spectators, giving the Women many Huzza's and Commendations for their Dexterity in the Work they were about'):

They gave out, that their Reason for so doing was owing to a Dislike they had to the Manager of the said Mills, whom they charge with engrossing, for some Time past, most of the Corn that should have been brought to the Weekly Markets at Taunton, and, after grinding it, with transporting the Flour to other Parts in Vessels, etc. whereby, they apprehended, Corn advanced to a higher Price in that Town than otherwise it would have done.[51]

Whatever the Corn Laws might condone, and whatever merchants might say about the freedom of trade, the labouring people held more sceptical ideas as to the legitimacy of exporting grain. This outlook was clearly articulated in November 1727 by the Cornish tin-miners, who were objecting to the exporting of grain from their county: a body of them, in search of provisions, entered Falmouth one day and 'cried aloud, *Corn we come for, and Corn we will have*; adding, the Merchants have no Commission from the King to send it to their Enemies'.[52] Occasionally such expressions of popular discontent induced the authorities to take some action. In May 1757, for example, there was a disturbance at the quay in Worcester 'on Account of between 20 and 30 Bags of Meal being put on board a Vessel, in order to be sent to Bridgnorth; but, by the Interposition of the Peace Officers, some Mischief was prevented; and, to appease the Clamours of the poor People, the Meal was re-landed for Home Consumption'.[53]

It is clear from the available evidence that these diverse popular actions were not simple instinctive rebellions: that is, they were not quasi-automatic, almost mechanical responses to physiological distress. Hunger, or the fear of hunger, was, of course, a primary stimulus for rioting. But the character of the actual social reactions to hunger was vitally determined by custom, inherited expectations and moral evaluation. These responses were, in other words, culturally mediated: they were significantly conditioned by learning, experience and interpretation. They were informed by a consciousness of moral purpose. Their objectives were usually selective and clearly defined, and the collective actions taken were commonly (though not always) conducted in a disciplined and reasonably discriminating manner.[54] And at the cultural centre of these popular grievances and protests was a keen sense of justice — a sense of correct morality being violated, and of injustice being tolerated or encouraged. The marketplace, as the people saw it, encompassed human relationships that were both moral and material in nature. Their moral economy was, I think, much like that which John Bunyan, the great Christian and popular writer, had advocated in his *The Life and Death of Mr. Badman* (1680). Bunyan, speaking of 'extortion', said that it was 'most commonly committed by men of Trade, who without all conscience, when they have the advantage, will make a prey of their neighbour'. He condemned traders who strove to maximize their profits, who were determined to set their prices as high as the market could bear. Trading, he thought, should be conducted with a good conscience: 'A man in dealing should as really design his Neighbours good, profit, and advantage, as his own: For this is to Exercise Charity in his dealing.' Hoarding and profiteering were clearly 'wicked': traders should show 'mercy to the poor' at times of scarcity.[55] This was very much the moral outlook that was inherited by the small consumer in the eighteenth century. Moreover, this popular morality often included as well (and here Bunyan might not have approved) a determination to see that justice was enforced, according to the law: by the established authorities if possible, by direct popular action if necessary. Direct action, on this popular view, was a legitimate means of redressing grievances, punishing transgressors and recalling gentlemen to their paternal responsibilities. An anonymous letter of March 1758 addressed 'To the Gentlemen of Birmingham' gave voice to the kinds of plebeian sentiments that must have been widely observed at times of scarcity:

As Whe ave Long Strugled for this twelvemonths Past for the scasety of provition whe think it very hard that the Gentlemen never Concidered it, for there is a Great meney that are starved for ye Whant of Provition and Whe think it But Our Dutys to Let you Know that if things are not Altered for the Better Whe shall make Bold to take it from them that Can Best Spar it for Whe are in Great Want. As it as plesed the Lord to Provide for Us Plentifull Crops and for the Baggers & millers and bakers to Surve Us so Whe think that they Are no Better than What you may call Rougs but there is a Company that will tend On them on the Next market Day so no more Till the Deed Proves itself.[56]

Standards and rights

The popular desire for a welfare-oriented management of economic affairs was not confined to the provisioning of foodstuffs. There was also a desire, largely on the part of industrial workers, for wages to be regulated in the interest of preserving certain minimum standards of subsistence. Just as there was though to be a 'fair' maximum for food prices, so too there was a 'fair' minimum for wages: a level determined by customary expectations and 'normal' human needs. This commitment to maintaining standards was central to the industrial relations of the period. According to this popular view, the forces of supply and demand should not be allowed to determine, without limit or restraint, the level of wages. From a strictly capitalist perspective labour was a factor of production whose price was determined by the mechanisms of the marketplace: and the market, of course, was not concerned with such notions as 'fairness' or the desire for a 'decent competence'. As one writer put it in 1733, 'Labour, as to its Price, is like every thing else, it rises or falls according to the Proportion that there is between the Demand and the Quantity then in the Market; all Restraints are unjust, let them be upon what Side they will.'[57] 'The Value of Labour has its Ups and Downs, according to the Demand there is for it, the same as any other Commodity', asserted another commentator in 1739.[58] Such views were completely incompatible with those of the people. For labouring people did not see themselves as akin to commodities, and they rejected this demoralized conception of their place in the social order. Price, to them, was not simply a mechanical mediator: price was fully meaningful only when it was related to 'needs', and 'just rewards', and other such morally informed ideas, and it could not be divorced from these sorts of evaluative considerations. Market forces should not be allowed to push wages down — down to levels below what was thought to be required for a decent subsistence. And here, as the people saw it, was a matter calling for active intervention on the part of the established authorities. For in their search for protection against these pressures of the competitive marketplace, many industrial workers looked to the justices of the peace to exercise their statutory authority to set wage rates and thereby ensure that minimum standards of pay would be observed. These powers available to magistrates derived originally from the protective social legislation of the Tudors and early Stuarts, and many labouring people expected these powers to be properly exercised, especially during years when wage-reductions were threatened.[59] And if the justices failed in their duty to regulate wages and to ensure that workmen were adequately compensated for their labour, then the people were liable to take direct action on their own behalf: action to redress their own grievances and to settle wages for themselves.

There were numerous instances of such disputes over wages. A prolonged strike by the colliers in Durham in 1730/31 was caused largely by the mine-owners' attempt to reduce their men's piece-wages by enlarging the size of the standard basket in which coal was carried: the miners complained 'that their Owners would not give them sufficient Subsistence for working their Coals' and demanded that the basket be 'reduc'd to its primary Size'.[60] A few years later, in 1738, it was reported that there were numerous murmurings among some of these Durham colliers 'about the Regulations that are making in the Coal-Trade, and it is probable, if what is done tends to lessen their Wages, there will be a rising among them, (which God forbid) and no Work done'.[61] In Kingswood Forest in Gloucestershire, another coal-mining district, a serious disturbance erupted in the autumn of 1738: a price war had broken out among the proprietors of the coal mines, and to reduce their costs as much as possible some of the employers were trying to lower the colliers' wages by 25 per cent (from 1s. 4d. to 1s. per day), a reduction which the colliers were determined to resist.[62] Such 'adjustments' in favour of property-owners (or at least some property-owners, usually the biggest) could spark off outraged reactions. It was reported, for example, that in Bocking, Essex, in the spring of 1740, a season of very high grain prices, a 'tumultuous Mob assembled before the house of an eminent Master Webster of that Town, threatening to kill him, and pull down his House to the Ground, for wanting to lower the Price of Spinning from seven Knots to nine Knots a Penny'.[63] The 'prices for work' (thought the people) must be kept up, reductions must be resisted: otherwise wage-earners would suffer a significant erosion of their customary living standards.

Weavers were particularly well represented in the various protests against wage reductions. It was said of the widespread weavers' riots in Wiltshire and Somerset in 1726/27 that the 'Difference they have with their Masters, the Clothiers, . . . is, that they have encreased their Work, and diminished their Wages'. On one occasion during this period of unrest, in late November 1726, the woollen town of Frome in Somerset was 'visited' by a large body of weavers from Wiltshire: they 'went into several Houses with a Paper to settle their Wages, and where their Demands were complied with, and smooth Words given, they did no harm, but where there was any Hesitation, or what they call uncivil Treatment, the Windows paid for it'. The weavers who were taking such direct actions referred to themselves as 'Regulators'.[64] Similar disturbances involving weavers and their resentment of wage deductions occurred in Bristol in 1729: they claimed that the 'Masters had combin'd to lower 6d. in a Piece of their Wages'. One weaver, who was capitally convicted for his part in these actions, declared at the time of his execution that 'these Riots were occasioned thro' the unreasonableness of their Masters, in abating the old Prices at a Time when Provisions were dear'.[65] (Direct action, of course, was only one possible response to such reduced circumstances: in 1750 it was reported that some 'forty or fifty Families of the Plush Weavers' in Bristol 'are come to a Resolution to go to the Settlement of Nova Scotia, on Account of their Masters going to abate their Wages, below what they can comfortably and honestly live by'.[66] In 1739 the weavers and other cloth-workers in Wiltshire were attempting to justify their recent direct actions against several clothiers on the grounds of the 'Barbarity and Cruelty of the Master Clothiers to us in general: Whereas our Pay was Eighteen-pence a Yard for fine Cloth, they have reduced it to fifteen, fourteen, thirteen, and some to Twelve; likewise lower'd the Price in every Branch belonging to the Trade which is *Starving us Inch by Inch*'. (There were also complaints about payment in truck.) They proposed that, in order to restore industrial peace, an Act of Parliament should be passed to establish a price list for work performed and 'a severe Penalty on any Clothier that shall act in Contempt thereof'.[67] A statutory regulation of wages, then, was the remedy they sought. The various actions of the Gloucestershire weavers in 1756/57 were all directed towards the goal of a satisfactory and successfully enforced rating of wages. As their petition to the House of Commons put it, they wanted to see 'some Power lodged in the said Justices of the Peace, or elsewhere, . . . to ascertain and settle the said Wages [in order] that the Petitioners may not be subject to the arbitrary Will and Power of the said Clothiers'.[68] (The clothiers were at this time petitioning for a repeal of all the statutory provisions that allowed magistrates to set wages.) James Wolfe, who commanded some troops that were sent to quell this weavers' rising, privately sympathized with their plight (he represented them as 'half-starved'): 'they say', he reported, 'the masters have beat down their wages too low to live upon; and I believe it is a just complaint'.[69]

The concern for maintaining standards of pay was also revealed on those occasions when individual workers were found to be employed for less than the customary rates. This was known as working 'under price', and it was very poorly regarded, for any willingness by one or two men to work for lower wages than usual would endanger the wages of all men in the trade. Men who disregarded this critical priority and worked under price were liable to be harshly dealt with. In March 1733, for instance, it was reported from Bristol that 'the Weavers being irritated against one of their Fraternity for working under Price, they rose in a great Body, and seiz'd the Delinquent, who underwent the Marks of their Revenge in the usual Manner of Ducking in the River, and a hearty Drubbing, by which Usage he had the Misfortune to have one of his Eyes beat out.'[70] Sometimes working under price was punished by means of a ritualized form of rough justice. In Bristol again, in October 1752, a number of journeymen sawyers 'seized a Man of the same Trade, as he was at Work in Mr. Tully's Yard, (under Pretence of his working under Price) and putting him across a Pole, they proceeded through different Parts of the City, in a Riotous Manner, sometimes dragging him on the Ground, and otherwise using him ill' (this was a form of *charivari* known as 'riding the stang').[71] Working under price, then, could arouse strong feelings. An incident that occurred in a blacksmith's shop in Bedfordshire suggests the potential strength of these sentiments. According to the testimony of one Nicholas Browne, a blacksmith, on the morning of 13 October 1679:

he beinge . . . at worke at his trade, John Winch, Thomas Crawley and others came into the shopp . . . and the said John Winch said, 'Hee's the Rogue that workes for eight pence a day when others have 12d. a day,' meaning Thomas Crawley, who reply'd, 'you lye you old Rogue I have 10d.' (which words of 'Lye' & 'Rogue', were spoken by them both severall tymes). The said John Winch being lighting a pipe of Tabacco with an iron rod being red hott, Did run the same into the Eye of the said Thomas Crawley, & told him that he would teach him to stare in his face, and further this informant saith not.[72]

An inspection of the evidence relating to industrial disputes — as, indeed, to most other forms of social conflict — reveals a strong sense of *popular rights*: of the right to a basic subsistence; of the right to have their interests considered and taken account of by the established authorities; of the right to resist the 'arbitrary will' of employers. Most manufacturing people claimed the right to exercise some degree of control over the conditions of their work and the terms of their employment. They rejected the newer, narrower and increasingly powerfully backed definition of their rights that considered only their 'freedom' to sell their labour, a kind of property, on the open market for whatever price they could get. Labouring people had a broader and much more morally informed conception of their own freedom. For their conception of freedom involved a high respect for 'independent' labour (as opposed to 'enslaved' labour), an expectation that their right to be paid 'decent' wages would be properly acknowledged, and a general presumption that, as 'free-born Englishmen', they enjoyed certain fundamental liberties that could not be taken from them. Industrial protesters saw nothing untoward about their claims: 'for we want nothing but what is honest and to work for selves and familers and you want to starve us', wrote some Manchester calico-printers in 1786 to one of their masters in the trade. A similar conviction of the justice of their cause — part natural justice, part biblical justice — was revealed in an anonymous weaver's letter of 1787 addressed to the clothiers of Newbury, Berkshire:

Gentlemen would you Think It a Crime in any one Liveing, To stand In His Own Defence Against His Enemy, You Gentlemen Are Agreed To Beat Down The Price of the Weavers Work, The Price of the weavers Work is already so Low They Cannot get A livelywood like Almost any Other Trade, why should you

wish To starve Us Quite, Yours Lives As Well as Ours are Not Insured One
Moment, Neither Can You Carry Your Ill Got Treasure with you Into The Next
Life, As For This Life I Look upon It as Nothing in Respect of The Life To Come,
If you, with Starveing The Poor, Could Gain The whole world And at the same
Time Greatly Indanger Your Precious soul's, In what Point Have You The
Advantage let me Desire of you Gentlemen To Take This Wicked Device Into
Consideration, Or Else Prepare your selves For A Good Bonfire at Both Ends At
Each Your Dwellings . . . was I sure To Dey For standing For My Right, I would
Dey Willingly . . . I May As well Dey with a Houlter, As Be starved To Death,
with Wicked Men's Devices . . . .[73]

This consciousness of possessing certain rights, along with a determination
to resist any fundamental attacks on these rights, were also made manifest in
the disputes that arose over the enclosure of common lands. Common rights,
as we have seen in Chapter 2, were highly valued in many regions, for they
were often of considerable importance in the functioning of the cottager's or
husbandman's household economy. Indeed, they were commonly considered
to be part of the 'patrimony of the poor'. Free access to Charnwood Forest in
Leicestershire, for example, was regarded by the commoners as 'their
inalienable right'.[74] But, as I shall discuss in Chapter 6, enclosure threatened
to eliminate all such rights — to eliminate them in favour of absolute *private*
rights of land-ownership — and these changes must have often aroused
intense feelings of injustice: a sense of the stark illegitimacy of the destruction
of a time-honoured popular right and its replacement by a property right.
John Clare, the Northamptonshire rural poet, was almost certainly giving
voice to widely felt and long-standing popular notions of justice when he
spoke of the 'lawless laws' of enclosure and charged that:

Inclosure came and trampled on the grave
Of labours rights and left the poor a slave.[75]

In July 1725, to take one instance of a collective action that was directed
against enclosure, it was reported that a 'great many poor People, both Men
and Women, in a tumultuous Manner, threw down a new Mill, and divers
Gates and Fences upon the Marsh' in Stokesby, Norfolk; they later said 'they
did it for Recovery of their Right, the Marsh being common till a certain
Gentleman had taken it away by fencing it in'.[76] Just as food should not be
engrossed by dealers, nor arbitrary power exercised by employers, so too
(according to the popular view) all land in a locality should not be engrossed
into the hands of one or two men, to the detriment of other men's legitimate
interests. For English labouring people, commoners and others, thought of
themselves as enjoying certain 'free-born' rights. In the course of the
prolonged struggle over the enclosure of Holland Fen in Lincolnshire, an
anonymous threatening letter was sent to one of the promoters of the

enclosure in the summer of 1769. It spoke of the Act of Parliament taking the 'poors Right from them By force and fraud' and demanded that 'the poor may ingoy their own wrights and libertyes'. The letter was signed:

A wel Wisher to peace
And liberty for Ever.[77]

A folk rhyme which was still being recited in the district of Blaxhall, Suffolk, in the twentieth century, and which had presumably been transmitted orally through several generations, reveals the same sense of moral injury, the same sort of awareness of the predatory attacks on the rights of the people and the partiality of the law, though in this case the social criticism was more ironically rendered:

They hang the man and flog the woman
Who steals the goose from off the Common;
But let the greater criminal loose
Who steals the Common from the goose.[78]

One of the most vigorous and revealing protests against a projected enclosure was that put forth by the commoners of Cheshunt, Hertfordshire, in an anonymous threatening letter of 27 February 1799. The letter was received by Oliver Cromwell, Esquire, of Cheshunt Park, though it was intended to be read as well by several other gentlemen. 'Whe right these lines', the letter opened, '. . . in the Defence of our Parish rights which you unlawfully are about to disinherit us of':

Resolutions is maid by the aforesaid Combind that if you intend of incloseing Our Commond Commond fields Lammas Meads Marshes &c Whe Resolve before you shall say & the rest of the heads of that bloudy and unlawful act it is finished to have your hearts bloud if you proceede in the aforesaid bloudy act Whe like horse leaches will cry give, give untill whe have spilt the bloud of every one that wishes to rob the Inosent unborn it shall not be in your power to say I am safe from the hands of the Enemy for Whe like birds of pray will prively lye in wait to spil the bloud of the aforesaid Charicters whose names and plaices of above are as putrified sores in our Nostrils Whe declair that thou shalt not say I am safe when thou goest to thy bead for beware that thou liftest not thine eyes up in the midst of flames . . . .

The foremost priority in the parish, according to these authors, was a satisfactory regulation of the commons:

the voice of Us and the maguor part of the parrish is for a regulation of commons rights is in the follow manner that Every one to turn on the Commonds in proportion to what they hold which to be deturmined by our superiors so that every one may have his alotment to do as he pleases to keep annerkey from our parrish so that if he dose not whish to keep anything let him or hur let those proportions to whome they like so that it may be an easement to them in the poors rates if thou had took this step then would thou had our hearts and our all at they survise.

'Whe leave if for thy consideration', they continued, 'Wheather thou would like to be sorted out from the land of the liveing or would like to have the poors hearts and there all if required.' They concluded by observing that 'if thou proceeds to inclose our blood will boil like a pot,' but 'if thou goist to regulate it then as aforesaid then will whe come and give our hearts and voices to it and to you for ever but no inclosure will whe agree to'.[79] (The imagery of the Old Testament and its concern for justice had not been lost on these parishioners.)

Finally, it should be noted that some protests and collective actions were expressions of popular resistance to a variety of personal exactions and restrictions on individual freedom, most of which were imposed on ordinary people (or their imposition sanctioned) by the central government. The initiatives of the eighteenth-century state, it would be fair to say, usually had little to offer to the labouring people. Indeed, the assertions of state authority were often regarded by the people with cold suspicion, and sometimes they were resisted with active hostility. The state was the source of the Game Laws; the people, who viewed this 'lawful' monopoly as illegitimate and oppressive, persisted in exercising what they saw as their right to hunt wild game, and thus came to be known as poachers. The state imposed high customs duties on certain imported goods, and as a result of these exactions some men were encouraged to engage in smuggling. Popular opinion on this matter overwhelmingly sympathized with the smugglers as against the customs officers. The excise, as a form of taxation, was probably even more poorly regarded, for its burdens weighed disproportionately heavily on the smaller consumers. Other new taxes which came to be levied, notably turnpike tolls, were sometimes resisted when they were seen as being responsible for a sharp increase in the cost of living, or for an unjust transference of some of the costs of road maintenance from the landowners, those who were best able to pay for these repairs, to the full range of road users, many of whom (in some regions) were men of small means. The state was also, of course, the organizer of military and naval conscription, and impressment was widely regarded as arbitrary and unjust and was often bitterly resisted. The keenly felt resentment of military recruitment was very much implicated in the widespread protests against the balloting for the newly approved militia in 1757, and as J. R. Western pointed out, this resentment was by no means ill-founded. 'The previous militia had been a burden on property', he wrote, 'but the new one, selecting men by lot from among the able-bodied, fell on rich and poor alike and might easily bear more heavily on a poor man than on his rich neighbour . . . . Bitter class feeling was aroused by the new system of ballots. It was said that gentlemen kept poor men alive only to fight for them.'[80] The state was increasingly seen by labouring people, not as a source of protection — as, in their view, it should be, and as they thought it had been in the past — but rather as a source of oppression and exploitation. The state did little or nothing to protect what the people saw as their traditional rights and liberties. Indeed, most of its initiatives and directives were seen as intrusive and restrictive and arbitrary — favourable to property and capital accumulation perhaps, but not to customary rights. And these rights, according to the people's view of the world, sometimes had to be vigorously defended: defended against the illegitimate demands of the state and the (to them) new, and unattractive, and officially approved interpretations of what was lawful and commendable behaviour, interpretations that were riddled through with ruling class interests.

Liberty and authority

Although collective actions were sometimes seen by gentlemen as symptomatic of a 'levelling' disposition among the populace, and as overt expressions of the people's fundamentally subversive intentions with respect to established authority,[81] it is clear that almost all popular protests were, in fact, intended to achieve strictly limited objectives. These actions were not, in other words, revolutionary in character; they were seldom, if ever during this period (that is, before the 1790s), part of any general insurrectionary movement.[82] The risings that occurred were intended to prevent enclosure in a Midland parish, to set weavers' wages in some woollen towns, to enforce traditional market regulations during a time of dearth, or to prevent the balloting for the militia in 1757. They were not, in short, motivated by any grand ambitions. Nor were the rioters looking forward to the creation of a fundamentally new sort of world of social relationships. Most of them wanted simply to preserve customary standards of living, to defend traditional rights and liberties, to resist what they took to be arbitrary and oppressive power.

The fundamental conservatism of the people is clearly revealed in their attitudes towards the local authorities, notably the justices of the peace. For few risings were rebellions against authority *per se*. Rather, they arose — and the people often saw them as arising — because the authorities that did exist, and whose powers were not essentially in question, had failed to do their duty, to act responsibly, to fulfil the people's expectations of them; and the people regarded their own direct actions as legitimate ways of forcing the authorities to act correctly, or of doing for themselves what the magistrates should have done but had neglected to do. Overt popular resentment of authority, then, was expressed, for the most part, only on those occasions when it was thought that power was being illegitimately, or negligently, exercised. Most riots, or demonstrations of force, or threatening utterances were intended to recall gentlemen to their obligations, not to undermine the whole social order. When grain was seized from dealers' wagons during the food riots of 1693 the people were reported to have said that 'they were resolved to put the law in execution since the magistrates neglected it'.[83] Similarly, in 1727, when the Kingswood colliers were protesting against the newly established turnpike tolls in the Bristol region, they alleged that the bad road conditions which the turnpike Act was supposed to remedy were partly a consequence of the *failure* of the magistrates to enforce the existing laws for repairing roads. These men of substance were accused, then, of having neglected to act properly in accordance with the authority and responsibiliy that were vested in them as justices. As the colliers put it in a letter they wrote (or commissioned to be written) on this subject, 'by the Omission of your Duty, and your Carelessnes and Over sight, you have lost your Honourable Magistracy, and brought your self under the reproach of a Turnpike'. The supposed 'necessity' for imposing road tolls was felt to stem from the previous failure of the authorities to behave responsibly; and the so-called 'riots' in which the colliers had been involved were represented by them as forms of corrective action, conduct that was intended to set things right (the colliers likened their actions to efforts to put out a fire that had been 'wilfully kindled' by others).[84] These colliers, then, like most other labouring people, did not (at least publicly) question the foundations of power and authority. But they did hold the authorities *accountable* for certain actions or inactions, and this notion of accountability included an assertion by the people of their right to exert pressure on the authorities, and to demand that popular interests be adequately considered and duly weighed. They claimed the right, in short, to twist gentlemen's arms.

It is clear that both the people and the authorities, in their relations with each other, behaved in accordance with a sense of certain political *limits*: limits as to what was possible, or desirable, or necessary. 'Authority' was not some adamantine presence, either ideologically or practically or in the eyes of the people. Rather, it was permeated with ambivalences and (on some occasions) uncertainties. Labouring people were, in certain respects, deferential towards authority and resigned to their positions of subordinaton. They often appealed to the gentry, after all, to exercise their authority, and to do the right thing. None the less, as their numerous direct actions clearly demonstrate, there were definite limits to this deference — points beyond which people could not be pushed around, times when respect for authority broke down (or was in danger of breaking down) and when outward plebeian quiescence could no longer be counted on by the magistrates. Gentlemen were certainly aware of these limits imposed on their actions. On many occasions, of course, they resorted to military assistance to help reinforce a crumbling local authority, but this was not a happy way of managing a crisis of public order, as many of them realized. For the legitimacy of their authority, both in their own eyes and (especially) in the eyes of the people, depended heavily on the performance of certain paternalist duties that were still widely assumed to be inherent in the exercise of power. Authority that could only be sustained through the presence of troops (and most people hated the army) was liable to be seen as a feeble, debased, morally impoverished kind of authority. Consequently, many gentlemen, when confronted with an actual or potential popular uprising, were disposed to negotiate with the protesters, to take quick action to redress some of their grievances, to engage in some form of appeasement. Actions of this sort — a sympathetic response to a delegation of aggrieved workers seeking price regulations, purchases of grain supplies for local sale at reduced rates, forcing farmers to bring their produce to market, substantial and well-publicized charitable donations during periods of hardship[85] — were frequently seen as the best means of restoring a proper respect for authority, subduing discontent and exacting from the common people some degree of public deference. The manner in which authority could or should be *exhibited*, then, was a matter to be seriously considered. And such considerations had to take into account the attitudes of the people: their sense of justice, their commitment to certain kinds of freedom, their expectations of the established authorities. As Edward Thompson has pointed out,

the tetchy sensibilities of a libertarian crowd defined, in the largest sense, the limits of what was politically possible. There is a sense in which rulers and crowd needed each other, watched each other, performed theater and countertheater to each other's auditorium, moderated each other's political behavior. This is a more active and reciprocal relationship than the one normally brought to mind under the formula 'paternalism and deference.'[86]

These libertarian sentiments of the people played an active role in this very unequal (but not undisciplined) relationship of power. For the common people held to many of the same (often loosely conceived) constitutionalist values that their rulers had come to espouse. Indeed, as Nicholas Rogers has written, the 'libertarian heritage was . . . *the* dominant political ideology of the eighteenth century, to which all groups subscribed': Whigs, Tories, dissenting radicals, plebeian protesters.[87] And it can be said, I think, that fundamentally and perhaps most importantly these constitutionalist values were anti-absolutist in character, resolutely hostile to arbitrary power. Thus one sees, especially in London, much evidence of popular xenophobia, for foreigners were frequently Roman Catholics, Catholicism was closely associated with absolutist power, and absolutism implied tyranny, enslavement and cultural darkness (French peasants having to wear wooden shoes, the Spanish Inquisition, Jesuitical intrigues against English Protestantism and the like). One also observes, as expressions of these libertarian values, the intense popular hatred of the press-gang, the standing army, excise taxes, and other manifestations of intrusive state power. In the 1760s John Wilkes became something of a popular hero as a result of his flamboyant and sensitively orchestrated opposition to just this sort of arbitrary power. Labouring people, in short, had a strong sense of the 'Englishman's birthright', a birthright that ensured them (as they thought) certain basic liberties, including the right to be left alone and enjoy a modicum of 'independence'.[88]

This commitment to a life of independence was, in fact, a vital component of the people's culture. It meant, for almost everyone, staying clear of dependence on parish poor relief and of the humiliation of being identified as a pauper; even if relief had to be sought, every effort would be made to avoid being confined in an institutional poor-house. For a manufacturing person independence meant exercising some degree of control over the immediate circumstances of his labour — setting his own rhythms of work (starting and stopping partly at his own pleasure), determining for himself other details of the work process, having his own work-place in his own cottage. Indeed, the popular attachment to these practical sorts of freedom helps to explain much of the early hostility to factory labour and its much tighter, and unself-determined, disciplinary regime.[89] For other people independence involved minimizing one's dependence on wage-labour and thereby limiting the constricting controls of employers. It was partly because of the freedom associated with more self-sustaining forms of labour that people particularly valued common rights, smallholdings and the various other kinds of material support that allowed for a degree of household self-sufficiency. A person might, by certain standards, be 'poor', but material hardship did not necessarily undermine his commitment to those modest, though in many respects fundamental, personal freedoms that were practicably within his grasp. The centrality of this popular view was only occasionally acknowledged by gentlemen — at least sympathetically: numerous observers went out of their way to condemn the fondness of the people for liberty and independence — but one who did, in 1788, put the case reasonably well (he was discussing the appropriateness of establishing workhouses for the poor):

The poor man is comforted under his poverty by thinking himself *free*. This freedom of his, God knows, is circumscribed by such a number of imperious necessities, that it is reduced to little in effect; but he pleases himself in imagining that he possesses it; and that he may go out or come in, work or play, at his own option. He likes to be the judge of his own wants, and to provide for them after his own manner .... Then he cannot be easy under *confinement*, abhors the thought of being under *lock and key*, and thinks no man deserves a *prison* who has not committed a crime.[90]

It is clear, in fact, that this commitment to independence, to possessing a certain social and psychological space of one's own — and it was often a very aggressive commitment — was of central importance in helping to determine the character of the people's relationships with their masters and employers and with the local authorities of church and state.

Conflict and social change

In any investigation of eighteenth-century social conflicts one confronts, time and time again, what Edward Thompson has referred to as 'alternative definitions of social reality'.[91] With respect to many matters of conduct there was an official, often legally sanctioned, definition as to what was proper or imperative, and also an unofficial and popular definition that embodied different priorities and other sorts of social aspiration. There was, in fact, no dominant consensus of opinion on many issues of importance. Rather, it would be more accurate to speak of a dominant view 'from above', the view of many gentlemen, merchants, large farmers and the like; and a dominant view 'from below', the view that was found mostly among labourers, artisans, smallholders, petty masters, and other ordinary working people. And here I am thinking, of course, in terms of probabilities, not of near universals. For neither view can be identified with the kind of precision that a natural scientist might hope to attain: there were fluidities of opinion, social cross-overs and overlapping cultural territories. But there were tendencies, and often strong tendencies: a tendency for men of property and privilege to see the social world in particular ways, and for the people's views to be both different from and often antagonistic towards these views from above. On the whole the official view favoured what was known as 'improvement' — economic innovation, managerial efficiency and capital accumulation (during the early Hanoverian decades this view was considerably more prominent among Whigs than among Tories, who commonly inclined to more paternalistic outlooks); the people, in contrast, were committed to the preservation of a traditional, custom-centred culture, as much of their rebelliousness makes clear. In the course of the century, Edward Thompson has written, 'capitalist logic and "non-economic" customary behaviour are in active and conscious conflict . . . . Hence we can read eighteenth-century social history', he suggests, 'as a succession of confrontations between an innovative market economy and the customary moral economy of the plebs.'[92] Now to see the problem in this way is, of course, to focus attention on the processes of social change and on the participation of the labouring people in these central processes. And understanding social change is clearly a fundamental duty of the social historian. Indeed, any social and cultural analysis that neglects to offer an explanation for the changes in people's experiences, patterns of behaviour and social relationships has failed to fulfil one of the critical responsibilities of historical inquiry. A social reconstruction of the relatively stable, continuous and recurrent dimensions of experience is an important and often essential aspect of the historian's task, but this bias towards a static analysis — the bias that has dominated this study thus far — cannot be allowed to remain largely dissociated from the attempt to understand the dynamics of a society. Let us turn, then, to concentrate on these questions of social change.

6 Changing experiences

Many of the changes that occurred in eighteenth-century England are well known, if not entirely well understood. Historians have often discussed the increasing elaboration of the market economy, the commercialization of agriculture and the innovations in industrial technology and organization. They have tried to account for the growth of population from the 1740s (and, more dramatically, after about 1780), the changing character of social relations, and the rise of evangelicalism. All of these questions can be, and have been, examined from various perspectives — though the perspective of 'economic growth' has very much predominated. In this chapter our concern is to assess the implications of some of these processes of change for the labouring people: to see how the conditions of plebeian life were altered in the course of the century. How were the labouring people affected by changes in the organization of productive activities? Did they benefit or did they lose? And what changes, if any, can be observed in their everyday social behaviour: their relations with men of property and authority, their involvement in a customary culture? Working men and women in the eighteenth century, like people at any time, had inherited (as we have seen) certain 'standards' of life, certain norms of experience, certain expectations about the future. But how successfully was this heritage preserved? And, while recognizing that cultures are always being in some ways 'revised', can we speak at all about this particular culture being 'impoverished' or 'enriched'? These, then, are the questions that dominate this final chapter, where, in contrast to the previous chapters, I will be extending my discussion to the years of the early nineteenth century.

Landlords, labourers and wages

It is clear that, in the course of the eighteenth century, landed property increasingly came to be regarded — by the gentry, by Parliament, by the courts — as absolute private property, that farming was increasingly being conducted in accordance with strictly capitalist principles (maximization of profits, an acute sensitivity to 'market forces', economies of scale and the like), and that customary laws and tenures and common rights were increasingly being undermined and swept aside. None of these processes, of course, was new. The commercialization of agriculture had been advancing steadily for several generations, and any serious investigation of these long-term changes in rural society must reach back to at least the early years of the Tudors, as R. H. Tawney did in his study of *The Agrarian Problem in the Sixteenth Century* (1912). But it took a long time for agrarian capitalism to triumph fully. In the later seventeenth century its development was still very incomplete: well advanced in some regions certainly (such as in many of the corn-growing districts near London), but much less deeply rooted in others (in forests and fenlands and other places with extensive common rights, and in regions where small farms could still be readily obtained). By around 1800, however, the triumph of agrarian capitalism was pretty nearly universal, and because of this triumph landed property had become much less freely accessible to labouring people. Their ease of access to the land had become severely constricted and their opportunities for some sort of 'independence' much reduced. The land came to be, overwhelmingly, something they worked *for others*. How, then, did these changes come about?

One kind of limitation on the ease of access to landed property stemmed from the process known as engrossing. In the later seventeenth century, in many parts of England, small tenant-farms were still very common. These were farms of around ten, fifteen or twenty-five acres, many of which were held by copyhold tenure. Their occupiers were known as husbandmen or smallholders: they were more likely to specialize in animal husbandry than corn-growing, and in some regions their livelihoods were heavily dependent on common grazing rights. However, in the course of the several generations up to 1800 these smallholders were dying out, largely because landlords were finding it more economically profitable to consolidate small farms into larger — and, in their view, more efficient and convenient — farming units. Large farms, it was thought, enjoyed the advantages of economy of scale; they could respond more effectively to market demand and, in the end, they would generate a better and steadier rent for the landlord. Small farms, in contrast, came to be seen as much less attractive: under-capitalized, inefficient, insufficiently market-oriented, and a nuisance for the rent collector. Consequently, the policy of landowners and their stewards on a growing number of estates came to favour the elimination of small farms and their amalgamation (or engrossing) into a smaller number of large farms. At the same time landlords were also assiduously buying up smaller freehold properties and absorbing them into their large estates. There is no doubt, certainly, that in the course of these several generations the total number of farms in England was substantially reduced. Farming came to be increasingly dominated by substantial and often quite prosperous farmers who worked large holdings, and as a result of these changes the possibilities for men of modest means to acquire and stock small farms very noticeably receded.[1]

This process of the consolidation of farms has been abundantly documented. One reads of it occurring in many parts of the country: in Shropshire and Staffordshire; in Herefordshire and Dorset; in Bedfordshire, Lincolnshire and Buckinghamshire. In the Lake District, because of 'an increase in the average size of farms' and 'the adoption of more intensive methods of cultivation', it is said that 'a larger proportion of the inhabitants of rural parishes became hired workers'. In Dorset small farms and copyhold tenancies were still very numerous in the later seventeenth century. However, in the following four or five generations

the 'engrossing' or throwing together of smallholdings to make larger, more economic and profitable farms, with the accompanying eviction of the tenants of the former smallholdings and the disappearance of common lands in the face of enclosures, deprived many labourers of the small plots of land or the grazing-rights which had previously given them a subsidiary income as well as a certain measure of independence.[3]

Similar changes were occuring in the parish of Myddle in Shropshire where, according to David Hey, there was 'a great deal of engrossing of the smaller tenements'. Here, as in many other places, security of tenure for smallholders was being persistently undermined.

As leases fell in, estate owners refused to renew them, for it was then [in the eighteenth century] more profitable to grow corn on larger farms. Some of the hedges were torn down, small farms were engrossed into larger ones, and the old pastures were ploughed up and converted to arable farming. The transformation of the agricultural system in the parish of Myddle not only exemplified the general trend throughout the county but reflected a national movement as a result of which the smaller landowner found it increasingly difficult to survive . . . the reports of the Board of Agriculture written at the close of the eighteenth century state that the size of farms had recently increased in all parts of the county, while the number of farms had diminished by about a third.

As a result of engrossing, he concludes, the 'small farmers were driven out, and a new society, more sharply divided between the rich and the poor, arose out of the old'.[4]

Such changes did not go unnoticed by eighteenth-century observers. Indeed, they were commonly seen as essential to those agricultural

'improvements' that many men of property so warmly condoned. ('Improvement' here meant the fostering of intensive, commercial farming.) A report
of 1790 on the recent improvements in Cumberland exemplifies this
attitude: it is suffused with the sort of progressive consciousness that was
commonplace by the end of the century:

The rust of poverty and ignorance is now wearing off. Estates are bought up into
fewer hands; and the poorer sort of people remove into towns, to gain a
livelihood by handicrafts and commerce. Lands increase in value: the houses (or
rather huts) of clay, which were small, and ill-built, are mostly thrown down;
instead of which, strong and roomy farm-houses are built, and building, with
hard durable stone....[5]

Other observers were less sanguine about the merits of engrossing. In 1758,
for instance, a contributor to the *Gentleman's Magazine* criticized the
'practice of throwing down the small and middling farms, and taking in the
commons', and in the 1770s both Samuel Rudder and William Chapple
spoke out against the 'laying of two or three farms into one' and the
'monopolizing farmer'.[6] These were not, of course, unprecedented criticisms:
the essential implications, and some of the causes, of engrossing had been
recognized by numerous commentators many years before. In the late
seventeenth century, for instance, Roger North had complained

that Gentlemen, of late Years, have taken up an Humour of destroying their
Tenements and Cottages, whereby they make it impossible that Mankind should
inhabit upon their Estates. This is done sometimes bare-faced, because they
harbour Poor that are a Charge to the Parish, and sometimes because the Charge
of Repairing is great, and if an House be ruinous, they will not be at the Cost of
rebuilding and repairing it, and cast their Lands into very great Farms, which are
managed with less Housing: And oftimes for Improvement, as it is called; which
is done by buying in all Freeholds, Copyholds, and Tenements that have
Common, and which harboured very many husbandry and labouring Families;
and then enclosing the Commons and Fields....[7]

As Roger North clearly recognized, the decline of small farms was closely
associated with another development — the demolishing of cottages, especially
those to which common rights were attached. For cottagers could be as
inconvenient to enterprising landlords as were small farmers, and for similar
reasons. A vigorous representation of this conflict of interest appeared in the
Northampton Mercury in 1726. 'You must know', this author argued,

there are a sort of Stewards in the World... that cannot endure to see a little
House or a little Farm,... and have therefore of late Years perswaded their
Lords and Masters, that little Houses and little Takings are every where

detrimental to great Estates; and that there is more Charge and Trouble in
supporting Cottages than they are worth; that they are impolitick Harbours for
poor People, and do even tempt them from other Parishes, to become troublesome,
if not chargeable, to theirs: and in short, that it is therefore more adviseable for his
Grace, his Lordship, or his Worship, utterly to abandon such Cottages, and let
them fall; especially considering that thereby the Right of Common, belonging to
such Cottages, (in some Places not inconsiderable) will be sunk to the Benefit of
larger Takings. . . . [8]

(Behind such stewards, we might suppose, eager landlords were likely to be
found. As one absentee landlord in Yorkshire wrote to his estate manager in
1730, 'I would rather have my Cottages diminished, than increased.'[9]) Other
observers were similarly unimpressed by these developments. Thomas
Alcock in 1752 spoke of gentlemen 'pulling down Cottages, and suffering no
Places of Inhabitation for Paupers, whereby the Estates are flung into a few
Hands' (he blamed the Poor Laws for these ills and others); and Samuel
Rudder noted that in Gloucestershire some landlords 'have pulled down their
cottage-houses, or suffered them to fall, on purpose to drive away the poor
miserable inhabitants'.[10] 'It has been the fashion for many years past',
according to a writer in 1785,

to destroy the cottages in the neighbourhood of commons, on the pretence of
their being injurious to the public, and serving only to harbour thieves, etc. And
tho' this may be sometimes the case, it is by no means general . . . . The real fact
is, that the great farmers dislike them, because they consider them as infringements
of their own rights of common; and I know many farmers who for that reason
will not employ any cottager who is possessed of any kind of beast, altho' he may
have a just right and conveniency to keep them. This added to the trouble they
give to many stewards of estates, who finding that the repairs and collecting the
rents of cottages create much trouble, are very ready to give way to the wishes of
the farmer, and are reasons among several others which might be assigned why
we see very few new cottages erected on commons, and many daily tumbling to
ruin for want of repair.[11]

Closely associated with these developments — the decline of cottages (in
some places) and of small farms (almost everywhere) — was the enclosure
movement. For although engrossing certainly could (and often did) occur
prior to an Act of enclosure, or entirely independently of enclosure, it is clear
that the enclosure of lands in a particular parish was sometimes associated
with, and at least partly a cause of, the consolidation of farms into larger
holdings. Often, admittedly, enclosure simply accentuated or completed a
process that had been going on for several generations. As G. E. Mingay has
observed, 'it is probable that in many cases enclosure merely reinforced,
rather than initiated, an old tendency towards larger farm units and sharper

social divisions'.[12] But sometimes enclosure did occasion a very substantial restructuring of tenancies in favour of large farmers. It was said, for instance, that in Merton, Oxfordshire, the enclosure of the parish 'annulled all leases, and the inclosure itself facilitated the plan of throwing several *small farms* into a *few large bargains*'.[13] Similarly, another writer thought that the 'ingrossing of land' was 'encouraged by inclosing':

But the poor, the tenant farmers, with their poorer dependants, and many others in the lower stations of life, suffer greatly by inclosing, as far as it is an encouragement to the monopoly of lands. The landholders . . . in most parishes that have been inclosed only fifteen or twenty years, are very few in comparison of [sic] the numbers who occupied them in their open-field state. It is no uncommon thing for four or five wealthy graziers to engross a large inclosed lordship, which was before in the hands of twenty or thirty farmers, and as many smaller tenants or proprietors.[14]

Enclosure was frequently the occasion for accelerated land sales, a substantial replacement of farming personnel and sometimes a reorganization of the local economy in favour of more intensive commercial farming. As Professor Mingay has said, 'engrossing was facilitated by the powers provided in enclosure Acts for the termination of leases', and 'it is obvious that a large-scale enclosure would give landlords a good opportunity for carrying out a radical change in farm sizes at the same time as land holdings were reallocated and made more compact'.[15] Moreover, the costs of enclosure also worked against smallholders: indeed, one recent study of Buckinghamshire has concluded that 'many landowners were forced by pressure of costs to sell their land upon enclosure'.[16]

Now it must be said right away that enclosure, which was an important component of the broader social changes of the century, has always been (and still remains) a controversial subject: its consequences have been condemned by some historians and applauded by others. These contrasting assessments stem in part from the different traditions of historical inquiry. For a perspective that attends primarily to matters of economic productivity, capital accumulation and market efficiency is likely to represent the consequences of enclosure in a mostly favourable light and to see them as a part of the generally beneficial process that has come to be known as the 'agricultural revolution'; while a primary concern to reconstruct the social history of the labouring people, as it was actually experienced by those who lived through the process of enclosure, and to understand how enclosure affected their lives and the lives of their children, is almost certain to render less comforting conclusions. There is little doubt, I think, that during the past generation the former perspective has dominated over the latter.

Enclosure has been seen mainly as a contributor to economic growth and improved farming; serious studies of common rights — their rationale, their implications, their significance in the culture of the people — have been much less frequently pursued. Consequently, the conventional wisdom at the moment is markedly 'optimistic' as to the consequences of enclosure. And yet there are other considerations and other evidence — considerations that alter the angle of vision on enclosure, evidence that is not entirely compatible with this optimism — that are in danger of being neglected or depreciated.

An elaborated discussion of such a complex and contentious subject as enclosure is not, I think, possible in a book of this kind, but there is one central proposition that does warrant at least passing consideration. This is the claim — a claim that I think is correct — that the termination of common rights caused substantial distress and dislocation among the labouring people. I have already examined the extent, character and importance of these common rights: in many regions, in the late seventeenth century, they continued to be vital components of the household economy of rural working people (cottagers, husbandmen, country craftsmen, forest-dwellers and the like), and they were certainly highly valued by these people. As Daniel Defoe once said, the 'right of commonage' was something 'which the poor take to be as much their property, as a rich man's land is his own'.[17] By the early nineteenth century, however, most of these common rights had been eliminated, and the clear consequence of this long-term undermining of such rights of access to landed property was the destruction — not total perhaps, but certainly substantial — of the kind of semi-self-sufficient household economy that I attempted to reconstruct in Chapter 2. Commons were of critical value to these people, and the loss of these rights accentuated their dependence on wage-labour and usually left them even more impoverished than they had been before.[18] Poor men, and men of very modest property, simply had little, if anything, to gain (directly and immediately) from enclosure. For enclosure extinguished use-rights: rights to use lands, for particular purposes and within certain limits, that belonged — though not absolutely — to others. It marked the triumphant realization of *exclusive* private rights of property — rights that were now unconstrained by any communal or public rights to enjoy certain benefits from this property. One critic of this process spoke of enclosure as the practice 'of taking in and discommoning publick Fields'.[19] There is no doubt that enclosure benefited large landowners, 'improving' farmers and the holders of clerical benefices. But others paid a price for these benefits. Enclosure exacted social costs, not all of which have been calculated in certain historians' accounts, and amongst the losers, as one recent study has concluded, the 'cottager class were certainly the most universal victims of enclosure'.[20]

Some contemporary observers were certainly well aware of the conflicts of interest that were imbedded in the process of enclosure. In 1700, for instance, Timothy Nourse reviewed some of the arguments in favour of enclosure, to which he clearly attached considerable weight, but he also acknowledged the interests of those cottagers to whom commons were important:

having liv'd Time immemorial in such Places, they have as good a Title to their Habitations, as if they had continu'd there from the Beginning of the World... to invade any Man's Private Interest without his Leave, or due Compensation had for his Loss, and for the Benefit purely of others, wherein the Loser himself is not concern'd, this is against Reason; so that we are carefully to distinguish between a Necessity and a Convenience. In Cases, I say, of Common Necessity, 'tis better a Part than a Whole should suffer; but in Cases of Convenience 'tis not so: For no Man ought to suffer for the Advantage of Others, when the Person suffering partakes not of that Advantage.[21]

Such attentiveness to matters of equity is also apparent in a remark by William Ellis, a farmer and agricultural writer. Ellis was not opposed on principle to enclosures, for he thought that they could be effected to the advantage of all, but he did complain of 'the great Disadvantages that have arisen from the unlawful and unjust Inclosing of Common Lands from the Poor, who had a proportionable Title with the greatest Farmer, and yet have been intirely excluded from such their just Right for ever'. He spoke of these commons as the 'Paternal Inheritance' of the poor.[22] Another writer, in the 1770s, conceded that there were drawbacks to enclosure (he seemed to admit that, in Lincolnshire, 'by inclosing the fens we deprive a number of cottagers of pasturage for their stock, and, by that means, of the method whereby to procure sustenance for themselves'), but he thought that the economic and moral advantages of enclosure outweighed these losses.[23] At the end of the century it was being stated as common knowledge that the 'prejudice amongst the lower classes of people against the inclosure of commons is very powerful and is almost universal', and schemes were being proposed to compensate these people for the loss of the benefits they had enjoyed from common rights.[24] In all of this commentary there is a clear recognition, as is reflected in the talk of trade-offs and of 'balancing' gains against losses, that the commoners' losses were tangible and (at least to them) of considerable importance. Even Arthur Young, who actively championed the cause of enclosure, acknowledged in his later years that enclosures had contributed substantially to the poverty and misery that, around 1800, were so widely observed in the English countryside.[25]

The reinterpretation of property rights during these several generations is beyond dispute. As C. B. Macpherson has said, we observe 'from the seventeenth century on . . . the replacement of the old limited rights in land and other valuable things by virtually unlimited rights': 'limited and not always saleable rights *in* things were being replaced by virtually unlimited and saleable rights *to* things'.[26] The 'ownership' of land, which had previously been constrained by the customary claims of non-owners to certain benefits from that land, came to be seen as an absolute and exclusive right. All other rights, especially those use-rights that small men highly valued, were steadily abrogated and swept aside. Indeed, it was often denied that these were proper rights at all. 'During the eighteenth century', writes Edward Thompson, 'one legal decision after another signalled that the lawyers had become converted to the notions of absolute property ownership, and that (wherever the least doubt could be found) the law abhorred the messy complexities of coincident use-right.'[27] Usages that had been, and still were (in the minds of the people), sanctioned by the force of custom were confronted by the challenges of capital accumulation and capitalist rationality — and in most places these challenges met with considerable, if not overwhelming, success. Such customary practices as gleaning, wood-gathering and the right of herbage were, in time, discovered to be incompatible with the absolute private possession of land. It has been remarked, for example, that 'Gleaning and the collection of firewood, both critical to the families of rural laborers, were among [those] rights increasingly denied in the slow transformation of rural society that accompanied the growth of commercial farming.'[28] And though country people often clung tenaciously to these rights and vigorously resisted their erosion or extinction, the law came to redefine them as 'crimes' against property, thereby discouraging their continuance. As John Beattie has observed of this process, the 'taking of certain perquisites, accepted earlier as customarily available to the rural community, came increasingly to be condemned as crimes and to be punished as such by magistrates.'[29] Direct access to the resources of the land, as a result, was further restricted.

One sees, then, a long-term erosion of subsistence-oriented local economies in which use-rights played a vital role. And as these rights were lost, and the possibilities for a moderate degree of self-sufficiency (or 'independence') were steadily reduced, country people inescapably became more dependent for their livelihoods on wage-labour. Self-employment diminished in importance and money-wages from employers increasingly became virtually the sole determinant of a plebeian household's material sustenance. It is important, then, that we attend directly to the changing value of these wages. Moreover, as we saw in Chapter 2, wage-dependence was no new thing around 1700. In many places — places where direct access to land was not an issue of immediate concern — wage-dependence was already the central reality of plebeian survival: in the already largely enclosed counties of the south-east corner of England, for example, or in the numerous scattered parishes elsewhere that had been enclosed in earlier generations, or among the roughly 20 to 25 per cent of the population that lived in towns and cities (half of them in London). Standards of living in all these places depended not on use-rights but on other circumstances, of which wages were certainly the most important.

The evidence on wages, however, is by no means straightforward, and many historians have contended with the difficulties involved in assembling and interpreting the relevant data. Numerous complexities have to be taken into account: the regularity of the wages received; regional variations in the movement of wages (for wages might have been rising in some areas while they were static or declining elsewhere); wage differentials from trade to trade (how can one satisfactorily determine general 'averages'?); the changing relations between wages and prices (for it is, of course, *real* wages that matter). Wage data cannot, it is clear, be properly understood in isolation. It cannot, on its own, be regarded as a reliable indicator of changing standards of living: to be of value it must be appreciated contextually, with due attention to those diverse circumstances that conditioned the actual experiences of wage-employment. And as yet studies of this sort — studies that present good evidence on wage rates over time and attend closely to the social and economic contexts of these changes — have been infrequently attempted. Such refinements are rarely attained, and few advances have been made in recent years.

Our present knowledge of wage-movements, as a consequence, is rather limited in character. We do know that during the first sixty to sixty-five years of the eighteenth century there was almost certainly no decline in real wages. In fact, in many places they seem to have improved moderately, especially during the 1730s and 1740s. Although the actual rates of money-wages were often fairly static, or moved upwards only very slowly, prices were generally low, sometimes very low, and consequently real wages were rarely threatened. Grain supplies, which were so vitally important to the sustenance of the labouring people, could be purchased very cheaply during most of these years (excepting a few years of dearth, notably 1709/10, 1740 and 1756/57). Because of this cheapness of provisions, then, real wages, at worst, held steady, or were often enhanced to varying (usually modest) extents. It can be said, I think, that the real wages of the labouring people were probably slightly higher around 1760 than they had been at the beginning of the century. However, from the 1760s provisions ceased to be cheap. Average annual grain prices rose significantly from the mid 1760s, reaching unprecedented heights during the last decade of the century. This price inflation is very well documented. It also seems — and here the evidence is less clear-cut — that wage rates, on the whole, though they increased almost everywhere, tended to lag behind prices, or at best just kept up with inflation (and even this was not common in the 1790s). The only districts that unquestionably experienced a general increase in real wages during the last third of the century were those with rapidly expanding industrial economies, notably the West Riding of Yorkshire, south Lancashire and the Birmingham region. Real wages in most country districts during these decades were undoubtedly eroded, and in London they were probably in decline by the 1790s, if not before. As the nineteenth century opened the real wages of most labouring people in most parts of England were probably lower — sometimes just slightly, sometimes quite strikingly — than they had been in the 1760s.[30]

There is abundant scattered evidence as to these pressures upon wages. Adam Smith, at an early point in this inflationary period, in 1776, remarked that the 'high price of provisions during these ten years past has not in many parts of the kingdom been accompanied with any sensible rise in the money price of labour'.[31] Around the same time a decline in real wages in the county of Devon was being noticed by an informed observer.[32] The depression of labourers' wages in various counties has been clearly represented in numerous local studies: Essex, Wiltshire, Herefordshire, Warwickshire and Notting-hamshire are five cases in point.[33] In Exeter, according to Professor Hoskins, real wages declined very noticeably between the 1760s and the 1790s; Professor Simmons remarked on a similar trend in the hosiery industry in Leicester; and in Bath it seems that real wages declined by at least 20 per cent during the quarter-century from 1780.[34] The circumstances in most parts of the Midlands, East Anglia, the South and the West were probably much like those that were described in 1792 by the vicar of Naseby, Northamptonshire, in a book about his own parish. The wages of labour, he said, 'are higher than they were twenty years ago, but by no means keep pace with the advancing price of provision'.[35] These were hard years for most wage-dependent people — even harder than the years of a half-century before. It is little wonder that a growing proportion of them resorted to poor relief in order to survive.

Social relations

As labouring people gradually lost their tenuous hold on the essential supports of semi-self-sufficiency, and as they became increasingly dependent on wages for their sustenance, they were also coming to experience a growing cleavage between their own culture and the culture of men of property. There was, it is clear, an increasing intolerance among propertied people of plebeian culture, and a growing disposition to challenge and undermine this customary culture. (These changes were particularly marked after the middle of the eighteenth century.) Moreover, certain long-standing social divisions were being widened even further, and social conflicts, in some important areas of experience, came to be considerably more pronounced during the later eighteenth century than they had been two or three generations before. What, then, are some of the signs of these important changes in social attitudes and relations?

In an earlier work I attempted to deal with some of these issues as they are revealed in the changing recreational culture of the labouring people. Before about 1750 most gentlemen had been prepared (at the least) to tolerate the common people's recreational customs; indeed, gentlemen often patronized and supported, or even sponsored, certain festivities and sporting events. Many gentlemen, with their respect for antiquity, were favourably disposed to tradition, to ritual and ceremony (especially when the ceremony reinforced their own authority), to robust and manly sports, to festive indulgences (as long as they were not too disorderly or expensive), to old, time-honoured customs; they were little inclined, during these years of vehement anti-puritanism, to meddle with the people's affairs on the grounds of religion or reforming morality. However, from around the mid eighteenth century these easy-going attitudes were noticeably in retreat. Customs which had previously been generally accepted came to be questioned and often vigorously condemned, and this newly mobilized hostility could hardly fail to have a significant impact on the recreational practices of plebeian society, especially when the strictures came from legislators and magistrates, employers and zealous clergymen. There is, indeed, much evidence of an increasing willingness among people of authority to intervene actively in opposition to these customary practices — and some of their attacks certainly succeeded. By around 1800 the undermining of popular recreations was already well underway, and the process was to continue for at least another half-century. The concern for moral 'improvement', refined manners, and orderly conduct steadily grew in prominence; these 'virtues' were accorded appreciating value by polite society; and consequently popular and genteel tastes became increasingly dissociated from each other. Upper and lower class standards for evaluating recreational behaviour came to have little in common — considerably less, certainly, than they had had around 1700 — and the customs that the people continued to honour were increasingly regarded from above as primitive, disorderly, often immoral, and usually at odds with certain elementary standards of social propriety. In 1777 John Brand, one of the best informed observers of popular culture, was able to speak of 'the present fashionable Contempt of old Customs'.[36]

Similar processes of change have been detected in other domains of experience. Consider, for instance, the Game Laws. As Peter Munsche has shown, the Game Laws were enforced rather leniently prior to the mid eighteenth century. 'No wholesale confiscation of guns, dogs or other "engines" took place; nor was there any sustained effort to punish violations of the game laws. Poachers were not, of course, allowed to operate with impunity, but the impact of the Game Act on the rural community as a whole was not as great as its provisions would suggest.' These lenient attitudes, however, were clearly being abandoned after about 1750; and, for a variety of reasons, all of which Mr Munsche attends to in his careful analysis, the Game Laws and their assertions of exclusive privileges became considerably more contentious and much more socially divisive in the later eighteenth century than they had ever been before.[37] Such changes in social relations were, I think, fairly common. Relations between country clergymen and their parishioners, for instance, which have been sensitively studied by Eric Evans, certainly became increasingly strained, and very frequently acrimonious, during the late eighteenth and early nineteenth centuries.[38] To take a further example: it seems to me that labourers' perquisites — those customary claims that working people made to part of the product of their own labour (servants' 'vails', shipwrights' 'chips', dockers' 'sweepings') — were subjected to increased attacks, and were much more likely to succumb to these attacks, during the second half than the first half of the century. This certainly appears to have been the case in the naval shipyards, where the taking of 'chips' by the workers became a serious issue of dispute after the middle of the century.[39] Employers were more and more intent on eliminating such customs (for by means of them labourers were able to exercise a certain degree of independent control over the work-place and the product of their own labour). The law increasingly came to the aid of men of capital, and helped to undermine the workers' claims, by redefining these perquisites as 'crimes' (just as it was doing with agrarian use-rights) and thus proscribing their continuance. One sees, then, once again, how, as Edward Thompson has suggested, 'capitalist logic and "non-economic" customary behaviour are in active and conscious conflict'.[40]

There is little doubt, I think, that the late eighteenth century was marked by a heightened sense of cultural dissociation based on class. This was partly a function of the strikingly differential benefits that resulted from capitalist expansion. For while there is abundant evidence throughout the eighteenth century of civic improvements, new public amenities and enlarged cultural opportunities, these fruits of 'progress' were predominantly enjoyed — at times even exclusively enjoyed — by genteel and middle-class people. As Jack Simmons has said of the improvements in eighteenth-century Leicester, 'these changes benefited only a minority. None of them brought much advantage to the poor, except indirectly through the increased trade and employment they entailed'.[41] This expanding culture of consumerism, of commercialized leisure, of what J. H. Plumb has referred to as 'the pursuit of happiness' — with its newly marketed pleasures and its capacity for handsomely satisfying the material aspirations of prospering families and for refining and agreeably embellishing their domestic routine[42] — this culture was certainly not accessible to all: in fact, it was almost entirely inaccessible to the great majority of the nation's population. Change was affording considerable benefits to a propertied few and virtually no immediate benefits to the unpropertied many. The patent inequalities that were imbedded in this process of cultural differentiation must have been noticed by many labouring people, especially since, at the same time as these changes were at work, their own customary culture was being persistently attacked and undermined. Around 1800 the cultural traditions of labouring people were probably held in greater contempt by polite society than ever before: they were obviously on the defensive, increasingly set off from the cultural identities of the 'better classes'. As Alan Everitt has written of these years, the 'increasing emphasis on the sanctity of the home and the growing tendency of gentlefolk to draw further apart from the common run of mankind were pronounced developments in provincial society in the late eighteenth and early nineteenth centuries: it was a time when divisions between class and class were clearly becoming deeper'.[43]

These deepening class divisions are also evidenced by the development of workers' combinations and the persistent efforts by manufacturers and legislators to suppress them. In certain industries the polarization of labour and capital was already well established by 1700, especially in London, the north-east coalfields and some of the larger provincial cities; and this polarization undoubtedly became more and more pervasive as the century advanced. An increasing proportion of working men found that they were destined to spend their whole lives as wage-dependent labourers. Craft traditions were breaking down, apprenticeship restrictions were becoming less enforceable and the habits of independent productive labour, to which many men were deeply attached, were being steadily eroded. Capitalist employers were coming to play an even larger role in industrial production and the scale of their enterprises grew dramatically in the course of the century, particularly during its last three or four decades. A classic division was emerging: on the one hand, wealthy manufacturers (or merchant-manufacturers) were in command of large capitalist enterprises; on the other, large bodies of full-time and lifelong wage-labourers were employed in these enterprises. (A few of these ventures, by the 1770s and 1780s, were for virtually the first time being run as recognizable 'modern' factories: that is, they involved a rigorous division of labour, a centrally administered and superintended organization of production, much stricter work discipline than ever before and sometimes a centralized source of power.) These were circumstances that inevitably encouraged the creation and development of working-men's clubs and societies; at times of conflict between the men and their employers these associations were liable to be transformed into 'combinations', whose principal objective was industrial action against the employers; and in response to these actions the employers were often disposed to resort to Parliament or the courts in order to confront the threat of workers' power and to destroy their unions. The law, in fact, as a critical mediator of industrial disputes, testifies to both the growing tensions between capital and labour and the manner in which these tensions were usually 'resolved' in capital's favour.

But let us pause for a moment to consider the testimony of a contemporary observer on a part of this question: testimony that brings a degree of particularity to this generalized argument concerning the growing separation between masters and men. The observer whose views are especially noteworthy is the economic writer, Josiah Tucker, a man who was certainly no admirer of plebeian culture. In a work first published in 1757, Tucker noted the persistence of small, independent manufacturing enterprises in Yorkshire and then went on to describe the character of the quite different industrial organization in the woollen districts of Gloucestershire, Wiltshire and Somerset, an area he knew well. His representation presses to the heart of some central social issues:

One Person, with a great Stock and large Credit, buys the Wool, pays for the Spinning, Weaving, Milling, Dying, Shearing, Dressing, etc. etc. That is, he is Master of the Whole Manufacture from first to last, and perhaps employs a thousand Persons under him. This is the Clothier, whom all the Rest are to look upon as their Paymaster. But will they not also sometimes look upon him as their Tyrant? And as great Numbers of them work together in the same Shop, will they not have it the more in their Power to vitiate and corrupt each other, to cabal and associate against their Masters, and to break out into Mobs and Riots upon every little Occasion? . . . Besides, as the Master is placed so high above the Condition of the Journeyman, both their Conditions approach much nearer to that of a Planter and Slave in our American Colonies, than might be expected in such a Country as England; and the Vices and Tempers belonging to each Condition are of the same Kind, only in an inferior Degree. The Master, for Example, however well-disposed in himself, is naturally tempted by his Situation to be proud and over-bearing, to consider his People as the Scum of the Earth, whom he has a Right to squeeze whenever he can; because they ought to be kept low, and not to rise up in Competition with their Superiors. The Journeymen on the contrary, are equally tempted by their Situation, to envy the high Station, and superior Fortunes of their Masters, and to envy them the more, in Proportion as they find themselves deprived of the Hopes of advancing themselves to the same Degree by any Stretch of Industry, or superior Skill. Hence their Self-Love takes a wrong Turn, destructive to themselves, and others. They think it no Crime to get as much Wages, and to do as little for it as they possibly can, to lie and cheat, and do any other bad Thing; provided it is only against their Master, whom they look upon as their common Enemy, with whom no Faith is to be kept.[44]

There is little doubt, I think, that discordant relations of this sort, and the structural underpinnings of such tensions, were becoming increasingly prevalent by the end of the century.[45] And we need not agree with all that Tucker says to recognize the truth of his basic contention: that capitalist accumulation was significantly responsible for the creation of a large and often disaffected proletariat.

Although much further research remains to be done on industrial relations, two further remarks can be offered with some degree of confidence. First, it is clear that the paternalistic policy of industrial regulation — that is, the willingness of the authorities to provide a certain level of protection and security for industrial workers — was being decisively jettisoned. (Indeed, the patrician retreat from paternalism, in its various forms, was central to the changing class relations of the century.) The workers' desire for the regulation of labour conditions, which I discussed in Chapter 5, was increasingly confronting the imperatives of *laissez-faire* economics; and from the middle of the century, during times of dispute, these latter values were almost always triumphant — triumphant in Parliament, among the magistrates, within genteel culture at large. As one authority has put it, 'the masters' argument that regulations were unnecessary and harmful now carried more weight than the labourers' appeal for protection: trade after trade was "freed" from restrictions'.[46] The new orthodoxy rejected the utility of such protective regulations. The wages of workers should be entirely dependent on the forces of supply and demand. The essence of this view had been clearly stated earlier in the century: 'the Workman', it was said in 1733, 'ought to be left at Liberty to take as much as he can get, but then the Magistrates ought to take a particular Care, that every Workman may be left at full liberty to work for as small Wages as he pleases'.[47] Government should not intervene — and increasingly it declined to intervene — in this individual, 'freely contracted' relationship.

At the same time — and this is a second important point — while discarding these remnants of paternalism, the public authorities, both legislative and magisterial, continued to be intent on preventing workers from combining together to defend their interests. Indeed, the efforts to proscribe trade unions became rather more pronounced later in the century, partly because by that time, with the accelerated expansion of industrial capitalism and the demise of industrial paternalism, the workers were finding good reasons for organizing themselves on a much more substantial scale. (As in the past, these combinations were mostly among skilled workers.) Henry Pelling, for instance, finds a 'sterner attitude displayed towards combinations in the later eighteenth century' and suggests that it was probably 'partly the extent and efficacy of combinations' during these years 'that provoked the active hostility of Government and Parliament'.[48] From the middle of the century government policy was unambiguously firm in its support of employers: new legislation strengthened their position in combating trade unions and enhanced their ability to impose effective discipline on their workers and restrict these workers' 'freedoms' — freedoms that were often spoken of as 'idleness' and 'lawlessness'. The Worsted Act of 1777, for example, which legalized a form of employers' association, significantly enlarged the powers of clothiers to regulate the industry as a whole in their own interest and to manage their work-force more rigorously.[49] Here, then, as in most other areas of life, property, not labour, was the overwhelming beneficiary of government protection.

The culture of class-confrontation that I have been pointing to in these pages became particularly acute in the 1790s. Indeed, the last decade of the century — a decade of revolution in France, of galloping inflation, of the heavy demands of warfare from 1793 — is well known for its turbulence. Democratic ideas were being widely discussed, Tom Paine became a celebrated figure and political radicalism sank deep roots in plebeian society. There is much evidence of widespread popular discontent, of overt social unrest and of unprecedented political agitation. The mood of the times is nicely reflected in a letter sent to the Home Secretary in July 1791 by two justices of the peace in south Lancashire. For although they acknowledged that 'the trade of this County is wonderfully prosperous', they expressed considerable anxiety about the influx of Irish workers ('estranged, unconnected, and in general composed of persons who are in a species of exile'), the 'unhappy party spirit about the Revolution in France', 'the general ill-humour', and the 'spirit of combination amongst all sorts of labourers and artisans, who are in a state of disaffection to all legal control'.[50] Genteel anxieties of this sort were commonplace. The authorities, through the 1790s, were becoming frightened: frightened about the possibility of serious public disorders, of conspiracies and insurrectionary movements, of internal subversion abetted by France. English Jacobins and their sympathizers, along with many other more straightforwardly discontented people, confronted 'loyalist' movements and the increasingly repressive power of the state. As Gwyn Williams has said of the 1790s, 'in these years it is the *polarisation* of English political society . . . that catches the historian's eye'.[51] There is little doubt, I think, that the divide between propertied and plebeian culture, and the conflicts between their interests and outlooks, had become more pronounced and more bitter and self-conscious than ever before in the century. Social and political relationships were being rapidly reconstructed and redefined; and these processes of transformation involved, inextricably, a heightened sense of class-consciousness and class-hostility and the emergence of some funda-mentally revised, and much more critical, popular conceptions of the realities of state power.

Standards of living

The discussion in this chapter has been, on the whole, 'pessimistic' in character. It has emphasized certain losses that labouring people experienced; it has pointed to the decline in their living standards in the later eighteenth century; and it has represented these people, for the most part, as victims rather than beneficiaries of various social changes and of capitalist expansion. There has been almost no suggestion that labouring people may have benefited at all from the growth of the economy or that their experiences of life may have improved in any way. But is this pessimistic emphasis justified? Is it not (a sceptic might ask) a rather exaggerated and highly selective representation of the history of the period? Were poverty and misery in no way reduced or ameliorated with the passage of time? Did labouring people really gain no benefits at all from the growing prosperity of the nation as a whole? Surely there is more to be said on these matters.

Now it must be admitted that this whole question of the 'standard of living', broadly conceived, is not, at present, satisfactorily understood. Some accounts are now clearly out of date and others are patently ideological; much further research remains to be done. Moreover, there are so many different considerations to take into account as one tackles such a large issue: considerations involving, for instance, regional and occupational differences, the availability and usefulness of quantitative information and the 'typicality' of whatever evidence is presented. The problems of interpretation, then, are very great. I am aware that this chapter is probably more provisional, and almost certainly more incomplete, than any of the previous chapters, and that future work is very likely to modify and to expose certain lacunae in the discussion I have offered. But one cannot always wait on the future. It is necessary to say something now, given the evidence currently available. But, again, is there more to say than has been said thus far?

One fundamental fact of life that undoubtedly warrants explicit consideration is the matter of life expectancy. For surely (it might be argued) the growth of population from the late 1740s, and especially after 1780, was partly a result of the decline of the death rate; and assuming that mortality rates did in fact decline, it may well be that these improvements in the biological chances of life were a consequence of certain economic and social changes that were much more widely beneficial than I have heretofore allowed. Indeed, evidence of increased life expectancy might be regarded as a strong indication of general environmental improvements: improvements, in effect, in the standard of living. Perhaps, then, there are other issues that remain to be explored: issues that would afford a less gloomy view of the social consequences of capitalist expansion? There is some evidence, certainly, and a substantial body of scholarly opinion, in support of the view that mortality rates declined after 1750 and that average life expectancy in many parts of the country was longer in the later eighteenth and early nineteenth centuries than it had been during the previous two or three generations. It is likely, moreover, that a substantial part of this reduction in mortality stemmed from a decline in the incidence and severity of certain epidemic diseases. Periods of 'crisis mortality' — that is, years when the death rate was, say, double or triple the normal level — certainly appear to have been less frequent in the second half than in the first half of the eighteenth century. But what does one make of this evidence? How is it to be interpreted? And how does it bear on an assessment of the labouring people's changing standard of living?

It can be said, I think, that the only aspect of the standard of living worth serious consideration in this demographic discussion is the possibility that nutritional conditions improved from around the mid eighteenth century. Indeed, this nutritional argument has been favourably reviewed in a recent book by Thomas McKeown: a major conclusion of his study is that 'the most acceptable explanation of the large reduction of mortality and growth of population which preceded advances in hygiene is an improvement in nutrition due to greater food supplies'.[52] This argument undoubtedly deserves further attention: perhaps food supplies did become more regular and malnutrition less common; perhaps, in particular, the rapidly expanding cultivation of the potato in England afforded a more widespread nutritional security and thus less susceptibility to disease.[53] However, there are some problems with this nutritional argument. First, there is not, as yet, at least as far as cereals are concerned, much direct evidence to support it. Indeed, the argument tends to be supported more by deductive reasoning than by hard empirical substantiation. One critic has even claimed that 'there is no solid historical evidence for improvements in the standard of diet before about the 1840s'.[54] Second, any fair-minded assessment of this problem has to come to terms with the rather puzzling fact that, during the first half of the eighteenth century, when grain prices were generally low, mortality rates appear to have been relatively high, while in the years from the 1760s, when grain prices rose (indeed, they became extraordinarily high during the years of the revolutionary and Napoleonic wars), life expectancy may well have been increasing. Is it possible that people came to be better fed in times when inflation was so severe? The issue clearly requires closer examination. Finally, while the best and most reliable evidence for a decline in mortality from the mid eighteenth century is derived from demographic studies of the gentry and aristocracy (and the evidence concerning their increased life expectancy after 1750 is certainly very striking), it is hard to imagine how nutritional changes could have had any such significant impact on the demographic experiences of such privileged, and already well-fed, social groups.[55] And if a nutritional explanation does little to account for these well-documented genteel experiences, it may be that scepticism is called for before applying it to the mortality experiences of the population at large. Perhaps genteel and aristocratic life expectancy improved largely for other reasons — reasons that might have some bearing on the biological state of the labouring people as well?

A possible alternative explanation might be found in the changes effected in health care. Indeed, it was once thought that various improvements in medical practice contributed significantly to the lowering of the death rate. These arguments, however, have been vigorously disputed and are now largely rejected[56] — though with one important exception. The exception, which has received considerable attention in recent years, concerns the extent and effectiveness of inoculation against smallpox. It has been argued by Peter Razzell, the principal student of this subject, that variolation came to be so generally practised in the last third of the eighteenth century that, given the destructive powers of smallpox and its near universality (prior to inoculation, he thinks, most people contracted it), this single medical advance was a major cause — probably *the* major cause — of increased life expectancy. During the first two generations of the eighteenth century, he thinks, smallpox was a devastating killer, but 'inoculation had become so widespread by the end of the eighteenth century that only a relatively small proportion of the population was left unprotected'.[57] Razzell's well-documented views deserve careful consideration. However, they are still very contentious. And even if they are granted some degree of credence, they may well be overstated: as one scholar has put it, the argument 'has the appearance of spoiling a good case by exaggeration', especially by exaggerating the weight of smallpox deaths in relation to total deaths during the period before inoculation came to be widely employed.[58] For even if inoculation against smallpox actually was as effective as Razzell contends, smallpox may not have been as prominent a killer as he suggests it was. It is possible, in short, that he is underestimating the importance of other causes of death. Here, then, is another issue on which further study will be needed before the merits of the case can be more precisely and judiciously assessed.

Two further considerations — considerations that bear on the possible connections between demographic changes and changes in living standards — deserve to be mentioned. First, it is possible that the declining rates of mortality during these years are not entirely explicable by reference solely to economic circumstances. For it may be that a reduction in the virulence of some infectious diseases occurred autonomously, or that with the passage of time the human hosts developed certain immunities to these pathogenic micro-organisms. Disease, then, may have functioned semi-independently of economic, and especially nutritional, conditions. These speculations have been prompted by the recognition on the part of demographic historians that years of high mortality were not always years of famine or other extraordinary economic hardship. One scholar, reflecting on certain long-term demographic changes in Europe, has noted that 'it is possible that plague and similar crises of public health were essentially biological in origin and not directly related to problems of subsistence'.[59] Similarly, a student of epidemics in early modern London has played down the impact of nutrition and other economic circumstances on the incidence and severity of disease. 'Largely independent of environmental factors', he concludes, 'the course of disease may have to be treated as an autonomous influence on population growth.'[60] If such suggestions are true, and if a significant part of the declining death rate was a consequence of 'fortuitous' biological changes, then increased life expectancy, though undoubtedly a benefit of a sort, cannot necessarily be interpreted as a clear indication of a generally improved standard of living. Moreover — and this is a second caveat — it is not even clear how much weight should be attached to declining mortality, as against increasing fertility, in any full explanation of population growth. For it may be that rising birth rates, largely as a result of a declining age of marriage, played a more vital role in England's demographic expansion than has been generally acknowledged. Indeed, the author of one recent and intensive demographic study has concluded that 'Changes in mortality appear to have affected population growth less than many earlier commentators have argued.'[61] And if a decline in the age of marriage was in fact responsible for an increase in the birth rate, these changing marital realities were probably mostly a function, not of growing prosperity, but of the increasing proletarianization of the labouring people.[62]

We can see, then, that this demographic literature leads to no clear conclusions with regard to the standard of living. Mortality rates — especially infant mortality and 'crisis' mortality — were almost certainly reduced in the later eighteenth century, but we do not have a satisfactory understanding of the extent of this decline or the reasons for whatever increased life expectancy there was. Perhaps one cause was clearly most important; or it may be that an adequate explanation of population growth will have to take account of a complex of relevant determinants. Possibly there were certain improvements in living conditions that reduced the risk of infection or increased the chance of survival among those who became infected, but at present there is no general agreement as to what these changes were. The whole discussion, in short, is full of uncertainty and conflicting interpretations. All we can say for now, I think, is that *if* an argument can be convincingly made to show an increased standard of living, it is likely to depend very heavily on evidence that demonstrates an increase in the expectation of life at birth. For life expectancy is not only of central importance to the 'quality of experience', it is also frequently (though not necessarily in all cases) very responsive to changes in material standards of life. Further studies of the standard of living question, then, would be wise to focus their attention on issues related to life expectancy; and it may be that findings will emerge that allow for more 'optimistic' interpretations than I have presented in much of this chapter. For the moment, though, firm pronouncements on these demographic matters would seem to be premature.

We are left, I think, with a pronounced sense of the ambiguities of social change and the complexities of interpreting the changing experiences of the labouring people. The testimonies of contemporary observers are often contradictory: some of them thought living standards were generally improving; others were sure that conditions were deteriorating, at least for large bodies of the labouring people. Employment opportunities were undoubtedly expanding rapidly in some parts of the country, but elsewhere (especially in southern, south-western and parts of central England) cottage by-employments were in decline, competition for jobs was becoming more acute, wages were severely depressed and unemployment was widespread. While numerous workers may have been enjoying a few new comforts and amenities (notably cotton clothing, which was cheap and easy to wash), there is much evidence that testifies to the pauperization of many other labouring people. During these years the state withdrew almost entirely from any attempt to regulate wages, food prices or conditions of employment, leaving the individual worker 'free' to pursue his own self-interest, as long as he did not combine in this pursuit with other workers. All men (theoretically) were to be subject to the same laws — the laws of the marketplace. And while some well-placed manufacturing workers undoubtedly benefited from this expanding market economy,[63] people in other trades and those employed as farm labourers certainly made no immediate gains, as we can see from the data on real wages from the late eighteenth and early nineteenth centuries. And yet the indications of decreased mortality suggest that there must have been other processes at work of a more favourable character. We still confront, then, many puzzling and unresolved issues, and much work remains to be done before satisfactory generalizations can be rendered.

But it would be inappropriate to conclude this inquiry on a note of such uncertainty. For while many questions certainly warrant more extensive examination, not all issues are equally ill-understood, and on some matters a substantial body of evidence is already available. And this evidence, in my view, tends to call into question many of the more optimistic interpretations of the immediate social consequences of capitalist expansion: consequences, that is, for the conditions of life of the labouring people during the (approximately) half-century from around 1770. At present the direct evidence as to improvements in living standards during these decades is spotty, frequently insubstantial and sometimes ambiguous, while the evidence of declining, or at least unimproving, living standards is extensive and often remarkably clear-cut. Undoubtedly the economy was vigorously expanding, but there is little evidence that much of this newly created wealth was trickling down to the working people. Labouring men and women certainly bore the brunt of the dislocations, disruptions and personal upheavals that were associated with economic growth — the agricultural revolution, the mechanization of manufacturing, the undermining of customary practices — while other people, in the short term (perhaps up to the 1840s), reaped most of the benefits of this growth. Moreover, there is no doubt at all that during these years the gap in living standards between propertied and un-propertied people noticeably widened. The inequalities in the distribution of wealth were accentuated, *relative* poverty increased and labour's share of the national income undoubtedly declined.[64] Indeed, the consciousness of these differential consequences of economic expansion — the discrepancy between the growing wealth of some men and the continuing (or increasing) poverty of others — actively informed much of the overt social criticism of these years, and probably much popular consciousness as well. The poet George Crabbe was habitually a rather morose commentator on social life, but in one passage he touched sensitively upon a fundamental fact of consciousness that must have been widely apparent, at least to those who looked:

Where Plenty smiles — alas! she smiles for few —
And those who taste not, yet behold her store,
Are as the slaves that dig the golden ore,
The wealth around them makes them doubly poor.[65]

These conditions of poverty and misery, in their various forms, as economically and culturally defined, were not to be unambiguously ameliorated for the bulk of England's population until the years from the 1840s, when the labouring people, for perhaps the first time, came to obtain some clear-cut material advantages from the economy of agrarian and industrial capitalism.

Notes and references

Abbreviations

PRO   Public Record Office
RO   Record Office
VCH   *Victoria County History*

Chapter 1: The labouring people in English society

1   Guy Miege, *The Present State of Great Britain* (London 1707), p. 264. This broad identification of the labouring people had a lengthy heritage: in the Elizabethan period William Harrison had reported that 'We in England divide our people commonly into four sorts, as gentlemen, citizens or burgesses, yeomen, and artificers or laborers.' This 'last sort of people', he later elaborated, 'are day laborers, poor husbandmen, and some retailers (which have no free land), copyholders, and all artificers, as tailors, shoemakers, carpenters, brickmakers, masons, etc.': William Harrison, *The Description of England*, ed. Georges Edelen (Ithaca, NY: Cornell University Press 1968, for the Folger Shakespeare Library), pp. 94 and 118.

2   *Covent-Garden Journal*, no. 47, 13 June 1752.

3   Henry Fielding, *An Enquiry Into the Causes of the late Increase of Robbers* (London 1751), reprinted in *The Complete Works of Henry Fielding*, ed. William E. Henley (16 vols., London: Frank Cass 1967), vol. 13: *Legal Writings*, p. 56.

4   John Brand, *Observations on Popular Antiquities* (Newcastle upon Tyne 1777), p. ix.

5   Daniel Defoe, *A Review of the State of the British Nation,* 25 June 1709.

6   *Parliamentary History*, vol. 15 (1753-65), col. 17 (debate of 7 May 1753).

7   *Gentleman's Magazine*, vol. 26 (1756), p. 557.

8   *Northampton Mercury*, 22 January 1739 (essay on the merits and usefulness of the poor).

9   Timothy Nourse, *Campania Foelix* (London 1700), p. 100.

10   A. Ruth Fry, *John Bellers, 1654-1725: Quaker, Economist and Social Reformer. His Writings Reprinted, With a Memoir* (London 1935), p. 124, from *An Essay Towards the Improvement of Physick* (1714); cf. pp. 38 and 64.

11   See especially Edgar S. Furniss, *The Position of the Laborer in a System of Nationalism: A Study in the Labor Theories of the Later English Mercantilists* (New York: A. M. Kelley 1965; first publ. 1920), ch. 2; and Ronald L. Meek, *Studies in the Labour Theory of Value* (London: Lawrence & Wishart 1956), ch. 1.

12   William C. Lehmann, *John Millar of Glasgow 1735-1801: His Life and Thought and his Contributions to Sociological Analysis* (Cambridge: Cambridge University Press 1960), p. 333; and Arthur Young, *A Six Months Tour Through the North of England* (4 vols., London 1770), vol. 4, p. 440.

13   *Reflexions Upon the Moral State of the Nation* (London 1701), pp. 18-19.

14   Henry Fielding, *A Proposal for Making an Effectual Provision for the Poor* (London 1753), reprinted in *Works of Henry Fielding*, ed. Henley, vol. 13: *Legal Writings*, p. 138.

15   George Hickes, *A Sermon Preached at the Church of St. Bridget . . . upon the Subject of Alms-giving* (London 1684), p. 7.

16   Soame Jenyns, 'A Free Inquiry Into the Nature and Origin of Evil', in his *Miscellaneous Pieces* (2 vols., London 1761), vol. 2, pp. 79-80.

17   For a discussion of many of these matters see Furniss, *Position of the Laborer in a System of Nationalism*, especially chs. 5 and 6. There were, of course, writers who favoured high wages, as a few economic historians have pointed out, but they were almost certainly much less numerous, much less influential and much less representative of the conventional wisdom on labour than the advocates of low wages.

18   Richard Burton (pseud. for Nathaniel Crouch), *The Apprentices Companion* (London 1681), pp. 2-3.

19   Richard Mayo, *A Present for Servants* (London 1693), p. 4; and Robert Moss, *The Providential Division of Men into Rich and Poor* (London 1708), p. 16.

20   Thomas Seaton, *The Conduct of Servants in Great Families* (London 1720), pp. 1-2.

21   Thomas Broughton, *A Serious and Affectionate Warning to Servants* (London 1746), p. 7.

22   [Resta Patching], *Four Topographical Letters* (Newcastle upon Tyne 1757), pp. 24-5.

23   Moss, *Providential Division of Men*, p. 5.

24   Samuel Smith, *A Sermon Preached to the Societies for Reformation of Manners* (London 1738), p. 18.

25   Hickes, *Sermon . . . upon the Subject of Alms-giving*, p. 7.

26 Mayo, *Present for Servants*, p. 4.
27 William Fleetwood, *The Relative Duties of Parents and Children, Husbands and Wives, Masters and Servants* (London 1705), p. 386.
28 Jenyns, *Miscellaneous Pieces*, vol. 2, pp. 58-9 and 60-1.
29 [Patching], *Four Topographical Letters*, pp. 24-5. In a similar manner, in 1722 a gentleman of Melksham, Wiltshire, after reflecting on the large number of poor people in his parish, and the misery among them, admitted that this harsh human reality 'is what is not by me to be comprehended, and must therefore be left, with true Acknowledgement that God is Wise, Just and Merciful': 'Diary of Thomas Smith, of Shaw House, 1721-22', in John Alexander Neale, *Charters and Records of Neales of Berkeley, Yate and Corsham* (Warrington 1907), p. 208. For some further discussion of the issues raised in this paragraph see Richard B. Schlatter, *The Social Ideas of Religious Leaders 1660-1688* (London 1940), pp. 106-10.
30 Fleetwood, *Relative Duties*, pp. 384-5. According to another writer, 'the Labour of a Poor man is more healthful, and many times more pleasant too, than the Ease and Softness of the Rich; to be sure much more easy than the Cares and Solicitudes, the Pride and Ambition, Discontents, and Envyings, and Emulations, which commonly attend an Exalted Fortune': William Sherlock, *A Discourse Concerning the Divine Providence* (London 1694), pp. 243-4.
31 Jenyns, *Miscellaneous Pieces*, vol. 2, p. 64.
32 Robert Nelson, *An Address to Persons of Quality and Estate* (London 1715), pp. 38-9.
33 Moss, *Providential Division of Men*, p. 11.
34 Although the well-known calculations of Gregory King from the late seventeenth century are useful for some purposes, they are only modestly helpful in trying to resolve the main question of this paragraph. Moreover, their reliability has been recently questioned: see G. S. Holmes, 'Gregory King and the social structure of pre-industrial England', *Transactions of the Royal Historical Society*, 5th series, vol. 27 (1977), pp. 41-68.
35 For an opinion supportive of these distinctions see Roger Howell, 'Hearth tax returns', *History*, vol. 49 (1964), p. 45; cf. W. G. Hoskins, *Industry, Trade and People in Exeter 1688-1800* (Manchester 1935), p. 118.
36 Evidence from the hearth tax returns of the 1670s may be found in *VCH Cambridgeshire*, vol. 4 (1953), pp. 277-80, and vol. 6 (1978), pp. 280-2; *VCH Essex*, vol. 4 (1956), pp. 306-10; *VCH Leicestershire*, vol. 2 (1954), p. 228, and vol. 4 (1958), p. 157; *VCH York, East Riding*, vol. 1: *The City of Kingston upon Hull* (1969), pp. 160-1; and Hoskins, *Exeter 1688-1800*, pp. 117-18. See also the estimates concerning the social structure of Essex in 1723 in A. F. J. Brown, *Essex at Work 1700-1815* (Chelmsford: Essex County Council 1969), p. 108: it would appear that around three-quarters of the heads of households were labouring persons. My own overall estimates take into account the often 'hidden' presence of servants in

eighteenth-century households: although they seldom appear in evidence that attends exclusively to the social or economic standing of household heads, servants in fact comprised at least 10 per cent of the total English population (see Chapter 3, pp. 65-6).

37   Lawrence Braddon, *The Miseries of the Poor are a National Sin* (London 1717), p. 18.

38   I am here restating with a different emphasis the estimate in E. A. Wrigley, 'A simple model of London's importance in changing English society and economy 1650-1750', *Past and Present*, no. 37 (July 1967), p. 49.

Chapter 2: Getting a living

1   Karl Marx and Friedrich Engels, *The German Ideology* (New York: International Publishers 1947), p. 16.

2   Richard Gough, *Antiquities and Memoirs of the Parish of Myddle, County of Salop* (Fontwell, Sussex: Centaur Press 1968), p. 34; Gough composed his work at the very beginning of the eighteenth century.

3   Sidney Webb and Beatrice Webb, *The Manor and the Borough* (London 1908), pp. 15-16 (cf. pp. 4, 9, 18-19, 64, 75-9 and 116).

4   T. R. Nash, *Collections for the History of Worcestershire* (2 vols., London 1781-82), vol. 1, p. xii.

5   *Northampton Mercury*, 17 October 1726.

6   The Swedish visitor Pehr Kalm described the economy of these 'sheepmen' in *Kalm's Account of His Visit to England on His Way to America in 1748*, trans. Joseph Lucas (London 1892), pp. 301-3.

7   Margaret Spufford, *Contrasting Communities: English Villagers in the Sixteenth and Seventeenth Centuries* (Cambridge: Cambridge University Press 1974), p. 142; see in general ch. 5 for a full study of Willingham. For similar evidence on three other Cambridgeshire fenland parishes — Cottenham, Landbeach and Waterbeach — see J. R. Ravensdale, *Liable to Floods: Village Landscape on the Edge of the Fens, AD 450-1850* (Cambridge: Cambridge University Press 1974), pp. 60-3 and 141.

8   David G. Hey, *An English Rural Community: Myddle under the Tudors and Stuarts* (Leicester: Leicester University Press 1974), p. 165.

9   J. A. Johnston, 'The probate inventories and wills of a Worcestershire parish 1676-1775', *Midland History*, vol. 1, no. 1 (Spring 1971), p. 25; C. W. Chalklin, *Seventeenth-Century Kent* (London: Longmans 1965), pp. 22 and 70; C. J. M. Moxon, 'Ashby-de-la-Zouch — a social and economic survey of a market town, 1570-1720' (unpubl. D Phil. thesis, Oxford University, 1971), p. 197; W. G. Hoskins, *The Midland Peasant: The Economic and Social History of a Leicestershire Village* (London: Macmillan 1957), pp. 200-1; Alan Harris, *The Open Fields of East Yorkshire* (York: East Yorkshire Local History Society 1959), p. 13; John Bridges, *The History and Antiquities of Northamptonshire*, compiled by Peter Whalley

(2 vols., Oxford 1791), vol. 1, p. 45, and vol. 2, p. 513 (based on material collected between 1719 and 1724); and William Baxter and Others, 'The Case of Atherstone, concerning Inclosure of the Common Fields' (1738), held in the Warwickshire RO, Compton-Bracebridge MSS, Box HR/35.

10   *The Case of the Greatest Number of the Freeholders, Charterers, and Inhabitants of Croston in the County of Lancaster, relating to the Inclosing of a large Town-Field there called Croston-Finney: With Reasons against Passing the Bill now depending for Inclosure thereof*, p. 2; held in Lincoln's Inn Library.

11   Chalklin, *Kent*, p. 70.

12   *Gentleman's Magazine*, vol. 33 (1763), p. 387; see also pp. 221-2 on Dorking, Surrey.

13   J. M. Neeson, 'Common right and enclosure in eighteenth-century Northamptonshire' (unpubl. Ph.D thesis, University of Warwick, 1977), pp. 279-80.

14   Samuel Rudder, *A New History of Gloucestershire* (Cirencester 1779), p. 854.

15   *Commons Journals*, vol. 52 (1796-7), p. 661.

16   John Dunkin, *Oxfordshire. The History and Antiquities of the Hundreds of Billington and Ploughley* (2 vols., London 1823), vol. 1, p. 121.

17   Stephen Addington, *An Inquiry into the Reasons For and Against Inclosing Open-Fields*, 2nd edn (Coventry 1772), p. 17; see also John Morton, *The Natural History of Northamptonshire* (London 1712), pp. 9-10.

18   Robert Masters, *A Short Account of the Parish of Waterbeach* (Cambridge 1795), p. 5; see also Ravensdale, *Liable to Floods*, pp. 52-3.

19   S. C. Roberts (ed.), *A Frenchman in England in 1784: Being the 'Mélanges sur l'Angleterre' of François de la Rochefoucauld* (Cambridge 1933), pp. 208-9; and *Kalm's Account of His Visit*, pp. 198-9, 249, 257, 260 and 355.

20   Neeson, 'Common right' (Ph.D), p. 56. Furze also 'provided litter for cattle and smaller livestock, and (when properly bruised) it could be fed as animal food over the winter' (ibid.).

21   See, for instance, William Stevenson, *General View of the Agriculture of the County of Dorset* (London 1812), pp. 333 and 335-6.

22   Neeson, 'Common right' (Ph.D), especially ch. 1. I am very grateful to Jeanette Neeson for allowing me to draw upon her unpublished findings in this paragraph and at several other points in this chapter.

23   For a discussion of common waste and pasturing rights in Northamptonshire see Neeson, 'Common right' (Ph.D), pp. 21-32.

24   *Northampton Mercury*, 17 October 1726.

25   Neeson, 'Common right' (Ph.D), pp. 35 and 75.

26   Gilbert White, *The Natural History of Selborne* (London: Dent Everyman's edn 1949), p. 22; first publ. in 1788.

27   John Hutchins, *The History and Antiquities of the County of Dorset* (4

vols., London 1861-70), vol. 3, p. 414 (first publ. in 1774); [Resta Patching], *Four Topographical Letters* (Newcastle upon Tyne 1757), p. 10; Douglas Hay, 'Poaching and the Game Laws on Cannock Chase', in Douglas Hay, Peter Linebaugh and E. P. Thompson (eds.), *Albion's Fatal Tree: Crime and Society in Eighteenth-Century England* (London: Allen Lane 1975), pp. 202-3; and William Salt Library (Stafford), Collection of Broadsheets, 20/6, 'The Case of the Petitioners against Parts of the Bill for inclosing the Forest or Chase of Needwood'.

28 T. R. Potter, *The History and Antiquities of Charnwood Forest* (London 1842), p. 23; Philip A. J. Pettit, *The Royal Forests of Northamptonshire: A Study in Their Economy 1558-1714*, Northamptonshire Record Society, vol. 23 (1968), pp. 158, 163 and 184; Rudder, *Gloucestershire*, p. 307; C. R. Tubbs, 'The development of the smallholding and cottage stockkeeping economy of the New Forest', *Agricultural History Review*, vol. 13 (1965), pp. 25-6; E. P. Thompson, *Whigs and Hunters: The Origin of the Black Act* (London: Allen Lane 1975), *passim*, and especially pp. 239-40; and E. P. Thompson, 'The grid of inheritance: a comment', in Jack Goody, Joan Thirsk and E. P. Thompson (eds.), *Family and Inheritance: Rural Society in Western Europe, 1200-1800* (Cambridge: Cambridge University Press 1976), pp. 339-40.

29 Tubbs, 'New Forest', p. 26.

30 For some evidence on gleaning see Vicars Bell, *To Meet Mr. Ellis: Little Gaddesden in the Eighteenth Century* (London: Faber & Faber 1956), pp. 142-3; William Ellis, *The Modern Husbandman* (8 vols., London 1750), vol. 5, pt 1, pp. 34-6; Ivy Pinchbeck, *Women Workers and the Industrial Revolution 1750-1850* (London 1930; reprinted 1969), p. 22; Daniel Hilman, *Tusser Redivivus: Being Part of Mr. Thomas Tusser's Five Hundred Points of Husbandry* (London 1710), 'August', p. 9; and Neeson, 'Common right' (Ph.D), pp. 70-5. By the later eighteenth century there was a growing tension between two conflicting opinions on the practice of gleaning: the traditional opinion regarded gleaning as a customary right, the newer view saw it as a privilege to be granted at the discretion of the farmer. This tension was reflected in an observation by Arthur Young in 1771. 'The custom of gleaning', he said, 'is universal, and very ancient: in this country, however, the poor have no right to glean, but by the permission of the farmer; but the custom is so old and common, that it is scarcely ever broken through.' He went on to warn against the 'excesses' and 'abuses' which gleaning sometimes involved, though he approved of the practice under suitably controlled conditions: *The Farmer's Kalendar* (London 1771), pp. 246-7.

31 'The Case of the Petitioners against the Bill for Dividing and Inclosing divers Parcels of Commons and Waste Grounds within the Manor of Bisleigh, alias Bisley, in the County of Gloucester' (1733), Br. Lib. (SPR) 356.m.5(7).

32 Chalklin, *Kent*, p. 22.
33 Cardanus Riders, *Riders British Merlin* (London 1683), under 'Observations on August'; and Arthur Young, *Farmer's Kalendar*, p. 231. See also Ellis, *Modern Husbandman*, vol. 5, pt 1, p. 2.
34 William Marshall, *The Rural Economy of the Southern Counties* (2 vols., London 1798), vol. 1, pp. 258 and 242; see also Peter Mathias, *The Brewing Industry in England 1700-1830* (Cambridge: Cambridge University Press 1959), pp. 491-3.
35 See, for instance, the explicit reference to this seasonality of employment in Westmorland in T. S. Willan, *An Eighteenth-Century Shopkeeper: Abraham Dent of Kirkby Stephen* (Manchester: Manchester University Press 1970), p. 64.
36 A. P. Wadsworth and J. de L. Mann, *The Cotton Trade and Industrial Lancashire 1600-1780* (Manchester 1931), pp. 314-23 and 337-8; and J. J. Cartwright (ed.), *The Travels Through England of Dr. Richard Pococke* (2 vols., Camden Society, n.s., vols. 42 and 44, 1888-9), vol. 1, pp. 203-4.
37 G. H. Tupling, *The Economic History of Rossendale* (Manchester 1927), ch. 6, especially p. 168
38 Herbert Heaton, *The Yorkshire Woollen and Worsted Industries from the Earliest Times up to the Industrial Revolution*, 2nd edn (Oxford: Clarendon Press 1965), pp. 290-4.
39 Joan Thirsk, 'Horn and thorn in Staffordshire: the economy of a pastoral county', *North Staffordshire Journal of Field Studies*, vol. 9 (1969), p. 11. For evidence on the dual occupations of the metalworkers see Marie B. Rowlands, *Masters and Men in the West Midland Metalware Trades before the Industrial Revolution* (Manchester: Manchester University Press 1975), pp. 41-3; and three works by David G. Hey: *The Village of Ecclesfield* (Huddersfield: Advertiser Press 1968), p. 57; 'A dual economy in south Yorkshire', *Agricultural History Review*, vol. 17 (1969), pp. 108-9; and *The Rural Metalworkers of the Sheffield Region: A Study of Rural Industry Before the Industrial Revolution*, Leicester University Department of English Local History Occasional Papers, 2nd series, no. 5 (Leicester University Press 1972), pts 1-3. Some general observations on dual occupations are offered by Joan Thirsk in 'Seventeenth-century agriculture and social change', in Thirsk (ed.), *Land, Church, and People: Essays Presented to Professor H. P. R. Finberg* (Reading: British Agricultural History Society 1970), pp. 171-2, and 'Roots of industrial England', in A. R. H. Baker and J. B. Harley (eds.), *Man Made the Land: Essays in English Historical Geography* (Newton Abbot, Devon: David & Charles 1973), pp. 106-8.
40 Hoskins, *Midland Peasant*, p. 204.
41 J. P. F. Broad, 'Sir Ralph Verney and his estates, 1630-1696' (unpubl. D Phil. thesis, Oxford University, 1973), pp. 191-4.
42 Neeson, 'Common right' (Ph.D), pp. 237-8.

43   *VCH Oxford*, vol. 10 (1972), p. 64.

44   John S. Moore (ed.), *The Goods and Chattels of Our Forefathers* (Chichester: Phillimore 1976), pp. 26-7.

45   J. H. Bettey and D. S. Wilde, 'The probate inventories of Dorset farmers 1573-1670', *Local Historian*, vol. 12, no. 5 (February 1977), pp. 231-2.

46   J. M. Martin, 'The parliamentary enclosure movement and rural society in Warwickshire', *Agricultural History Review*, vol. 15 (1967), pp. 23-4.

47   Numerous accounts of forests allude to the woodworking industries that were conducted in their vicinity. See, for instance, J. E. Linnell, *Old Oak: The Story of a Forest Village* (London 1932), pp. 3-4, on Whittlewood Forest in southern Northamptonshire. In King's Cliffe, Northamptonshire, a small market town on the edge of Rockingham Forest, twenty-six of the able-bodied men who were liable for the militia in the 1760s were listed as wood turners (Pettit, *Forests of Northamptonshire*, pp. 160-1; see also p. 182). It may be noteworthy that the large and prominent Boughton Green Fair, which was held in central Northamptonshire, about midway between Rockingham Forest to the north and Whittlewood and Salcey Forests to the south, was said to be noted for (among other things) the sale of 'timber, poles, ladders, cooper's ware, and tunnery': John Ogilby and William Morgan, *The Traveller's Pocket-Book*, 19th edn (London 1778), p. 186. See also Alan Everitt, 'Urban growth, 1570-1770', *Local Historian*, vol. 8, no. 4 (1968), p. 120.

48   Chalklin, *Kent*, p. 45; see also p. 150.

49   John G. Rule, 'The labouring miner in Cornwall *c.* 1740-1870: a study in social history' (unpubl. Ph.D thesis, University of Warwick, 1971), pp. 76 and 96.

50   Arthur Young, *A Six Weeks Tour, Through the Southern Counties of England and Wales*, 2nd edn (London 1769), p. 132.

51   T. S. Ashton, *Iron and Steel in the Industrial Revolution* (Manchester 1924), p. 197. Similarly, Cornish miners commonly had small plots of land — perhaps a couple of acres — attached to their cottages: Rule, 'Labouring miner' (Ph.D), pp. 95-100.

52   David C. Levine, *Family Formation in an Age of Nascent Capitalism* (New York: Academic Press 1977), pp. 19-20.

53   B. A. Holderness, ' "Open" and "close" parishes in England in the eighteenth and nineteenth centuries', *Agricultural History Review*, vol. 20 (1972), p. 129.

54   K. J. Allison, *The East Riding of Yorkshire Landscape* (London: Hodder & Stoughton 1976), pp. 193-4.

55   See for instance Arthur Young, *Political Arithmetic* (London 1774), pp. 102-3; Charles Brears, *Lincolnshire in the 17th and 18th Centuries* (London 1940), p. 105; Martin, 'Parliamentary enclosure in Warwickshire', pp. 22-3; and Joan Thirsk (ed.), *Suffolk Farming in the Nineteenth Century*, Suffolk Records Society, vol. 1 (1958), p. 31.

56   Joseph Hunter (ed.), *The Diary of Ralph Thoresby (1677-1724)* (2 vols., London 1830), vol. 2, p. 207.

57   Pinchbeck, *Women Workers, passim*, provides some evidence on most of these trades. See also G. F. R. Spenceley, 'The origins of the English pillow lace industry', *Agricultural History Review*, vol. 21 (1973), pp. 90-2; and John G. Dony, *A History of the Straw Hat Industry* (Luton 1942), pp. 24-5.

58   For a local study that illustrates this argument see S. R. H. Jones, 'The development of needle manufacturing in the West Midlands before 1750', *Economic History Review*, 2nd series, vol. 31 (1978), pp. 361-5.

59   J. D. Chambers, *Nottinghamshire in the Eighteenth Century,* 2nd edn (London: Frank Cass 1966), p. x. See also J. D. Chambers, 'Economic change in the Vale of Trent, 1700-1800', *Renaissance and Modern Studies*, vol. 2 (1958), p. 88; and E. L. Jones, 'Agricultural origins of industry', *Past and Present*, no. 40 (July 1968), pp. 62-3.

60   Hoskins, *Midland Peasant*, pp. xv, 212 and 228.

61   Levine, *Family Formation*, pp. 19-20.

62   Adam Smith, *The Wealth of Nations* (New York: Modern Library 1937), p. 226.

63   Arthur Young, *Tours in England and Wales (Selected from the Annals of Agriculture)*, London School of Economics and Political Science Series of Reprints of Scarce Tracts in Economic and Political Science, no. 14 (London 1932), pp. 144 and 162.

64   White, *History of Selborne*, pp. 15-16.

65   Francis W. Steer (ed.), *The Memoirs of James Spershott*, Chichester Papers, no. 30 (Chichester 1962), p. 15.

66   White, *History of Selborne*, pp. 189-92. For further evidence on home lighting see Winifred M. Bowman, *England in Ashton-Under-Lyne* (Ashton-Under-Lyne 1960), p. 547, and William Rollinson, *Life and Tradition in the Lake District* (London: Dent 1974), pp. 41-2.

67   Christopher Merret, 'An Account of several Observables in Lincolnshire, not taken Notice of in Camden, or any other Author', *Philosophical Transactions of the Royal Society*, vol. 19 (November and December 1696), p. 349.

68   Young, *Tours in England and Wales*, pp. 140-2.

69   Rudder, *Gloucestershire*, p. 711. For an excellent account of the woollen industry in Devon during the earlier eighteenth century, which was a dominating economic presence in some eastern portions of the county, see W. G. Hoskins, 'The rise and decline of the serge industry in the south-west of England, with special reference to the eighteenth century' (unpubl. MSc. thesis, University of London 1929), ch. 2.

70   [Patching], *Four Topographical Letters*, pp. 62-3; cf. *VCH Warwick*, vol. 7 (1964), p. 95.

71   See, for instance, Neil McKendrick, 'Josiah Wedgwood and factory discipline', *Historical Journal*, vol. 4, no. 1 (1961), pp. 30-4.

72   Chalklin, *Kent*, p. 150.

73   James M. Haas, 'The royal dockyards: the earliest visitations and reform 1749-1778', *Historical Journal*, vol. 13, no. 2 (1970), p. 191.

74   W. R. Sullivan, *Blyth in the Eighteenth Century* (Newcastle upon Tyne: Oriel Press 1971), pp. 85-92.

75   John Ehrman, *The Navy in the War of William III 1689-1697* (Cambridge: Cambridge University Press 1953), p. 111; cf. Ralph Davis, *The Rise of the English Shipping Industry in the Seventeenth and Eighteenth Centuries* (London: Macmillan 1962), p. 116.

76   *VCH York: East Riding*, vol. 1 (1969), pp. 148-9.

77   *VCH Warwick*, vol. 7 (1964), pp. 7-8; and C. W. Chalklin, *The Provincial Towns of Georgian England* (London: Edward Arnold 1974), pp. 13, 49.

78   *VCH Somerset*, vol. 3 (1974), p. 142; *VCH Wiltshire*, vol. 10 (1975), p. 260; and *VCH Gloucester*, vol. 11 (1976), p. 273.

79   In considering the position of craftsmen in provincial society, I have found particularly useful the evidence in Victor Hatley (ed.), *Northamptonshire Militia Lists 1777*, Northamptonshire Record Society, vol. 25 (1973). See also G. H. Dannatt, 'Bicester in the seventeenth and eighteenth centuries', *Oxoniensia*, vol. 26/27 (1961/62), pp. 248-51 and 268; and A. F. J. Brown, *Essex at Work 1700-1815* (Chelmsford: Essex County Council 1969), pp. 51-7.

80   For evidence on one riverside suburb and its trades see Michael Power, 'Shadwell: the development of a London suburban community in the seventeenth century', *London Journal*, vol. 4, no. 1 (May 1978), pp. 36-8.

81   For a discussion of the trades of London see M. Dorothy George, *London Life in the Eighteenth Century* (London 1925; reprinted 1964), ch. 4. See also R. Campbell, *The London Tradesman* (London 1747), which is available in a modern reprint (Newton Abbot, Devon: David & Charles 1969).

82   J. U. Nef, *The Rise of the British Coal Industry* (2 vols., London 1932), vol. 2, p. 140.

83   See, for instance, *VCH Stafford*, vol. 2 (1967), p. 101; cf. John Rhodes, *Derbyshire Lead Mining in the Eighteenth Century*, University of Sheffield, Institute of Education Local History Series, pamphlet no. 7 (1973), pp. 22-3.

84   For evidence on customary perquisites see Walter M. Stern, *The Porters of London* (London: Longmans 1960), p. 64; Ehrman, *Navy in the War of William III*, pp. 92-3; T. S. Ashton, *An Economic History of England: The 18th Century* (London: Methuen 1955), p. 208; Peter Linebaugh, in 'Conference Report', *Bulletin of the Society for the Study of Labour History*, no. 25 (Autumn 1972), p. 13; and Chapter 6, p. 148.

85   Llewellyn Jewitt (ed.), *The Life of William Hutton* (London 1872), pp. 105-6.

86   N. L. Tranter, 'Demographic change in Bedfordshire 1670-1800' (unpubl. Ph.D thesis, Nottingham University, 1966), pp. 293-7.

Chapter 3: Facts of life

1   From Book 2, ch. 13; quoted in Charles W. Kennedy, *Early English Christian Poetry* (New York: Oxford University Press 1963), p. 6.

2   My statements concerning infant mortality are based on the following sources: N. L. Tranter, 'Population and social structure in a Bedfordshire parish: the Cardington listing of inhabitants, 1782', *Population Studies*, vol. 21 (1967), p. 276; David C. Levine, 'The demographic implications of rural industrialization: a family reconstitution study of two Leicestershire villages, 1600-1851' (unpubl. Ph.D thesis, Cambridge University, 1975), p. 161; David C. Levine, 'The demographic implications of rural industrialization: a family reconstitution study of Shepshed, Leicestershire, 1600-1851', *Social History*, no. 2 (May 1976), p. 188; R. E. Jones, 'Infant mortality in rural north Shropshire, 1561-1810', *Population Studies*, vol. 30 (1976), pp. 313-14; F. West, 'Infant mortality in the east fen parishes of Leake and Wrangle', *Local Population Studies*, no. 13 (Autumn 1974), p. 43; T. H. Hollingsworth, *The Demography of the British Peerage*, supplement to *Population Studies*, vol. 18 (1964), pp. 53-7; and Penelope J. Corfield, 'The social and economic history of Norwich, 1650-1850: a study in urban growth' (unpubl. Ph.D thesis, University of London, 1976), pp. 164-5 and 197-202.

3   M. Dorothy George, *London Life in the Eighteenth Century* (New York: Harper Torchbook edn 1964), p. 406. See also Corfield, 'Norwich, 1650-1850' (Ph.D), pp. 164, 201-2 and 481*n.*; and J. D. Chambers, 'Population change in a provincial town: Nottingham 1700-1800', in L. S. Pressnell (ed.), *Studies in the Industrial Revolution Presented to T. S. Ashton* (London: Athlone Press 1960), pp. 114-15.

4   See for instance J. M. Martin, *The Rise of Population in Eighteenth-Century Warwickshire*, Dugdale Society Occasional Papers, no. 23 (1976), p. 29.

5   Joan Simon, 'Was there a charity school movement? The Leicestershire evidence', in Brian Simon (ed.), *Education in Leicestershire 1540-1940* (Leicester: Leicester University Press 1968), p. 88.

6   As a guide to what little is known about elementary education see Derek Robson, *Some Aspects of Education in Cheshire in the Eighteenth Century* (Manchester: Chetham Society 1966), pp. 11-13, 42-3, 109, 113-14, 115, 117-18 and 160; Simon (ed.), *Education in Leicestershire*, pp. 55-89; Thomas W. Laqueur, 'Working-class demand and the growth of English elementary education, 1750-1850', in Lawrence Stone (ed.), *Schooling and Society: Studies in the History of Education* (Baltimore and London: Johns Hopkins University Press 1976), pp. 192 and 196; and Richard S. Tompson, *Classics or Charity? The dilemma of the 18th century grammar school* (Manchester: Manchester University Press 1971), pp. 1-2. See also Margaret Spufford, 'First steps in literacy: the reading and writing experiences of the humblest seventeenth-century spiritual autobiographers', *Social History*, vol. 4. no. 3 (October 1979), pp. 407-35. For evidence on particular parishes see David G. Hey, *An English Rural Community: Myddle under the Tudors*

and Stuarts (Leicester: Leicester University Press 1974), p. 189; and David Baker, *The Inhabitants of Cardington in 1782*, Publications of the Bedfordshire Historical Record Society, vol. 52 (1973), pp. 63-6.

7   See ch. 4. p. 95. In the parish of Cardington, Bedfordshire, in 1782 just over half of the boys between 5 and 9 years of age were attending school, and just under a third of the girls: R. S. Schofield, 'Age-specific mobility in an eighteenth-century rural English parish', *Annales de Démographie Historique* (1970), pp. 265-6.

8   *The Autobiography of William Stout of Lancaster 1665-1752*, ed. J. D. Marshall (Manchester: Manchester University Press 1967), p. 70.

9   My account of apprenticeship has been helpfully informed by the valuable research of Joan Lane, which is presented in her study of 'Apprenticeship in Warwickshire, 1700-1834' (unpubl. Ph.D thesis, University of Birmingham, 1977). See also Christabel Dale (ed.), *Wiltshire Apprentices and their Masters 1710-1760*, Wiltshire Archaeological and Natural History Society, Records Branch, vol. 17 (1961), and K. J. Smith (ed.), *Warwickshire Apprentices and their Masters 1710-1760*, Publications of the Dugdale Society, vol. 29 (1975).

10   A. P. Wadsworth and Julia de L. Mann, *The Cotton Trade and Industrial Lancashire 1600-1780* (Manchester 1931), pp. 330-1, 333-4 and 336-7. See also Lane, 'Apprenticeship in Warwickshire' (Ph.D), pp. 167-8, 340-1 and 350-1.

11   Marie B. Rowlands, *Masters and Men in the West Midland Metalware Trades before the Industrial Revolution* (Manchester: Manchester University Press 1975), pp. 39-41.

12   See, for instance, Philip Styles, 'A census of a Warwickshire village in 1698', *University of Birmingham Historical Journal*, vol. 3 (1951-52), p. 42.

13   J. U. Nef, *The Rise of the British Coal Industry* (2 vols., London 1932), vol. 2, p. 143; and T. S. Ashton and Joseph Sykes, *The Coal Industry of the Eighteenth Century*, 2nd edn (New York: A. M. Kelley 1967), pp. 156-7.

14   Peter Laslet (ed.), *Household and Family in Past Time* (Cambridge: Cambridge University Press 1972), p. 152.

15   My discussion of farm service is heavily dependent on the excellent study by Ann Sturm Kussmaul, 'Servants in husbandry in early-modern England' (unpubl. Ph.D thesis, University of Toronto, 1978). I am grateful to Ms Kussmaul for allowing me to make use of her unpublished findings. See also her substantially revised study, tentatively entitled *Servants in Husbandry*, to be published by Cambridge University Press in 1981.

16   E. P. Thompson, 'The grid of inheritance: a comment', in Jack Goody, Joan Thirsk and E. P. Thompson (eds.), *Family and Inheritance: Rural Society in Western Europe, 1200-1800* (Cambridge: Cambridge University Press 1976), p. 359.

17   G. Eland, ed., *Purefoy Letters 1735-1753* (2 vols., London 1931), vol. 1, p. 147.

18 William Ellis, *The Modern Husbandman* (8 vols., London 1750), vol. 5, pt 2, p. 92.

19 J. M. Martin, 'An investigation into the small size of the household as exemplified by Stratford-on-Avon', *Local Population Studies*, no. 19 (Autumn 1977), p. 19.

20 *A Political Enquiry into the Consequences of Enclosing Waste Lands* (London, 1785), p. 44.

21 Kussmaul, 'Servants in husbandry' (Ph.D), pp. 181-4.

22 F. G. Stokes (ed.), *The Blecheley Diary of the Rev. William Cole 1765-67* (London 1931), p. 41.

23 J. M. Martin, 'Marriage and economic stress in the felden of Warwickshire during the eighteenth century', *Population Studies*, vol. 31 (1977), pp. 528-9 and 533-5 (see also Martin's *Population in Eighteenth-Century Warwickshire*, pp. 24-7); Levine, 'Reconstitution study of Shepshed, Leicestershire', p. 185; C. J. M. Moxon, 'Ashby-de-la-Zouch — a social and economic survey of a market town, 1570-1720' (unpubl. DPhil. thesis, Oxford University, 1971), p. 46; and Peter Laslett, *Family Life and Illict Love in Earlier Generations* (Cambridge: Cambridge University Press 1977), p. 40.

24 See for instance E. A. Wrigley, 'Family limitation in pre-industrial England', *Economic History Review*, 2nd series, vol. 19 (1966), p. 87.

25 Levine, 'Reconstitution study of Shepshed, Leicestershire', pp. 178 and 191-2.

26 George Sturt, *Change in the Village* (1912; reprinted New York: A. M. Kelley 1969), p. 29.

27 For evidence on the duration of marriage see Peter Laslett, 'Philippe Ariès and "La Famille" ', *Encounter* (March 1976), p. 81; Lawrence Stone, *The Family, Sex and Marriage in England 1500-1800* (New York: Harper & Row 1977), pp. 55-6; and N. L. Tranter, 'Demographic change in Bedfordshire 1670-1800' (unpubl. Ph.D thesis, University of Nottingham, 1966), pp. 362 and 370.

28 Laslett, *Family Life*, pp. 57-8; see also Baker, *Inhabitants of Cardington*, p. 37.

29 Peter Laslett, *The World We Have Lost*, 2nd edn (London: Methuen 1971), p. 103.

30 Peter Laslett, 'Parental deprivation in the past: a note on the history of orphans in England', *Local Population Studies*, no. 13 (Autumn 1974), pp. 12-15 (cf. Laslett's *Family Life*, pp. 162-9); Baker, *Inhabitants of Cardington*, pp. 40-2; and J. R. Holman, 'Orphans in pre-industrial towns — the case of Bristol in the late seventeenth century', *Local Population Studies,* no. 15 (Autumn 1975), pp. 41-4.

31 Kussmaul, 'Servants in husbandry' (Ph.D), pp. 106-8.

32 Robert W. Malcolmson, *Popular Recreations in English Society 1700-1850* (Cambridge: Cambridge University Press 1973), pp. 23-4, 78-9 and 87.

33 Kussmaul, 'Servants in husbandry' (Ph.D), pp. 137-42, 148 and 173-4. My

discussion of the mobility of servants is heavily dependent on Ms Kussmaul's unpublished research, and I am indebted to her for allowing me to make use of her findings. Much of this research will be presented in her forthcoming article in the *Economic History Review*, 'The ambiguous mobility of farm servants'.

34   Kussmaul, 'Servants in husbandry' (Ph.D), p. 113.

35   ibid., pp. 114-15.

36   ibid., p. 113.

37   Peter Clark, 'The migrant in Kentish towns 1580-1640', in Peter Clark and Paul Slack (eds.), *Crisis and Order in English Towns 1500-1700* (London: Routledge & Kegan Paul 1972), pp. 137-8.

38   Robert W. Malcolmson, ' "A set of ungovernable people": the Kingswood colliers in the eighteenth century', in John Brewer and John Styles (eds.), *An Ungovernable People: The English and their Law in the Seventeenth and Eighteenth Centuries* (London: Hutchinson 1980), pp. 90-1.

39   Schofield, 'Age-specific mobility', p. 264.

40   For further details on the extent of geographical mobility see R. E. Jones, 'Population and agrarian change in an eighteenth century Shropshire parish', *Local Population Studies*, no. 1 (Autumn 1968), p. 28; Laslett, *Family Life*, pp. 65-74; A. F. J. Brown, *Essex at Work 1700-1815* (Chelmsford: Essex County Council 1969), pp. 106-7; J. A. Johnston, 'The probate inventories and wills of a Worcestershire parish 1676-1775', *Midland History*, vol. 1, no. 1 (Spring 1971), pp. 29-30; J. D. Chambers, *Population, Economy, and Society in Pre-Industrial England* (London: Oxford University Press 1972), pp. 44-6; David Levine, *Family Formation in an Age of Nascent Capitalism* (New York: Academic Press 1977), pp. 37-43; and Peter Clark, 'Migration in England during the late seventeenth and early eighteenth centuries', *Past and Present*, no. 83 (May 1979), pp. 64-75.

41   For evidence on the regional character of these patterns of migration see Tranter, 'Social structure in a Bedfordshire parish', p. 277; Schofield, 'Age-specific mobility', pp. 263-4 and 268-74; R. Speake, 'The historical demography of the ancient parish of Audley, 1538-1801', *North Staffordshire Journal of Field Studies*, vol. 11 (1971), pp. 77-9; E. A. Wrigley, 'A note on the life-time mobility of married women in a parish population in the later eighteenth century', *Local Population Studies*, no. 18 (Spring 1977), pp. 22-6; Levine, *Family Formation*, p. 36; E. J. Buckatzsch, 'Places of origin of a group of immigrants into Sheffield, 1624-1799', *Economic History Review*, 2nd series, vol. 2 (1949-50), pp. 303-6; and Clark, 'Migration', pp. 66-70.

42   E. A. Wrigley, 'A simple model of London's importance in changing English society and economy 1650-1750', *Past and Present*, no. 37 (July 1967), pp. 46-9; D. George, *London Life*, pp. 109-10 and 140-41; and Peter Spufford, 'Population movement in seventeenth century England', *Local Population Studies*, no. 4 (Spring 1970), pp. 43-5.

43 D. E. C. Eversley, 'Epidemiology as social history', introduction to Charles Creighton, *A History of Epidemics in Britain*, 2nd edn (2 vols., London: Frank Cass 1965), vol. 1, p. 35. See also Keith Thomas, *Religion and the Decline of Magic* (Harmondsworth: Penguin 1973), pp. 5-17.

44 Robert Mandrou, *Introduction to Modern France 1500-1640: An Essay in Historical Psychology* (London: Edward Arnold 1975), p. 34.

45 For evidence concerning the mortality crises of the late 1720s see J. A. Johnston, 'The impact of the epidemics of 1727-1730 in south west Worcestershire', *Medical History*, vol. 15 (1971), pp. 278-92; A. Gooder, 'The population crisis of 1727-30 in Warwickshire', *Midland History*, vol. 1, no. 4 (Autumn 1972), pp. 1-22; Ransom Pickard, *The Population and Epidemics of Exeter in Pre-Census Times* (Exeter: James Townsend 1947), pp. 63 and 65-8; J. D. Chambers, *The Vale of Trent 1670-1800*, Supplement no. 3 to *Economic History Review* (1957), pp. 28-9; Martin, *Population in Eighteenth-Century Warwickshire*, pp. 30-1; David Hey, *The Rural Metalworkers of the Sheffield Region: A Study of Rural Industry before the Industrial Revolution*, Leicester University Department of English Local History, Occasional Papers, 2nd series, no. 5 (Leicester 1972), pp. 54-7; and Tranter, 'Demographic change in Bedfordshire' (Ph.D), ch. 3, pt 2. The newspapers of the period include numerous references to the sickliness of these years.

46 The evidence from William Stout is drawn from his *Autobiography*, pp. 176, 179, 182, 193-4, 201 (and 276n.), 206, 211, 213, 217, 221 and 227-9. See also E. L. Jones, *Seasons and Prices: The Role of the Weather in English Agricultural History* (London: Allen & Unwin 1964), pp. 137-9.

47 Ellis, *Modern Husbandman*, vol. 6, pt 3, p. 141; see also vol. 3, pt 1, p. 158, and vol. 4, pt 1, p. 106.

48 William George Maton, *Observations Relative Chiefly to the Natural History, Picturesque Scenery, and Antiquities, of the Western Counties of England, Made in the Years 1794 and 1796* (2 vols., Salisbury, 1797), vol. 1, p. 233; see, for the tinners, vol. 1, pp. 238-9, and for the Mendip miners, vol. 2, p. 133. For another comment on the hazards of mining in Cornwall see [Edward D. Clarke], *A Tour Through the South of England, Wales and Part of Ireland, Made During the Summer of 1791* (London 1793), pp. 93-4. The *Gentleman's Magazine*, vol. 55 (1785), pt 2, pp. 938-9, drew attention to the impaired health of many lace-makers. For secondary accounts of the hazards of industrial employment see George, *London Life*, pp. 202-5, and Lane, 'Apprenticeship in Warwickshire' (Ph.D), pp. 126-32.

49 Peter Clark and Paul Slack, *English Towns in Transition 1500-1700* (London: Oxford University Press 1976), p. 43.

50 Roger North, *A Discourse of the Poor* (London 1753), p. 54 (written around the late seventeenth century and published posthumously).

51 *Reflexions upon the Moral State of the Nation* (London 1701), p. 18. 'If we

were to make a progress through the outskirts of this town', wrote Henry
Fielding of London in 1753, 'and look into the habitations of the poor, we
should there behold such pictures of human misery as must move the
compassion of every heart that deserves the name of human.' The observer
would see, he said, 'whole families in want of every necessary of life,
oppressed with hunger, cold, nakedness, and filth; and with diseases, the
certain consequences of all these': *A Proposal for Making an Effectual
Provision for the Poor*, reprinted in *The Complete Works of Henry Fielding*,
ed. William E. Henley (16 vols., London: Frank Cass 1967), vol. 13: *Legal
Writings*, p. 141. cf. Joseph Massie, *Considerations Relating to the Poor and
the Poor's Laws of England*, appended to his *A Plan for the Establishment of
Charity-Houses* (London 1758), p. 50.

52 Laslett (ed.), *Household and Family in Past Time*, pp. 145 and 147; and
    J. R. Holman, 'Orphans in pre-industrial towns', p. 41. See also Tranter,
    'Social structure in a Bedfordshire parish', p. 269; and D. V. Glass, 'Two
    papers on Gregory King', in D. V. Glass and D. E. C. Eversley (eds.),
    Population in History (London: Edward Arnold 1965), pp. 181 and 209.

53 For evidence on the prominence of widows among the recipients of poor
    relief see Brown, *Essex at Work*, p. 145; Baker, *Inhabitants of Cardington*, p.
    47; Geoffrey C. Edmonds, 'Accounts of eighteenth-century overseers of the
    poor of Chalfont St Peter', *Records of Buckinghamshire*, vol. 18, pt 1
    (1966), pp. 3-23; F. G. Emmison, 'The relief of the poor at Eaton Socon,
    1706-1834', *Publications of the Bedfordshire Historical Record Society*, vol.
    15 (1933), pp. 12 and 14-15; John A. Redwood, 'Pauper fortunes in Oxford-
    shire, 1660-1760', *Oxoniensia*, vol. 37 (1972), p. 208; A. W. Ashby, *One
    Hundred Years of Poor Law Administration in a Warwickshire Village*
    (Oxford 1912), pp. 142-5; and Geoffrey W. Oxley, *Poor Relief in England
    and Wales 1601-1834* (Newton Abbot, Devon: David & Charles 1974), p.
    59.

54 William Cobbett, *Cottage Economy* (London 1828), paragraph 6.

Chapter 4: Beliefs, customs and identities

1 Peter Laslett, *The World We Have Lost*, 2nd edn (London: Methuen 1971),
   p. 74.

2 John H. Pruett, *The Parish Clergy under the Later Stuarts: The Leicestershire
   Experience* (Urbana, Illinois: University of Illinois Press 1978), pp. 115-18.

3 G. V. Bennett, 'The seven bishops: a reconsideration', in *Studies in Church
   History*, vol. 15, ed. Derek Baker (Oxford: Blackwell 1978), pp. 269-70.

4 Christopher Hill, 'Plebeian irreligion in 17th century England', in Manfred
   Kossok (ed.), *Studien über die Revolution* (Berlin: Akademie-Verlag 1969),
   pp. 46-61; and Keith Thomas, *Religion and the Decline of Magic: Studies in
   Popular Beliefs in Sixteenth- and Seventeenth-Century England* (Harmondsworth: Penguin 1973), pp. 189-97 and 200-5.

5　See, for instance, John Redwood, *Reason, Ridicule and Religion: The Age of Enlightenment in England 1660-1750* (London: Thames & Hudson 1976), pp. 18-19 and 39-40; Geoffrey Holmes, *Religion and Party in Late Stuart England*, Historical Association pamphlet (1975), p. 7; Alan D. Gilbert, *Religion and Society in Industrial England: Church, Chapel and Social Change, 1740-1914* (London: Longman 1976), pp. 3-12; and A. W. Smith, 'Popular religion', *Past and Present*, no. 40 (July 1968), pp. 181-6.

6　*A Foreign View of England in the Reigns of George I and George II: The Letters of Monsieur César de Saussure to his Family*, ed. Madame van Muyden (London 1902), p. 220.

7　Robert Currie, Alan Gilbert and Lee Horsley, *Churches and Churchgoers: Patterns of Church Growth in the British Isles Since 1700* (Oxford: Clarendon Press 1977), p. 139.

8　*Diary of Viscount Percival, Afterwards First Earl of Egmont*, vol. 1: *1730-1733*, publ. by the Historical Manuscripts Commission (London 1920), p. 400. In 1700 one writer alleged that many of the inhabitants in places with substantial common rights, where agricultural 'improvements' had not been effected, succeeded in distancing themselves from the normal institutions of social discipline: 'Such People … being remote from Neighbours of Reputation and Fortune, may be accounted for Heathens and Savages, living in a manner without all Knowledge of God; there being little Encouragement for able Ministers from a lean and hungry Soil, so that living remote from Churches, and no Officers or Magistrates being near them, they seem to be a Brood of … Lawless Rogues': Timothy Nourse, *Campania Foelix. Or, A Discourse of the Benefits and Improvements of Husbandry* (London 1700), p. 98. See also Chapter 5, pp. 110-12.

9　Thomas, *Religion and the Decline of Magic*, pp. 761-62.

10　William Henderson, *Notes on the Folk-Lore of the Northern Counties of England and the Borders* (Folk-Lore Society 1879; repr. 1967), p. 1.

11　James Obelkevich, *Religion and Rural Society: South Lindsey 1825-1875* (Oxford: Clarendon Press 1976), ch. 6.

12　Thomas, *Religion and the Decline of Magic*, p. 215.

13　*Gloucester Journal*, 12 September 1736.

14　*Northampton Mercury*, 15 October 1759.

15　*Felix Farley's Journal*, 25 April 1752; quoted in John Latimer, *The Annals of Bristol in the Eighteenth Century* (Bristol 1893), p. 294 (cf. p. 56). See also Francis Grose, 'Popular superstitions', in *A Provincial Glossary*, 2nd edn (London 1790), p. 41. Grose reported that 'the chips or cuttings of a gibbett or gallows, on which one or more persons have been executed or exposed, if worn next the skin, or round the neck, in a bag, will cure the ague, or prevent it' (p. 42). Further evidence on these beliefs may be found in Peter Linebaugh, 'The Tyburn Riot against the surgeons', in Douglas Hay, Peter Linebaugh and E. P. Thompson (eds.), *Albion's Fatal Tree* (London: Allen Lane 1975), pp. 109-10.

16   Gilbert White, *The Natural History of Selborne* (London: Dent 1949), pp. 194-5. Another detailed account of this custom of 'drawing a child through a cleft tree', which parallels White's, is recorded in Sir John Cullum, *The History and Antiquities of Hawsted, in the County of Suffolk* (London 1784), pp. 233-4.

17   John Brand, *Observations on Popular Antiquities* (Newcastle upon Tyne 1777), p. 405.

18   Lewellyn Jewitt (ed.), *The Life of William Hutton* (London 1872), p. 18.

19   See, for instance, Caesar Caine (ed.), *Strother's Journal: Written by a Tradesman of York and Hull, 1784-1785* (London n.d. [c. 1912]), p. 59; and Francis Grose, 'Popular superstitions', pp. 38-9 and 55.

20   Some further details on omens are provided in Henry Bourne, *Antiquitates Vulgares; or, the Antiquities of the Common People* (Newcastle 1725), pp. 70-1.

21   *Felix Farley's Bristol Journal*, 28 June 1760.

22   *Northampton Mercury*, 26 April 1731; see also Daniel Defoe, *A System of Magick* (London 1727), p. 359.

23   *Northampton Mercury*, 26 April 1731.

24   Defoe, *A System of Magick*, p. 258.

25   J. S. Fletcher, *Recollections of a Yorkshire Village* (London 1910), pp. 102-3; cf. John MacKinnon, *Account of Messingham in the County of Lincoln*, ed. Edward Peacock (Hertford 1881), p. 13, and J. C. Atkinson, *Forty Years in a Moorland Parish* (London 1892), pp. 110-25. Some evidence on an eighteenth-century conjurer is reported in W. Harbutt Dawson, 'An old Yorkshire astrologer and magician, 1694-1760', *Reliquary*, vol. 23 (1882/83), pp. 197-202. See also the important discussion of cunning men in Thomas, *Religion and the Decline of Magic*, ch. 8.

26   See, for instance, Brand, *Popular Antiquities*, pp. 102-22; and *Northampton Mercury*, 13 February 1769.

27   *Felix Farley's Bristol Journal*, 15 May 1762.

28   *Felix Farley's Bristol Journal*, 16 May 1752.

29   Thomas, *Religion and the Decline of Magic*, especially ch. 18; and W. B. Carnochan, 'Witch-hunting and belief in 1751: the case of Thomas Colley and Ruth Osborne', *Journal of Social History*, vol. 4, no. 4 (Summer 1971), pp. 389-403. The story of the witch-trial at Tring may be followed through the files of various newspapers, such as the *Northampton Mercury*, between April and September 1751.

30   *Salisbury Journal*, 26 August and 2 September 1751; cf. *Northampton Mercury*, 26 August 1751. The *Northampton Mercury* for 18 September 1752 reports on several attempts to conduct 'trials' of witches in Suffolk, and notes the genteel oppostion to these efforts. Later indications of the resilience of witchcraft beliefs may be found in the *Mercury* for 26 February 1759, 28 July 1760 and 2 July 1770.

31   *Ipswich-Journal*, 29 January 1731.

32 Keith Thomas, 'An anthropology of religion and magic, II', *Journal of Inter-disciplinary History*, vol. 6, no. 1 (Summer 1975), pp. 101-2. Similarly, Malinowski suggested that the 'integral cultural function of magic ... consists in the bridging-over of gaps and inadequacies in highly important activities not yet completely mastered by man': Bronislaw Malinowski, *Magic, Science and Religion, And Other Essays* (New York: Anchor Books 1954), p. 140.

33 Defoe, *System of Magick*, pp. 262-75. See also Atkinson, *Forty Years in a Moorland Parish*, pp. 110-25.

34 *Gentleman's Magazine*, vol. 58, pt 1 (1788), p. 455. For a discussion of the involvement of conjuring in the detection of theft see Thomas, *Religion and the Decline of Magic*, pp. 252-64.

35 Margaret Baker, *Folklore and Customs of Rural England* (Newton Abbot, Devon: David & Charles 1974), p. 170.

36 Malinowski, *Magic, Science and Religion*, p. 90; cf. p. 79. In preparing this discussion of popular magic I have benefited at several points from the researches of Heather A. Cameron, which were presented in her unpublished essay, 'Popular beliefs in magic in eighteenth and nineteenth century England' (Honours BA essay, Department of History, Queen's University at Kingston, 1973). Her paper focuses largely on nineteenth-century sources.

37 One observer, for instance, reported on the alleged ill consequences of a visit by a fortune-teller to Hatfield, Yorkshire, in 1695. 'He told about fifty people in this parish that they should come to suddain death, some be hang'd, some be drown'd, and he told several people the divel would fetch them, others that they should be bewitched, and named the witches, which were poor good harmless women. In a word, he has done incredible mischief in this parish, and rob'd the people of above five pound.... He should have been whipp'd, but that the women of this town begg'd his pardon, and help him to contrive his escape.' The last remark acknowledges the differences in contemporary evaluation of conjurers: Charles Jackson (ed.), *The Diary of Abraham de la Pryme*, Publications of the Surtees Society, vol. 54 (1870), pp. 56-7.

38 Thomas, *Religion and the Decline of Magic*, p. 761.

39 See for instance Deborah M. Valenze, 'Prophecy and popular literature in eighteenth-century England', *Journal of Ecclesiastical History*, vol. 29, no. 1 (January 1978), especially pp. 86-8.

40 Quoted in Henderson, *Folk-Lore of the Northern Counties*, p. 15. See also Alan Smith, *The Established Church and Popular Religion 1750-1850* (London: Longman 1971), pp. 19-20.

41 J. W. Tibble and Anne Tibble (eds.), *The Prose of John Clare* (London: Routledge & Kegan Paul 1951), p. 20 (from the 'Autobiography 1793-1824').

42 *An Exmoor Scolding; In the Propriety and Decency of Exmoor Language*, 7th edn (Exeter 1771), pp. iii-iv. The author said of the Exmoor dialect that 'none but the very lowest Class of People generally speak the Language here

exemplified, but were it more commonly spoken by their Betters, perhaps it might not be so much to their Discredit as some may imagine; most of the antiquated Words being so expressive as not to be despised' (p. iii).

43   Daniel Defoe, *The Great Law of Subordination consider'd* (London 1724), p. 48.

44   Daniel Defoe, *A Tour Through the Whole Island of Great Britain* (2 vols., London: Dent Everyman's edn 1962), vol. 1, pp. 218-19.

45   William Stukeley, *Itinerarium Curiosum*, 2nd edn (2 vols., London 1776), vol. 2, p. 65. For similar testimony to the existence of a distinctive dialect in, respectively, Lincolnshire, Shropshire and Devon, see J. W. F. Hill, *Tudor and Stuart Lincoln* (Cambridge: Cambridge University Press 1956), p. 5; *Gentleman's Magazine*, vol. 34 (1764), p. 263; and William Chapple, *A Review of Part of Risdon's Survey of Devon* (Exeter 1785), p. 55.

46   William Marshall, *The Rural Economy of Yorkshire* (2 vols., London 1788), vol. 2, p. 303. See also Marshall's *The Rural Economy of Norfolk* (2 vols., London 1795), vol. 2, p. 373.

47   R. S. Schofield, 'Dimensions of illiteracy, 1750-1850', *Explorations in Economic History*, vol. 10 (1972/73), p. 445.

48   Nicholas Rogers, 'London politics from Walpole to Pitt: patriotism and independency in an era of commercial imperialism, 1738-63' (unpubl. Ph.D thesis, University of Toronto, 1974), pp. 509-14.

49   Robert W. Malcolmson, 'Some aspects of the society of north-west Bedfordshire during the eighteenth century' (unpubl. MA thesis, University of Sussex, 1966), pp. 46-7.

50   Victor A. Hatley, 'Literacy at Northampton, 1761-1900: a third interim report', *Northamptonshire Past and Present*, vol. 5, no. 4 (1976), p. 347. See also W. B. Stephens, 'Illiteracy and schooling in the provincial towns, 1640-1870: a comparative approach', in D. A. Reeder (ed.), *Urban Education in the Nineteenth Century* (New York: St Martin's 1978), pp. 30-4.

51   J. E. Linnell, *Old Oak: The Story of a Forest Village* (London 1932), p. 173. The statement was made about Silverstone, Northamptonshire, in the early nineteenth century.

52   For some helpful reflections on the limitations imposed on critical thinking in an oral culture see Jack Goody, *The Domestication of the Savage Mind* (Cambridge: Cambridge University Press 1977), pp. 43-4. John Brewer kindly drew this work to my attention.

53   Leon Trotsky, *Problems of Everyday Life* (New York: Monad Press 1973), p. 32.

54   Samuel Johnson, *A Dictionary of the English Language* (2 vols., London 1755).

55   Robert W. Malcolmson, *Popular Recreations in English Society 1700-1850* (Cambridge: Cambridge University Press 1973), pp. 17-18; E. P. Thompson, 'Patrician society, plebeian culture', *Journal of Social History*, vol. 7, no. 4 (Summer 1974), p. 392; and Bodleian Library, MSS Top. Devon b. 1-2 (2

vols.). See also Francis Hill, *Georgian Lincoln* (Cambridge: Cambridge University Press 1966), pp. 52-4.

56 Much of the documentation bearing on this summary discussion of sports and festivities will be found in various parts of my *Popular Recreations* (for this paragraph, especially chs. 2 and 3).

57 *Sketches in the Life of John Clare, Written by Himself*, ed. Edmund Blunden (London 1931), p. 48.

58 Most gardens were cultivated for food, but it is noteworthy that when Richard Pococke was travelling outside Nantwich, Cheshire in July 1750 he 'observed in this country the common people have their little gardens before their houses, full of carnations, which they keep in neat order, and some of them appear very beautiful': J. J. Cartwright (ed.), *The Travels Through England of Dr. Richard Pococke* (2 vols., Camden Society, n.s., vols. 42 and 44, 1888-9), vol. 1, p. 6.

59 Peter Mathias, *The Brewing Industry in England 1700-1830* (Cambridge: Cambridge University Press 1959), pp. 100-1; cf. J. A. Chartres, 'The place of inns in the commercial life of London and western England 1660-1760' (unpubl. D.Phil thesis, Oxford University, 1973), p. 439.

60 Just outside Nottingham was a well, popularly known as 'Robin Hood's Well', and it was said that the people who kept the nearby public house, 'to promote a Holy-day Trade, shew an old wickered Chair, which they call *Robin Hood's* Chair, a Bow, and an old Cap, both these they affirm to have been this famous Robber's Property; this little Artifice takes so well with the People in low-Life, That at Christmas, Easter and Whitsuntide, it procures them a great deal of Business, for at Those Times great Numbers of young Men bring their Sweethearts to this Well, and give them a Treat, and the Girls think themselves ill-used, if they have not been saluted by their lovers in *Robin Hood's* Chair': Charles Deering, *Nottinghamia Vetus et Nova: or An Historical Account of the Ancient and Present State of the Town of Nottingham* (Nottingham 1751), p. 73.

61 For further details on the involvement of public houses in recreational life see Malcolmson, *Popular Recreations*, pp. 71-4; and Chartres, 'Inns 1660-1760' (Ph.D), pp. 417-22. A valuable analysis of the position of public houses in plebeian social life before the eighteenth century may be found in an unpublished paper by Keith Wrightson (University of St Andrews), 'Alehouses, order and reformation in rural England, 1590-1660'. One literary source that richly documents the importance of the alehouse in everyday life is *The Diary of Roger Lowe of Ashton-in-Makerfield, Lancashire, 1663-74*, ed. William L. Sachse (London 1938). I have omitted from this account any discussion of the negative consequences of drinking, partly because the polemics against alehouses are well known, and partly because it is not at all clear what should be made of them. However, it is worth taking note of one partly critical commentator. John Clare, who was employed as a farm labourer when he was around 18 to 20 years of age, complained of his

workmates that their 'whole study was continual striving how to get beer & the bottle was the general theme from week-end to week-end such as had got drunk the oftenest fancied themselves the best fellows & made a boast of it as a fame'. He recalled that 'though I joined my sixpence towards the bottle as often as the rest I often missed the tot that was handed round for my constitution would not have borne it'. 'Saturday nights', he added, 'used to be what they called randy nights which was all meeting together at the public-house to drink & sing & every new beginner had to spend a larger portion than the rest which they called "colting" a thing common in all sorts of labour': Tibble and Tibble (eds.), *Prose of John Clare*, pp. 34-5.

62 *Life of John Clare*, ed. Blunden, p. 46.

63 A. L. Lloyd, *Folk Song in England* (London: Panther 1969), p. 32. The culture of the people should be seen, I think, as a complex amalgam of literate and pre-literate components. John Clare, for instance, before noting his father's love of ballad-singing, spoke of him as 'illiterate'; and yet he also reported that his father 'could read a little in a Bible, or testament, and was very fond of the superstitious tales that are hawked about a street for a penny, such as old Nixon's Prophesies, Mother Bunches Fairy Tales, and Mother Shipton's Legacy, etc., etc.': *Life of John Clare*, ed. Blunden, p. 46.

64 Quoted in Ralph Arnold, *A Yeoman of Kent: An Account of Richard Hayes (1725-1790) and the Village of Cobham in which he Lived and Farmed* (London: Constable 1949), p. 177.

65 Quoted in Victor E. Neuburg, *Popular Literature: A History and Guide* (Harmondsworth: Penguin 1977), p. 56. Very much later, in 1874, Richard Jefferies recalled that 'In the old days there was another character in most villages; this was the rhymer. He was commonly the fiddler too, and sang his own verses to tunes played by himself. Since the printing-press has come in, and flooded the country with cheap literature, this character has disappeared, though many of the verses these men made still linger in the countryside': Richard Jefferies, *The Toilers of the Field* (London 1898), p. 84. William Marshall had noticed the importance of balladry in rural culture in the late eighteenth century: *The Rural Economy of the Midland Counties* (2 vols., London 1790), vol. 2, pp. 20-1.

66 PRO, SP 36/32, fols. 72 and 74.

67 See especially K. H. Macdermott, *The Old Church Gallery Minstrels: An Account of the Church Bands and Singers in England from about 1660 to 1860* (London: SPCK 1948); and Nicholas Temperley, *The Music of the English Parish Church* (2 vols., Cambridge: Cambridge University Press 1979), vol. 1, pp. 148-62 and 196-201 (the quotation appears on p. 157). For evidence on church choirs and orchestras in parts of Leicestershire in the late eighteenth century, see William Gardiner, *Music and Friends* (2 vols., London, 1838), vol. 1, pp. 44-7; for references from the counties of Wiltshire, Somerset and Dorset see J. H. Bettey, *Rural Life in Wessex 1500-1900* (Bradford-on-Avon: Moonraker Press 1977), pp. 92-3. cf. Thomas

Sanderson, 'An essay on the character, manners, and customs of the peasantry of Cumberland', in *The Poetical Works of Robert Anderson* (2 vols., Carlisle 1820), vol. 1, p. xlvi; and Arthur Warne, *Church and Society in Eighteenth-Century Devon* (Newton Abbot: David & Charles 1969), pp. 47-8.

68   Malcolmson, *Popular Recreations*, pp. 24, 32 and 44-5.

69   These and other functional dimensions of sports and festivities are discussed in greater detail in my *Popular Recreations*, pp. 52-5 and ch. 5. The fairground setting for courtship and flirtation is highlighted in two contemporary poems: 'The Holyday Gown', in John Cunningham, *Poems, Chiefly Pastoral* (London 1766), pp. 117-18; and 'A Description of Rosaly-hill Fair', in Ewan Clark, *Miscellaneous Poems* (Whitehaven 1779), pp. 37-45.

70   Sidney Gilpin (ed.), *The Songs and Ballads of Cumberland* (London 1866), p. 338; cf. James Clarke, *A Survey of the Lakes of Cumberland, Westmorland, and Lancashire*, 2nd edn (London 1789), p. xxv.

71   James Mott, 'Miners, weavers and pigeon racing', in Michael A. Smith, Stanley Parker and Cyril S. Smith (eds.), *Leisure and Society in Britain* (London: Allen Lane 1973), pp. 94-5.

72   For a discussion of customary recreational practices, with special reference to the right claimed to the enjoyment of certain 'playing fields', see my *Popular Recreations*, pp. 110-16.

73   W. K. Clay, 'A history of the parish of Landbeach in the County of Cambridge', *Publications of the Cambridge Antiquarian Society*, vol. 6 (1861), p. 60*n*.; *Hull Advertiser*, 1 November 1817; and Samuel Rudder, *A New History of Gloucestershire* (Cirencester 1779), p. 619.

74   *Leicester and Nottingham Journal*, 1 March 1766.

75   William Marshall, *The Rural Economy of the Midland Counties* (2 vols., London 1790), vol. 1, pp. 215-16.

76   See the essay on 'The sale of wives' in his forthcoming book, *Customs in Common*. My account is based largely on notes taken from his public talks on this subject, and I am grateful for his permission to summarize some of his provisional findings, and for his advice on my handling of the topic.

77   *Sarah Farley's Bristol Journal*, 11 September 1784. A report of 1790 stated that 'instances of the sale of wives have of late frequently occurred among the lower class of people, who consider such sales lawful': *Felix Farley's Bristol Journal*, 6 March 1790. Most of the recorded instances of wife sales date from the late eighteenth and early nineteenth centuries.

78   The principal investigator of bridal pregnancy is P. E. H. Hair: see his 'Bridal pregnancy in rural England in earlier centuries', *Population Studies*, vol. 20 (1966-7), pp. 233-43; 'Bridal pregnancy in earlier rural England further examined', *Population Studies*, vol. 24 (1970), pp. 59-70; and 'Puritanism and bridal pregnancy: some doubts', *Journal of Interdisciplinary History*, vol. 7, no. 4 (Spring 1977), pp. 739-44. See also Laslett, *World We Have Lost*

(1971), p. 148, and Peter Laslett, *Family Life and Illicit Love in Earlier Generations* (Cambridge: Cambridge University Press 1977), p. 130.

79   Jonas Hanway, *The Defects of Police the Cause of Immorality* (London 1775), p. 163; and Jonas Hanway, *A Candid Historical Account of the Hospital for the Reception of Exposed and Deserted Young Children* (London 1759), p. 43.

80   John Smeaton, *A Narrative of the Building and a Description of the Construction of the Edystone Lighthouse with Stone* (London 1791), p. 65*n*. It was also said that some workers who came down from London 'were much struck and mightily pleased with the facility of the Portland ladies, and it was not long before several of the women proved with child: but the men being called upon to marry them, this part of the lesson they were uninstructed in; and on their refusal, the Portland women arose to stone them out of the island; insomuch that those few who did not chuse to take their sweethearts for *better, or for worse*, after so fair a trial, were in reality obliged to decamp: and on this occasion some few bastards were born: but since then matters have gone on according to the ancient custom' (ibid.). This whole account, though interesting and suggestive, should not yet be regarded as representative of plebeian courtship customs, for Portland was a relative isolated district, and it may have preserved certain customary practices with unusual vigour. Further evidence on courtship practices should be sought from other regions.

81   See especially E. P. Thompson, ' "Rough music": Le Charivari anglais', *Annales*, 27e année (1972), pp. 285-312.

82   *Salisbury Journal*, 29 September 1755 (an article reprinted from the *World*, no. 142). John Brand reported that 'there is a vulgar Custom in the North, called *riding the Stang*, when one in Derision is made to ride on a Pole for his Neighbour's Wife's Fault': *Popular Antiquities*, p. 409.

83   E. P. Thompson, 'Eighteenth-century English society: class struggle without class?', *Social History*, vol. 3, no. 2 (May 1978), p. 153.

Chapter 5: Authority, legitimacy and dissension

1   For some comments on the popular counter-culture of irreverence — ridicule, mockery, ceremonial parodies of authority, ritualized disdain for the symbols of class hegemony — see Robert W. Malcolmson, *Popular Recreations in English Society 1700-1850* (Cambridge: Cambridge University Press 1973), pp. 81-2; John Brewer, *Party Ideology and Popular Politics at the Accession of George III* (Cambridge: Cambridge University Press 1976), pp. 190-1; and John Redwood, *Reason, Ridicule and Religion: The Age of Enlightenment in England 1660-1750* (London: Thames & Hudson 1976), p. 183.

2   Richard Mayo, *A Present for Servants, From their Ministers, or Other Friends, Especially in Country Parishes* (London 1693), pp. 57-8.

3   Timothy Nourse, *Campania Foelix. Or, A Discourse of the Benefits*

and Improvements of Husbandry (London 1700), p. 15.

4 Bernard Mandeville, *The Fable of the Bees*, ed. Phillip Harth (Harmondsworth: Penguin 1970), pp. 159-60.

5 *Cobbett's Parliamentary History*, vol. 9 (1733-37), col. 1295 (debate of 10 February 1737).

6 Nicholas Rogers, 'London politics from Walpole to Pitt: patriotism and independency in an era of commerical imperialism, 1738-63' (unpubl. Ph.D thesis, University of Toronto, 1974), p. 498. See also the pertinent observations in J. M. Beattie, 'The criminality of women in eighteenth-century England', *Journal of Social History*, vol. 8 (Summer 1975), pp. 99-100; and Geoffrey M. Sill, 'Rogues, strumpets, and vagabonds: Defoe on crime in the city', *Eighteenth-Century Life*, vol. 2, no. 4 (June 1976), p. 77.

7 Thomas Broughton, *A Serious and Affectionate Warning to Servants* (London 1746), p. 13.

8 Batista Angeloni (pseud. for John Shebbeare), *Letters on the English Nation* (2 vols., London 1755), vol. 2, p. 6.

9 According to Arthur Young, 'miners in general, I might almost say universally, are a most tumultuous, sturdy set of people, greatly impatient of controul, very insolent, and much void of common industry': *A Six Months Tour Through the North of England* (4 vols., London 1770), vol. 2, p. 288. A disgruntled clergyman, the rector of Market Deeping in Lincolnshire, complained to his bishop in 1721 of the smallholder inhabitants of the fen parishes that they 'are . . . very poor, yet very proud. . . . [They] love a great deal of respect, but will give none, and what difficulties a Minister must meet with amongst such people I leave your Lordship to judge': R. E. G. Cole (ed.), *Speculum Dioceseos Lincolniensis Sub Episcopis Gul: Wake et Edm: Gibson A.D. 1705-1723*, pt 1: *Archdeaconries of Lincoln and Stow*, Publications of the Lincoln Record Society, vol. 4 (1913), p. 185. 'Forrests and great Commons', according to John Bellers in 1714, 'make the Poor that are upon them too much like the *Indians*', and are 'a hindrance to Industry, and . . . Nurseries of Idleness and Insolence': A. Ruth Fry, *John Bellers, 1654-1725: Quaker, Economist and Social Reformer. His Writings Reprinted, With a Memoir* (London 1935), p. 128.

10 Alan Everitt has been specially responsible for drawing attention to these characteristics of forest settlements. See his observations in Joan Thirsk (ed.), *The Agrarian History of England and Wales*, vol. 4: *1500-1640* (Cambridge: Cambridge University Press 1967), pp. 411-12 and 463; *Change in the Provinces: the Seventeenth Century* (Leicester: Leicester University Press 1969), pp. 22-3 and 36; and Joan Thirsk (ed.), *Land, Church, and People: Essays Presented to Professor H. P. R. Finberg* (Reading: British Agricultural History Society 1970), pp. 188-193. See also Christopher Hill, *The World Turned Upside Down* (London: Temple Smith 1972), ch. 3.

11 E. P. Thompson, *Whigs and Hunters: The Origin of the Black Act* (London: Allen Lane 1975); and Douglas Hay, 'Poaching and the Game Laws in

Cannock Chase', in Douglas Hay, Peter Linebaugh and E. P. Thompson (eds.), *Albion's Fatal Tree: Crime and Society in Eighteenth-Century England* (London: Allen Lane 1975), pp. 189-253.

12   William West, *A History of the Forest or Chase, known by the Name of Cranborn Chase* (Gillingham 1816), pp. vi, 122 and 131; and John Hutchins, *The History and Antiquities of the County of Dorset* (4 vols., London 1861-70), vol. 3, pp. 411-12.

13   On Kingswood see my essay '"A set of ungovernable people": the Kingswood colliers in the eighteenth century', in John Brewer and John Styles (eds.), *An Ungovernable People: The English and their Law in the Seventeenth and Eighteenth Centuries* (London: Hutchinson 1980), pp. 85-127.

14   John Collinson, *The History and Antiquities of the County of Somerset* (3 vols., Bath, 1791), vol. 2, p. 194.

15   Arthur Young, *General View of the Agriculture of Oxfordshire* (London 1813), p. 239, cf. Philip A. J. Pettit, *The Royal Forests of Northamptonshire: A Study in their Economy 1558-1714*, Northamptonshire Record Society, vol. 23 (1968), pp. 162-3 and 182, on the forest parish of Brigstock.

16   For general discussions of the extent and timing of eighteenth-century food riots see R. B. Rose, 'Eighteenth century price riots and public policy in England', *International Review of Social History*, vol. 6 (1961), pp. 277-92; Robert F. Wearmouth, *Methodism and the Common People of the Eighteenth* Century (London: Epworth Press 1945), ch. 1; and George Rudé, *The Crowd in History: A Study of Popular Disturbances in France and England 1730-1848* (New York: John Wiley 1964), ch. 2. For a regional study see Michael Thomas, 'The rioting crowd in Derbyshire in the 18th century', *Derbyshire Archaeological Journal*, vol. 95 (1975), pp. 37-47.

17   The statement about 1740 draws on my own unpublished research into the food riots of that year. For 1766 see Walter J. Shelton, *English Hunger and Industrial Disorders: A Study of Social Conflict During the First Decade of George III's Reign* (London: Macmillan 1973), ch. 1.

18   Jeremy N. Caple, 'Popular protest and public order in eighteenth century England: the food riots of 1756-7' (unpubl. MA thesis, Queen's University at Kingston 1978), pp. 38-40.

19   Roger A. E. Wells, *Dearth and Distress in Yorkshire 1793-1802*, University of York Borthwick Papers no. 52 (1977); Alan Booth, 'Food riots in the north-west of England 1790-1801', *Past and Present*, no. 77 (November 1977), pp. 84-107; Roger Wells, 'The revolt of the south-west, 1800-1801: a study in English popular protest', *Social History*, no. 6 (October 1977), pp. 713-44; and J. Stevenson, 'Food riots in England, 1792-1818', in R. Quinault and J. Stevenson (eds.), *Popular Protest and Public Order: Six Studies in British History 1790-1920* (London: Allen & Unwin 1974), ch. 1.

20   Two recent efforts to collect and interpret some of the scattered evidence on industrial disputes may now be consulted: John Stevenson, *Popular*

Disturbances in England 1700-1870 (London: Longman, 1979), chap. 6; and C. R. Dobson, *Masters and Journeymen: A Prehistory of Industrial Relations 1717-1800* (London: Croom Helm, 1980).

21   On the west of England see J. de L. Mann, 'Clothiers and weavers in Wiltshire during the eighteenth century', in L. S. Pressnell (ed.), *Studies in the Industrial Revolution* (London: Athlone Press 1960), pp. 66-96; J. de L. Mann, *The Cloth Industry in the West of England from 1640 to 1880* (Oxford: Clarendon Press 1971), ch. 4; W. E. Minchinton, 'The beginnings of trade unionism in the Gloucestershire woollen industry', *Transactions of the Bristol and Gloucestershire Archaeological Society*, vol. 70 (1951), pp. 126-41; and E. A. L. Moir, 'The gentlemen clothiers: a study of the organization of the Gloucestershire cloth industry 1750-1835', in H. P. R. Finberg (ed.), *Gloucestershire Studies* (Leicester: Leicester University Press 1957), especially pp. 246-66. The principal disturbance in East Anglia involved the Norwich wool-combers in 1752/53; see the columns of the *Norwich Mercury* for the year after the winter of 1752. See also K. H. Burley, 'A note on a labour dispute in early eighteenth-century Colchester', *Bulletin of the Institute of Historical Research*, vol. 29 (1956), pp. 220-30. On Yorkshire see Herbert Heaton, *The Yorkshire Woollen and Worsted Industries*, 2nd edn (Oxford: Clarendon Press 1965), pp. 312-21.

22   A. P. Wadsworth and J. de L. Mann, *The Cotton Trade and Industrial Lancashire 1600-1780* (Manchester 1931), chs. 18 and 19.

23   Respectively: J. M. Fewster, 'The keelmen of Tyneside in the eighteenth century', *Durham University Journal*, n.s., vol. 19 (1957/58), pp. 24-33, 66-75 and 111-23; J. D. Chambers, *Nottinghamshire in the Eighteenth Century*, 2nd edn (London: Frank Cass 1966), pp. 35-44 (framework-knitters); *Norwich Mercury*, 7 April, 28 April and 19 May 1753, and *Felix Farley's Bristol Journal*, 1 May 1762 (tailors); *Worcester Journal*, 26 July 1753 (building workers); *Salisbury Journal*, 13 March 1738 (nailers); ibid., 7 November 1737 (button-makers); *Northampton Mercury*, 26 March 1759 (needle-makers); J. U. Nef, *The Rise of the British Coal Industry* (2 vols., London 1932), vol. 2, pp. 177-80; T. S. Ashton and Joseph Sykes, *The Coal Industry of the Eighteenth Century*, 2nd edn (New York: A. M. Kelley 1967), ch. 6, and Edward Hughes, *North Country Life in the Eighteenth Century: The North-East, 1700-1750* (London: Oxford University Press 1952), pp. 249-57 (colliers and other coal workers).

24   See B. McL. Ranft, 'Labour relations in the royal dockyards in 1739', *Mariner's Mirror*, vol. 47 (1961), pp. 281-91; James M. Haas, 'The introduction of task work into the royal dockyards, 1775', *Journal of British Studies*, vol. 8, no. 2 (May 1969), pp. 44-68; John Ehrman, *The Navy in the War of William III, 1689-1697* (Cambridge: Cambridge University Press 1953), pp. 91-3; Daniel A. Baugh, *British Naval Administration in the Age of Walpole* (Princeton, NJ: Princeton University Press 1965), pp. 321-31; and Peter Linebaugh, 'Tyburn: a study of Crime and the Labouring Poor in

London during the first half of the eighteenth century' (unpubl. Ph.D thesis, University of Warwick, 1975), ch. 4.

25   See George Rudé, *Hanoverian London 1714-1808* (Berkeley and Los Angeles: University of California Press, 1971), ch. 10; Shelton, *English Hunger and Industrial Disorders*, pt 2; Linebaugh, 'Tyburn', chs. 9 and 10; and Alfred Plummer, *The London Weavers' Company 1600-1970* (London: Routledge & Kegan Paul 1972), chs. 14 and 15.

26   For accounts of some of the various conflicts over customs duties see Edward Carson, *The Ancient and Rightful Customs: A History of the English Customs Service* (London: Faber & Faber, 1972), ch. 5; and Cal Winslow, 'Sussex smugglers', in Hay *et al.* (eds.), *Albion's Fatal Tree*, pp. 119-66. It has been said that in Suffolk smuggling was in its heyday during the eighteenth century and that 'it was a highly organized business whose roots extended through the whole community': George Ewart Evans, *Ask the Fellows Who Cut the Hay*, 2nd edn (London: Faber & Faber 1962), pp. 186 and 188.

27   For an excellent discussion of the Game Laws and some of their social consequences see Peter B. Munsche, 'The Game Laws in England, 1671-1831' (unpubl. Ph.D thesis, University of Toronto, 1978). See also his essay, 'The Game Laws in Wiltshire 1750-1800', in J. S. Cockburn (ed.), *Crime in England 1550-1800* (London: Methuen 1977), pp. 210-28.

28   Accounts of turnpike riots are available in D. G. D. Isaac, 'A study of popular disturbances in Britain 1714-1754' (unpubl. Ph.D thesis, University of Edinburgh, 1953), pp. 104-21; and Malcolmson, 'Kingswood colliers', pp. 93-113. For details on the major risings in the West Riding in the summer of 1753 see *Felix Farley's Bristol Journal*, 14 July 1753; Br. Lib., Add. MSS 32,732, fols. 111-12 and 182-83; John James, *Continuations and Additions to the History of Bradford, and its Parish* (London 1866), pp. 86-87; and PRO, SP 36/122, fol. 188.

29   For discussions of the popular resistance to impressment see Baugh, *British Naval Administration*, ch. 4, *passim*; and Arthur N. Gilbert, 'Army impressment during the war of the Spanish Succession', *Historian*, vol. 38, no. 4 (August 1976), pp. 692-4. New evidence on this subject is presented in Fenela A. Childs, 'Naval impressment in eighteenth century England: the social, economic, and legal ramifications' (unpubl. MA essay, University of Toronto, 1979). Accounts of the popular protests against the Militia Act in 1757 may be found in Joyce Godber (ed.), 'Some documents relating to riots', *Publications of the Bedfordshire Historical Record Society*, vol. 49 (1970), pp. 154-6; David Neave, 'Anti-militia riots in Lincolnshire, 1757 and 1796', *Lincolnshire History and Archaeology*, vol. 11 (1976), pp. 21-2 and 25-6; and J. R. Western, *The English Militia in the Eighteenth Century* (London: Routledge & Kegan Paul 1965), pp. 290-302.

30   See George Rudé, *Wilkes and Liberty: A Social Study of 1763 to 1774* (Oxford: Clarendon Press 1962); and the stimulating analysis in John

Brewer, *Party Ideology and Popular Politics*, ch. 9. For an admirable discussion of an earlier period see Nicholas Rogers, 'Popular protest in early Hanoverian London', *Past and Present*, no. 79 (May 1978), pp. 70-100.

31 For an account of the character and extent of the opposition to enclosure in one county see J. M. Neeson, 'Common right and enclosure in eighteenth-century Northamptonshire' (unpubl. Ph.D thesis, University of Warwick, 1977), chs. 6 and 7.

32 In offering this reconstruction I am very much indebted to the discussion in E. P. Thompson, 'The moral economy of the English crowd in the eighteenth century', *Past and Present*, no. 50 (February 1971), pp. 76-136.

33 *Worcester Journal*, 19 May 1757.

34 Ibid., and *Salisbury Journal*, 9 May 1757; *Northampton Mercury*, 9 May 1757; and *Worcester Journal*, 2 June 1757.

35 *Jackson's Oxford Journal*, 27 September 1766.

36 *Northampton Mercury*, 2 May 1757.

37 *Worcester Journal*, 15 December 1757.

38 *Felix Farley's Bristol Journal*, 4 October 1766.

39 *Sarah Farley's Bristol Journal*, 16 May 1795.

40 *Worcester Journal*, 24 November 1757.

41 *Jackson's Oxford Journal*, 27 September 1766.

42 ibid.

43 *Jackson's Oxford Journal*, 16 August 1766.

44 John G. Rule, 'The labouring miner in Cornwall *c.* 1740-1870: a study in social history' (unpubl. Ph.D thesis, University of Warwick, 1971), pp. 119-20 and 123.

45 *Jackson's Oxford Journal*, 9 August 1766.

46 *Ipswich-Journal*, 12 March 1726; cf. *Farley's Bristol Newspaper*, 19 March 1725/26.

47 *Worcester Journal*, 24 November 1757.

48 *Ipswich-Journal*, 17 May 1740.

49 *Jackson's Oxford Journal*, 9 August 1766.

50 *Salisbury Journal*, 16 May 1737.

51 *Gloucester Journal*, 17 July 1753.

52 *Ipswich-Journal*, 2 June 1757.

53 *Worcester Journal*, 2 June 1757.

54 The least restrained crowd actions in the eighteenth century often focused on disputes concerning religion: and gentlemen were sometimes abettors of these actions. See, for instance, Geoffrey Holmes, 'The Sacheverell riots: the crowd and the church in early eighteenth-century London', *Past and Present*, no. 72 (August 1976), pp. 55-85; John Walsh, 'Methodism and the mob in the eighteenth century', in G. J. Cuming and Derek Baker (eds.), *Studies in Church History*, vol. 8: *Popular Belief and Practice* (Cambridge: Cambridge University Press 1972), pp. 213-27; and George Rudé, 'The Gordon riots: a study of the rioters and their victims', in his *Paris and London in the*

Eighteenth Century: Studies in Popular Protest (London: Collins 1970), pp. 268-92.

55 John Bunyan, *The Pilgrim's Progress and The Life and Death of Mr. Badman* (n.p.: Nonesuch Press 1928), pp. 354, 360 and 368-9 (and in general pp. 354-69).

56 *Northampton Mercury*, 27 March 1758. Two slight alterations have been made in the text of this letter to render it more easily intelligible.

57 *The Political State of Great-Britain*, vol. 45 (January-June 1733), p. 355.

58 *Gloucester Journal*, 30 January 1739. The essay in which this comment is found was one contribution to a prolonged debate over the character of industrial relations in the Wiltshire woollen industry; this essay, by 'A Manufacturer in Wilts.', was written in defence of the clothiers. The issues of the *Salisbury Journal* and the *Gloucester Journal* between December 1738 and June 1739 are full of evidence concerning these difficult relations and their implications.

59 On this general subject see W. E. Minchinton (ed.), *Wage Regulation in Pre-Industrial England* (Newton Abbot, Devon: David & Charles 1972).

60 *Gloucester Journal*, 24 February 1730, 9 February and 2 March 1731.

61 ibid., 16 May 1738.

62 Malcolmson, 'Kingswood colliers', pp. 114-16.

63 *Ipswich-Journal*, 7 June 1740.

64 *Northampton Mercury*, 5 December 1726; *Ipswich-Journal*, 10 December 1726; and *Farley's Bristol Newspaper*, 10 December 1726. Similarly, in the spring of 1738 a body of woolcombers and weavers marched on Tiverton in Devon, complaining that the merchants there did not give a 'Price for Goods to the Masters who employ'd them, sufficient for Masters to give Wages whereby a poor Man can live', and on their arrival in town they 'oblig'd the Merchants to promise they would give a better Price for their Goods' (since a detachment of soldiers reached Tiverton shortly thereafter, it may well be that this commitment made under duress was quickly abandoned): *Gloucester Journal*, 16 May 1738.

65 *Gloucester Journal*, 9 September 1729 and 28 July 1730.

66 *Bristol Weekly Intelligencer*, 21 July 1750.

67 'The humble Petition of the poor distressed Weavers and Clothworkers in Bradford, Trowbridge, and Melksham, in Wiltshire, to his Most Gracious Sovereign Lord King George, and to the Honourable both Houses of Parliament, etc.', printed in the *Salisbury Journal*, 12 March 1739. The reduction in wages was admitted by an apologist for the clothiers, though excused with the explanation that the 'Master Clothiers cannot now afford to give the Manufacturer as good a Price for his Work as he Heretofore could, by Reason of the present sinking Condition of our Trade' (ibid). For accounts of these disturbances in Wiltshire see especially the issues of the *Salisbury Journal* for 11 December 1738, 8 January 1739 and 17 April 1739.

68 *Journals of the House of Commons*, vol. 27 (1754-57), p. 741 (1 March

1757). For accounts of these disputes see the *Salisbury Journal*, 25 October 1756; E. Lipson. *The History of the Woollen and Worsted Industries* (London 1921), pp. 114-16, and *The Economic History of England*, vol. 3: *The Age of Mercantilism*, 3rd edn (London 1943), pp. 266-71; and Moir, 'Gentlemen clothiers', pp. 255-7.

69 Robert Wright, *The Life of Major-General James Wolfe* (London 1864), p. 351. For some testimony to the constitutional orderliness and concern for due process among aggrieved woollen workers see Mann, *Cloth Industry in the West of England*, pp. 109-13.

70 *Gloucester Journal*, 13 March 1733.

71 *Bristol Weekly Intelligencer*, 28 October 1752; cf. *Felix Farley's Bristol Journal*, 28 October 1752.

72 Bedfordshire RO, HSA 1680 W105. I am grateful to Miss Patricia Bell for bringing this item to my attention.

73 These letters are printed in full in the appendix to E. P. Thompson's essay, 'The crime of anonymity', in Hay *et al.* (eds.), *Albion's Fatal Tree*, pp. 318-20.

74 T. R. Potter, *The History and Antiquities of Charnwood Forest* (London 1842), p. 23.

75 'The Mores', in *Clare: Selected Poems and Prose*, ed. Eric Robinson and Geoffrey Summerfield (London: Oxford University Press 1966), pp. 188-90.

76 *Ipswich-Journal*, 31 July 1725.

77 *Northampton Mercury*, 7 August 1769. For further evidence on these conflicts see W. Marrat, *The History of Lincolnshire, Topographical, Historical, and Descriptive* (3 vols., Boston 1814), vol. 1, pp. 138-46; and Joan Thirsk, *English Peasant Farming: The Agrarian History of Lincolnshire from Tudor to Recent Times* (London: Routledge & Kegan Paul 1957), pp. 212-15.

78 Quoted in Evans, *Ask the Fellows Who Cut the Hay*, p. 253.

79 This document is printed in full in Hay *et al.* (eds.), *Albion's Fatal Tree*, pp. 313-14.

80 Western, *English Militia*, p. 299.

81 In 1757, for example, the Dean of Lincoln wrote of the recent militia disturbances that the rioters' 'behaviour showed the greatest licenciousness and cowardice, and an utter contempt of the public authority and welfare. "We will not fight", they said, "for what does not concern us, and only belongs to our landlords: let the worst happen, we can but be tenants and labourers, as we are at present." A divine here preached on the obedience due to civil governors: "aye", said his hearers, "he fetches that doctrine out of a book, which our governors do not believe in, and why shoud we?" ': quoted in Francis Hill, *Georgian Lincoln* (Cambridge: Cambridge University Press 1966), p. 107.

82 Perhaps the only such insurrectionary movement was the Monmouth rebellion of 1685: see Peter Earle, *Monmouth's Rebels: The Road to Sedgemoor 1685* (London: Weidenfeld & Nicolson 1977).

83   Quoted in Max Beloff, *Public Order and Popular Disturbances 1660-1714* (London: Frank Cass 1963; first publ. 1938), p. 64.
84   Malcolmson, 'Kingswood colliers;, pp. 95-7.
85   Thompson, 'Moral economy', pp. 122-6; and Caple, 'Food riots of 1756-7', ch. 4. It was reported that Sir Richard Acton, Bart, 'attended in Person' at the market in Bridgnorth, Shropshire, one day in November 1756 and 'recommended it to the Farmers to sell their Wheat that Day at 5s. per Bushel, to the Poor only, which gave them a general Satisfaction, and prevented the expected Riot'. A year later, with high food prices persisting in some districts, the Earl of Warrington was advising his tenant farmers that they should 'gradually thresh up their Corn, supply the Wants of their poor Neighbours, and afterwards bring what they have to spare to be sold in the Publick Markets on reasonable Terms, which I hope will be a Means to silence and put a stop to all future Riots and Disturbances': *Worcester Journal*, 25 November 1756 and 15 December 1757. It was said in 1728 that in Cornwall 'the Tinworkers murmur'd very much at the high Price of Corn, and that to quiet them several Dealers therein had afforded them some Quarters of Grain [at] the prime Cost, their Rising having been much fear'd': *Ipswich-Journal*, 25 May 1728. During seasons of dearth and popular protest the newspapers were full of reports of such timely accommodations.
86   E. P. Thompson, 'Patrician society, plebeian culture', *Journal of Social History*, vol. 7, no. 4 (Summer 1974), p. 396.
87   Rogers, 'London politics', pp. 508-9.
88   This paragraph is especially indebted to the observations in E. P. Thompson, *The Making of the English Working Class* (Harmondsworth: Penguin 1968), pp. 86-8; E. P. Thompson, 'Eighteenth-century English society: class struggle without class?', *Social History*, vol. 3, no. 2 (May 1978), p. 158; Rudé, *The Crowd in History*, pp. 229-30; and Nicholas Rogers, 'Popular disaffection in London during the Forty-Five', *London Journal*, vol. 1, no. 1 (May 1975), pp. 22-3.
89   One author, having noted the numerous hardships that were faced by the domestic manufacturers in the Gloucestershire woollen industry, was also at pains to point out that 'in spite of all these hazards and fluctuations, the workers clung tenaciously to their independence, even though it might amount to no more than a semblance of freedom. They worked at home on their own looms, supplied their own tools and some of the minor raw materials, and refused to bind themselves to one master but accepted work from several. Their greatest dread was of being driven from their homes and compelled to work under the clothier's roof. The very thought of a factory aroused feelings of the deepest hatred': Moir, 'Gentlemen clothiers', p. 248. cf. Wadsworth & Mann, *Cotton Trade and Industrial Lancashire*, pp. 391-2.
90   *Gentleman's Magazine*, vol. 58, pt 1 (1788), p. 41.
91   Thompson, *Whigs and Hunters*, p. 183.
92   Thompson, 'Eighteenth-century English society', p. 155.

Chapter 6: Changing experiences

1　These changes in the size of farms have been noticed by numerous authorities: see for example Paul Mantoux, *The Industrial Revolution in the
Eighteenth Century*, 2nd edn (London: Methuen 1961), pp. 172-3; W.
Hasbach, *A History of the English Agricultural Labourer* (London: Frank
Cass 1966; first publ. 1908), pp. 59-60 and 107-8; *VCH Wiltshire*, vol. 4
(1959), pp. 57-8; Joan Thirsk, *The Restoration* (London: Longman 1976),
pp. 153-4; Roger A. E. Wells, 'The development of the English rural
proletariat and social protest, 1700-1850', *Journal of Peasant Studies*, vol.
6, no. 2 (January 1979), pp. 117-18; Ann Sturm Kussmaul, 'Servants in
husbandry in early-modern England' (unpubl. Ph.D thesis, University of
Toronto, 1978), pp. 215-17; H. J. Habakkuk, 'English landownership,
1680-1740', *Economic History Review*, vol. 10 (1940), pp. 15-16; J. D.
Chambers, *Nottinghamshire in the Eighteenth Century*, 2nd edn (London:
Frank Cass 1966), p. ix; and G. E. Mingay (ed.), *Arthur Young and His
Times* (London: Macmillan 1975), pp. 112-13. The most sustained modern
discussions of this problem may be found in G. E. Mingay, 'The size of
farms in the eighteenth century', *Economic History Review*, 2nd series,
vol. 14 (1961-2), pp. 469-88; and H. J. Habakkuk, 'La disparition du
paysan anglais', *Annales Economies-Sociétés-Civilisations*, 20e année,
no. 4 (Juillet-Août 1965), pp. 649-63.

2　C. M. L. Bouch and G. P. Jones, *A Short Economic and Social History of
the Lake Counties 1500-1830* (Manchester: Manchester University Press
1961), p. 239.

3　J. H. Bettey, *Rural Life in Wessex 1500-1900* (Bradford-on-Avon: Moonraker
Press 1977), p. 63 (cf. p. 66); see also the remarks concerning Dorset in
Bettey's 'Agriculture and rural society in Dorset 1570-1670' (unpubl. Ph.D
thesis, University of Bristol, 1976), pp. 354-5, and R. Machin, 'The great
rebuilding: a reassessment', *Past and Present*, no. 77 (November 1977),
pp. 53-4. Similar circumstances prevailed in Herefordshire: see M. A.
Faraday (ed.), *Herefordshire Militia Assessments of 1663*, Royal Historical
Society, Camden 4th series (1972), p. 19, and E. L. Jones, 'Agricultural
conditions and changes in Herefordshire, 1660-1815', in his *Agriculture
and the Industrial Revolution* (Oxford: Blackwell 1974), pp. 53-4.

4　David G. Hey, *An English Rural Community: Myddle Under the Tudors
and Stuarts* (Leicester: Leicester University Press 1974), pp. 5, 11 and 231-
2. For similar evidence on engrossing in the parish of Moreton Say, also in
Shropshire, see R. E. Jones, 'Population and agrarian change in an
eighteenth century Shropshire parish', *Local Population Studies*, no. 1
(Autumn 1968), pp. 10 and 24-6. Further evidence on engrossing in
various regions is presented in Joan Thirsk, *English Peasant Farming: The
Agrarian History of Lincolnshire from Tudor to Recent Times* (London:

Routledge & Kegan Paul 1957), p. 299; Robert W. Malcolmson, 'Some aspects of the society of north-west Bedfordshire during the eighteenth century' (unpubl. MA thesis, University of Sussex, 1966), pp. 22-30; J. P. F. Broad, 'Sir Ralph Verney and his estates, 1630-1696' (unpubl. DPhil. thesis, Oxford University 1973), pp. 188-90 (on Middle Claydon, Buckinghamshire); and J. R. Wordie, 'Social change on the Leveson-Gower Estates, 1714-1832', *Economic History Review*, 2nd series, vol. 27 (1974), pp. 593-609 (on Shropshire and Staffordshire).

5   *Gentleman's Magazine,* vol. 60, pt 1 (1790) p.506. Another example of a positive assessment of large farms is the tract by John Arbuthnot, *An Inquiry Into the Connection between the present Price of Provisions, and the Size of Farms* (London 1773).

6   *Gentleman's Magazine,* vol. 28 (1758), p. 509; Samuel Rudder, *A New History of Gloucestershire* (Cirencester 1779), p.vii; and William Chapple, *A Review of Part of Risdon's Survey of Devon* (Exeter 1785), pp. 43n.-44n. (probably written in the 1770s).

7   Roger North, *A Discourse of the Poor* (London 1753), pp. 57-8 (written in the late seventeenth century). A later observer thought that some land-lords, 'in refusing to let their Copy and Lease-holders Renew, or raising their Fines so high', were preventing the common people from working their own small allotments of land: A Gentleman of Wilts. [Thomas Andrews Jnr], *Country Common-Sense* (Gloucester 1739), p. 71.

8   *Northampton Mercury,* 22 August 1726.

9   Peter Roebuck (ed.), *Constable of Everingham Estate Correspondence 1726-43,* Yorkshire Archaeological Society Record Series, vol. 136 (1976), p. 28.

10 Thomas Alcock, *Observations on the Defects of the Poor Laws* (London 1752), p. 19; and Rudder, *Gloucestershire,* p. vii.

11 *A Political Enquiry into the Consequences of Enclosing Waste Lands* (London 1785), pp. 48-9.

12 G. E. Mingay, *Enclosure and the Small Farmer in the Age of the Industrial Revolution* (London: Macmillan 1968), p. 21; cf. M. E. Turner, 'Parliamentary enclosure and landownership change in Buckinghamshire', *Economic History Review,* 2nd series, vol. 28 (1975), p. 566, and J. A. Yelling, *Common Field and Enclosure in England 1450-1850* (London: Macmillan 1977), ch. 6.

13 John Dunkin, *Oxfordshire. The History and Antiquities of the Hundreds of Billington and Ploughley* (2 vols., London 1823), vol. 2, p. 2. Similar evidence from Gloucestershire may be found in Rudder, *Gloucestershire,* p. vii, and *Inclosure in Gloucestershire* (Gloucester: Gloucestershire Record Office 1976), pp. vii and ix.

14 Stephen Addington, *An Inquiry into the Reasons For and Against Inclosing Open-Fields,* 2nd edn (Coventry 1772), pp. 37-8 and 40.

15 Mingay, *Enclosure and the Small Farmer,* p. 21.

16   Turner, 'Parliamentary enclosure in Buckinghamshire', p. 573 (the whole
      article is relevant to this paragraph); cf. J. M. Martin, 'The cost of
      parliamentary enclosure in Warwickshire', in E. L. Jones (ed.), *Agriculture
      and Economic Growth in England 1650-1815* (London: Methuen 1967),
      especially pp. 143-4. An admirable account of some of the implications of
      enclosure in Northamptonshire may be found in J. M. Neeson, 'Common
      right and enclosure in eighteenth-century Northamptonshire' (unpubl.
      Ph.D thesis, University of Warwick, 1977), ch. 4.
17   Daniel Defoe, *A Tour Through the Whole Island of Great Britain* (2 vols.,
      London: Dent Everyman's edn 1962), vol. 2, p. 16.
18   J. D. Chambers aptly summarized some of the circumstances of those
      people who had lost their common rights: 'the sudden disappearance of the
      common unaccompanied by an adequate substitute that could be turned to
      immediate use, was felt not merely by the squatter on the waste, but the day
      labourers, handicraftsmen and the very small farmers and cottagers who
      looked to the common to eke out their livelihood'. Moreover, 'Compensation
      for the irregular use of the common by labourers and others was not given,
      except very occasionally, in the form of allotments for the poor. In any case,
      the occupant of a cottage with rights of common would have to stand by and
      see the common, which might easily be the most important part of his
      livelihood, exchanged for an allotment which the owner would probably
      sell rather than go to the expense of enclosing it': *Nottinghamshire in the
      Eighteenth Century*, pp. 182-4. Similarly, in a later study he emphasized
      that he did not want 'to minimize the social consequences of the loss of the
      commons. The appropriation to their own exclusive use of practically the
      whole of the common waste by the legal owners meant that the curtain
      which separated the growing army of labourers from utter proletarianization
      was torn down. It was, no doubt, a thin and squalid curtain, . . . but it was
      real, and to deprive them of it without providing a substitute implied the
      exclusion of the labourers from the benefits which their intensified labour
      alone made possible': 'Enclosure and labour supply in the industrial
      revolution' (1953), reprinted in E. L. Jones (ed.), *Agriculture and Economic
      Growth in England 1650-1815* (London: Methuen 1967), p. 117.
19   *Northampton Mercury*, 17 October 1726.
20   J. M. Martin, 'The small landowner and parliamentary enclosure in War-
      wickshire', *Economic History Review*, 2nd series, vol. 32 (1979), p. 343n.
      For some Warwickshire evidence on the relationship between enclosure
      and the increased cost of fuel see Joan Lane, *The Administration of an
      Eighteenth-century Warwickshire Parish: Butlers Marston*, Dugdale Society
      Occasional Papers, no. 21 (1973), pp. 12-13; cf. Thomas Rudge, *General
      View of the Agriculture of the County of Gloucester* (London 1807), p.
      332.
21   Timothy Nourse, *Campania Foelix. Or, A Discourse of the Benefits and
      Improvements of Husbandry* (London 1700), pp. 104-5.

22   William Ellis, *The Modern Husbandman* (8 vols., London 1750), vol. 6, pt
      1, p. 151. 'If ever a general inclosing of this Parish should be agreed upon',
      wrote the rector of Bolnhurst, Bedfordshire in the 1750s, 'I would willingly
      hope that the restoring & confirming the benefit of the Commons to the
      poor Cottagers will be remembered and made at least One of the Conditions
      of such Agreement': *Bedfordshire Parish Registers*, ed. F. G. Emmison,
      vol. 11 (Bedford 1935), p. C30.

23   [Thomas Quincey], *A short Tour in the Midland Counties of England*
      (London 1775), pp. 12-13.

24   *Monthly Magazine*, vol. 7 (May 1799), pp. 358-61.

25   Arthur Young, *An Inquiry into the Propriety of applying Wastes to the
      Better Maintenance and Support of the Poor* (Bury 1801), pp. 16-21; and
      Arthur Young, *General Report on Enclosures* (London 1808), pp. 150-63.

26   C. B. Macpherson (ed.), *Property: Mainstream and Critical Positions*
      (Toronto: University of Toronto Press 1978), pp. 7-8.

27   E. P. Thompson, *Whigs and Hunters: The Origin of the Black Act*
      (London: Allen Lane 1975), p. 241.

28   J. M. Beattie, 'The criminality of women in eighteenth-century England',
      Journal of Social History, vol. 8 (Summer 1975), p. 88.

29   J. M. Beattie, 'The pattern of crime in England 1660-1800', *Past and
      Present*, no. 62 (February 1974), p. 80.

30   The principal authority on wages is Elizabeth W. Gilboy, *Wages in
      Eighteenth Century England* (Cambridge, Mass. 1934). Some of her
      conclusions, in my view, are considerably more optimistic than her evidence
      warrants, especially for London and its region. This deficiency, however,
      was partly corrected in her later study, 'The cost of living and real wages in
      eighteenth century England', *Review of Economic Statistics*, vol. 18
      (1936), pp. 134-43. See also Rufus S. Tucker, 'Real wages of artisans in
      London, 1729-1935', in Arthur J. Taylor (ed.) *The Standard of Living in
      Britain in the Industrial Revolution* (London: Methuen 1975; first publ.
      1936), pp. 21-35; and Elizabeth Boody Schumpeter, 'English prices and
      public finance, 1660-1822', *Review of Economic Statistics*, vol. 20 (1938),
      pp. 21-37. Further price data are presented in B. R. Mitchell and Phyllis
      Deane, *Abstract of British Historical Statistics* (Cambridge: Cambridge
      University Press 1962), ch. 16.

31   Adam Smith, *The Wealth of Nations*, ed. Edwin Cannan (New York:
      Modern Library 1937), p. 74.

32   Chapple, *Review of Risdon's Survey of Devon*, pp. 51-3.

33   A. F. J. Brown, *Essex at Work 1700-1815* (Chelmsford: Essex County
      Council 1969), pp. 132-4; *VCH Wiltshire*, vol. 4 (1959), p. 63; P. B.
      Munsche, 'The Game Laws in Wiltshire 1750-1800', in J. S. Cockburn
      (ed), *Crime in England 1550-1800* (London: Methuen 1977), pp. 215-16;
      E. L. Jones, 'Agricultural conditions and changes in Herefordshire, 1660-
      1815', in his *Agriculture and the Industrial Revolution* (Oxford: Blackwell

1974), p. 56; A. W. Ashby, *One Hundred Years of Poor Law Administration in a Warwickshire Village* (Oxford 1912), pp. 179 and 183; and Chambers, *Nottinghamshire in the Eighteenth Century*, ch. 9. For a well-documented study of one county during the French revolutionary and Napoleonic wars see T. L. Richardson, 'The agricultural labourer's standard of living in Kent 1790-1840', in Derek Oddy and Derek Miller (eds.), *The Making of the Modern British Diet* (London: Croom Helm 1976), pp. 103-16.

34 W. G. Hoskins, *Industry, Trade and People in Exeter 1688-1800* (Manchester 1935), p. 141; Jack Simmons, *Leicester Past and Present*, vol. 1: *Ancient Borough to 1860* (London: Eyre Methuen 1974), p. 113; and R. S. Neale, 'The standard of living, 1780-1844: a regional and class study', *Economic History Review*, 2nd series, vol. 19 (1966), pp. 599-600.

35 John Mastin, *The History and Antiquities of Naseby, in the County of Northampton* (Cambridge 1792), pp. 54-5.

36 John Brand, *Observations on Popular Antiquities* (Newcastle upon Tyne 1777), p. 333. The evidence and elaborated arguments that support these generalizations may be found in my *Popular Recreations in English Society 1700-1850* (Cambridge: Cambridge University Press 1973), chs. 4 and 6-8. An authority on folk songs, having noted the interest displayed by seventeenth-century gentlemen in balladry and other forms of popular literature, suggests that there was a growing dissociation between elite and popular culture in the eighteenth century. 'With the coming of newspapers containing accounts of foreign wars, Stock Exchange dealings, society scandals, the broadside ceased to interest the "polite" classes and became more and more exclusively associated with farmhands and farriers, milkmaids and muckmen': A. L. Lloyd, *Folk Song in England* (London: Panther 1969), p. 29.

37 Peter B. Munsche, 'The Game Laws in England, 1671-1831' (unpubl. Ph.D thesis, University of Toronto, 1978), pp. 195-6 and ch. 4 *passim*. See also his forthcoming book to be published by Cambridge University Press in 1981, *Gentlemen and Poachers: The English Game Laws 1671-1831*, especially ch. 2; and his essay 'The Game Laws in Wiltshire'.

38 Eric J. Evans, 'Some reasons for the growth of English rural anti-clericalism *c.* 1750—*c.* 1830', *Past and Present*, no. 66 (February 1975), especially pp. 101-9.

39 See especially R. J. B. Knight, 'The royal dockyards in England at the time of the American War of Independence' (unpubl. Ph.D thesis, University of London, 1972), pp. 153-4, 164-5 and 181-99; and Peter Linebaugh, 'Tyburn: a study of crime and the labouring poor in London during the first half of the eighteenth century' (unpubl. Ph.D thesis, University of Warwick, 1975), ch. 4. While my suspicion is that perquisites in general declined most noticeably after the middle of the century, I must admit that the chronology of these long-term changes is, as yet, not clearly established. See also Linebaugh's brief observations in 'Conference report', *Bulletin of the*

Society for the Study of Labour History, no. 25 (Autumn 1972), p. 13; Beattie, 'Pattern of crime', pp. 79-80; and the preface to *Albion's Fatal Tree*, ed. Douglas Hay, Peter Linebaugh and E. P. Thompson (London: Allen Lane 1975), p. 13.

40   E. P. Thompson, 'Eighteenth-century English society: class struggle without class?', *Social History*, vol. 3, no. 2 (May 1978), p. 155.

41   Simmons, *Leicester Past and Present*, vol. 1, p. 123.

42   On these themes see J. H. Plumb, *The Commercialisation of Leisure in Eighteenth-century England* (University of Reading 1973); *The Pursuit of Happiness: A View of Life in Georgian England* (Yale Center for British Art 1977); and *Georgian Delights* (London: Weidenfeld & Nicolson 1980). See also Peter Borsay, 'The English urban renaissance: the development of provincial urban culture *c.* 1680−*c.*1760', *Social History*, no. 5 (May 1977), pp. 581-603.

43   Alan Everitt, 'Kentish family portrait: an aspect of the rise of the pseudo-gentry', in C. W. Chalklin and M. A. Havinden (eds.), *Rural Change and Urban Growth 1500-1800* (London: Longman 1974), p. 192. In some places the growing social and cultural distance between propertied and unpropertied people was already apparent during the seventeenth century: see Keith Wrightson and David Levine, *Poverty and Piety in an English Village: Terling, 1525-1700* (New York: Academic Press 1979), especially ch. 7.

44   Josiah Tucker, 'Instructions for Travellers' (1757), in Robert L. Schuyler (ed.), *Josiah Tucker: A Selection from His Economic and Political Writings* (New York 1931), pp. 244-5. For a modern discussion of combinations in one part of this region see W. E. Minchinton, 'The beginnings of trade unionism in the Gloucestershire woollen industry', *Transactions of the Bristol and Gloucestershire Archaeological Society*, vol. 70 (1951), pp. 126-41.

45   See, for instance, the relevant discussion in Alfred P. Wadsworth and Julia de Lacy Mann, *The Cotton Trade and Industrial Lancashire 1600-1780* (Manchester 1931), chs. 18 and 19.

46   G. D. H. Cole and A. W. Filson, *British Working Class Movements: Select Documents 1789-1875* (London: Macmillan 1951), pp. 83-4; cf. A. Aspinall, *The Early English Trade Unions* (London: Batchworth Press, 1949), p. ix, and Henry Pelling, *A History of British Trade Unionism* (Harmondsworth: Penguin 1963), pp. 18-19. For evidence from one industry see J. D. Chambers, 'The Worshipful Company of Framework Knitters (1657-1778)', *Economica*, no. 27 (November 1929), pp. 327-9. By the later eighteenth century, according to Sidney and Beatrice Webb, 'The abandonment of the operatives by the law, previously resorted to under pressure of circumstances, and, as we gather, not without some remorse, was now carried out on principle, with unflinching determination': *The History of Trade Unionism* (1920; reprinted New York: A. M. Kelley

1965), p. 55. The Act of 1773 for the regulation of the Spitalfields weavers' wages is the major exception to this trend.

47 *Political State of Great Britain*, vol. 45 (January-June 1733), p. 355.
48 Pelling, *British Trade Unionism*, p. 24.
49 Herbert Heaton, *The Yorkshire Woollen and Worsted Industries*, 2nd edn, (Oxford: Clarendon Press 1965), pp. 418-37. On the increasing severity of the laws concerning 'embezzlement' see Michael Ignatieff, *A Just Measure of Pain: The Penitentiary in the Industrial Revolution, 1750-1850* (New York: Pantheon 1978), pp. 26-7.
50 Document printed in Aspinall, *Early English Trade Unions*, p. 1.
51 Gwyn A. Williams, *Artisans and Sans-Culottes: Popular movements in France and Britain during the French Revolution* (London: Edward Arnold 1968), p. 63. The principal authorities on the popular radicalism of the 1790s are E. P. Thompson, *The Making of the English Working Class* (Harmondsworth: Penguin 1968), pt 1; and Albert Goodwin, *The Friends of Liberty: The English Democratic Movement in the Age of the French Revolution* (London: Hutchinson 1979).
52 Thomas McKeown, *The Modern Rise of Population* (London: Edward Arnold 1976), p. 153; see especially his discussion in ch. 7.
53 In 1778 Gilbert White said of the region around Selborne in Hampshire that 'Potatoes have prevailed in this little district, by means of premiums, within these twenty years only; and are much esteemed here now by the poor, who would scarce have ventured to taste them in the last reign'; and it was said of the Lake District a decade later that potatoes, which had been recently introduced, had 'superseded the old-fashioned dishes [of the region] . . . so entirely as in a manner to render their names, and the manner in which they were cooked, obsolete, even in so short a space of time as that of fifty or sixty years': Gilbert White, *The Natural History of Selborne* (London: Dent Everyman's edn 1949), pp. 211-12 (from a letter of 1778); and James Clarke, *A Survey of the Lakes of Cumberland, West-morland, and Lancashire*, 2nd edn (London 1789), p. xxiv. Adam Smith had observed in the 1770s that 'Potatoes . . . do not at present, through the greater part of the kingdom, cost half the price which they used to do thirty or forty years ago': *Wealth of Nations*, p. 78. There is much evidence concerning the depressed condition of the agricultural labourers in Dorset during the late eighteenth and early nineteenth centuries, and yet one local observer was reported to believe that 'the state of the poor is much altered for the better within the last twenty years, and principally by the introduction of potatoes, which were scarcely known thirty years since': William Stevenson, *General View of the Agriculture of the County of Dorset* (London 1812), p. 454. Further evidence on the spread of potato cultivation from the mid eighteenth century may be found in Redcliffe N. Salaman, *The History and Social Influence of the Potato* (Cambridge: Cambridge University Press 1949), chs. 25 *passim* and 27. For broadly conceived

discussions of the impact of New World foods on European population growth see Alfred W. Crosby, *The Columbian Exchange: Biological and Cultural Consequences of 1492* (Westport, Conn.: Greenwood Press 1972), ch. 5; and W. L. Langer, 'American foods and Europe's population growth 1750-1850', *Journal of Social History*, vol. 8 (Winter 1975), pp. 51-66.

54   Peter Razzell in a review of McKeown's book in the *Economic History Review*, 2nd series, vol. 30 (1977), p. 193.

55   The principal authority on the mortality experiences of these people is T. H. Hollingsworth, *The Demography of the British Peerage*, Supplement to *Population Studies*, vol. 18 (1964), ch. 4. McKeown's attempt to confront this evidence and its implications in *The Modern Rise of Population*, pp. 139-42, is, in my view, unconvincing.

56   The most important contribution to this discussion has been by Thomas McKeown and R. G. Brown, 'Medical evidence related to English population changes in the eighteenth century' (1955), reprinted in Michael Drake (ed.), *Population and Industrialization* (London: Methuen 1969), pp. 40-72.

57   P. E. Razzell, 'Population change in eighteenth century England: a re-appraisal' (1965), reprinted in Drake (ed.), *Population and Industrialization*, pp. 128-56 (quote from p. 147). Razzell's arguments have recently been elaborated in greater detail in his book, *The Conquest of Smallpox: The Impact of Inoculation on Smallpox Mortality in Eighteenth Century Britain* (Firle, Sussex: Caliban Books 1977).

58   M. W. Flinn, *British Population Growth 1700-1850* (London: Macmillan 1970), p. 44.

59   John D. Post, 'Famine, mortality, and epidemic disease in the process of modernization', *Economic History Review*, 2nd series, vol. 29 (1976), p. 14; cf. J. D. Chambers, *Population, Economy, and Society in Pre-Industrial England* (London: Oxford University Press 1972), ch. 4 *passim*. Post's article focuses on the dearth of 1816-17, by which time European population growth was already well underway: his own findings, for the early nineteenth century, are largely incompatible with the notion of an 'autonomous death-rate', for he emphasizes the importance of improved governmental responses to the threat of disease.

60   Andrew B. Appleby, 'Nutrition and disease: the case of London, 1550-1750', *Journal of Interdisciplinary History*, vol. 6 (Summer 1975), p. 19.

61   David Levine, *Family Formation in an Age of Nascent Capitalism* (New York: Academic Press 1977), p. 147.

62   For discussions of some of the economic circumstances underlying the declining age of marriage see especially Levine's book, which is the most important work on the subject; J. M. Martin, 'Marriage and economic stress in the felden of Warwickshire during the eighteenth century', *Population Studies*, vol. 31, no. 3 (November 1977), pp. 519-35; Kussmaul,

'Servants in husbandry' (Ph.D), ch. 7 *passim*; and Chambers, *Population, Economy, and Society*, ch. 3.

63 For a good account of London's skilled artisans, many of whom maintained or even improved their standards of living during the war years of the late eighteenth and early nineteenth centuries, see I. J. Prothero, *Artisans and Politics in Early Nineteenth-Century London: John Gast and his Times* (Folkestone, Kent: Dawson 1979), ch. 2. Ch. 4, however, points to some of the distress they experienced during the second decade of the nineteenth century.

64 The 'steepening pyramid of wealth' may have been developing by around 1760: Peter Mathias, 'The social structure in the eighteenth century: a calculation by Joseph Massie', *Economic History Review*, 2nd series, vol. 10 (1957-8), p. 38. The most judicious summary of these trends in the distribution of income may be found in Sidney Pollard, 'Labour in Great Britain', in *The Cambridge Economic History of Europe*, vol. 7, pt 1, ed. Peter Mathias and M. M. Postan (Cambridge: Cambridge University Press 1978), pp. 161-4. He concludes that during the years from the 1770s to the 1840s 'wages remained somewhere near a level which had come to be accepted as subsistence. This betokens an economy operating essentially in conditions of abundant labour, and it is clear that an elastic labour supply at low cost and a transfer of income from labour to capital were two basic features of the British industrial revolution . . . . The labour market was rigged in such a way as to allow the labour supply to react sensitively to detailed attractions and repulsions while remaining in a state of overabundance as a whole. It was only when labour found its feet, in the second half of the nineteenth century, that a true labour market — one in which the supplier had at least a semblance of power — began slowly to emerge' (p. 164).

65 George Crabbe, 'The village' (1783), in *George Crabbe: Tales, 1812, and other Selected Poems*, ed. Howard Mills (Cambridge: Cambridge University Press 1967), p. 4.

Index